Masses, Classes, and the Public Sphere

Masses, Classes, and the Public Sphere

Edited by MIKE HILL

and WARREN MONTAG

VERSO

London • New York

First published by Verso 2000
© in the collection Verso 2000
© in individual contributions the contributors 2000
All rights reserved

Verso
UK: 6 Meard Street, London W1V 3HR
US: 180 Varick Street, New York, NY 10014–4606

Verso is the imprint of New Left Books

ISBN 1–85984–777–3

British Library Cataloguing in Publication Data
A catalogue record for this book is available from the British Library

Library of Congress Cataloging-in-Publication Data
Masses, classes and the public sphere / edited by Mike Hill and Warren Montag.
     p. cm.
ISBN 1–85984–777–3 (cloth)
1. Sociology—Methodology. 2. Social classes. 3. Social structure. 4. Mass soscieity. 5.
Public interest. 6. Political sociology. I Hill, Mike, 1964–. II. Montag, Warren.
HM511.M37 2000
301′.01—dc21

                                                                    00–061438

Typeset in 10/12pt Baskerville by SetSystems Ltd, Saffron Walden, Essex
Printed by Biddles Ltd, Guildford and King's Lynn

This volume is dedicated to the memory of Michael Sprinker

Contents

Introduction
What Was, What Is, the Public Sphere? Post-Cold War Reflections

Mike Hill and Warren Montag

In September 1989 a conference was held to celebrate the appearance, in English translation, of *The Structural Transformation of the Public Sphere*.[1] The featured speaker was none other than Jürgen Habermas himself. As Craig Calhoun, editor of the published proceedings of the conference, noted, the event coincided with the transformation of Central and Eastern Europe, a fact that gave it a doubly celebratory air.[2] Indeed, Habermas himself cited this transformation as a triumph of civil society and the public sphere (if only as an ideal or "norm"—to use Habermas's term) over the despotism of the state that ought to be regarded as cause for optimism. In keeping with such a mood, the participants debated whether the public sphere was best understood as a fact or as a norm, as existing in some form today or in the past, or rather as a political ideal never quite realized but always nevertheless to be pursued. In the published transcript of the discussion with which the conference concluded, the usually voluble Habermas, who was able generously to acknowledge the various critiques of his work offered by the assembly of philosophers, historians, and sociologists, was caught short only once, by an entirely unexpected question that seemed to have appeared out of another historical epoch, an epoch which the events frequently alluded to by the conference's participants had rendered irrevocably past. It was left to Nancy Fraser to ask what once would have seemed an obligatory question: if, as Habermas has argued, "markets and state bureaucracies are a necessary feature of life in complex societies" (*HPS*, 468) must we not ask whether capitalism is compatible with a "non-exclusionary and genuinely democratic public sphere" (*HPS*, 468)?

However obvious such a question might once have been and however relevant it might continue to be for some people, it caught Habermas off guard, momentarily disrupting his composure: "I'll have to get over the shock to answer such a question" (*HPS*, 469). The response that follows in the published proceedings is relatively disjointed; the first three sentences are separated by ellipses and it is not clear whether the three editors of the "Concluding Remarks" deleted certain phrases (although ellipses appear in only one other place in the text) or whether the ellipses represent pauses in Habermas's speech. But the disjunction that appears is thematic as well; Habermas declares himself "the last Marxist" while simultaneously postulating the impossibility of "any type of revolution in societies that have such a degree of complexity" (*HPS*, 469).

Since Fraser did not raise the issue of revolution or the question of how a people might rid itself of capitalism, but only the question of capitalism itself, we are left to conclude that the impossibility of revolution here is a substitute for the impossibility of there existing (at least in complex societies) anything other than capitalism. Whatever the accuracy of such an assertion, it is not an answer to Fraser's question. Capitalism may be the only possible economic system but that does not render it any more compatible with Habermas's norm. It is not too fine a point to suggest that the present collection takes shape in the theoretical and political space opened by Habermas's discursive feint, as well as by the test, both theoretical and practical, to which the concept of the public sphere has been put over the last decade or more.

From the time of its publication in 1989, the English translation of *The Structural Transformation of the Public Sphere* (originally published in German in 1961) had an immediate and far-reaching impact on the understanding of the Enlightenment and its continued relationship to contemporary political life. Even as moderate criticism has emerged since its appearance, the fundamental concepts that informed the book remain prominent and distinctly influential. Indeed, the term "public sphere," as Habermas introduced it, has today become an ultimately foundational (and therefore underinterrogated) concept for assessing everything from intellectual civility and "public access" criticism, to the function of race, gender, and sexual difference. After more than a decade of perceived "attacks" on the Enlightenment (Michel Foucault,

Edward Said, *et al.*, and, more recently, progenitors of gender studies and multiculturalism), Habermas seems to have provided "modernity" with its most theoretically sophisticated defense. An account of early-eighteenth-century Britain as one blissful and all-too-fleeting moment in the history of capitalist societies, by virtue of the fact that unlike anti-capitalist utopias, it actually existed, seemed to Habermas originally, and to leading U.S. intellectuals at present, to offer a set of realistic objectives for liberal social reform.

What sustains the public sphere today as the object of a certain historical longing is the apparent emergence in the eighteenth century of a civil society independent of the state in which autonomous individuals exchanged arguments in a manner analogous to the way they exchanged commodities in the market. For Habermas the market, liberated from the artificial interference of the mercantile system but not yet compromised by the formation of monopolies, would necess-arily give rise to an abundance that would neutralize class antagonisms, as well as to an economic rationality whose primary characteristic would be the optimization of products and services. In the same way, a public sphere, liberated from the state and from any threat of coercion but not yet the site of class conflict, permitted the emergence of a world of rational critical exchange in which the merely ornamental discourses of wit and aristocratic *bons mots* gave way to genuine arguments which were adjudicated solely according to the criteria of reason.

More recently, Habermas has responded to the objection that his early work has privileged the bourgeois public sphere which in reality was or is only one among others (proletarian, feminine, etcetera) by pluralizing the concept.[3] The public sphere as discussed in the work of the 1990s is no longer "bourgeois" either in its origins or in its actual functioning at present. Instead, Habermas has come to recognize that if there is indeed a plurality of spheres, there is also a sphere of all spheres. The public sphere thus conceived is the totality formed by the communicative interaction of all groups, even nominally dominant and subaltern. For the early Habermas, the constant concourse of these groups in the communicative realm (where rational–critical debate stands above relations of power, and an intellectual contest of ideas is fundamentally independent of and even opposed to the materiality of forces) has worn away their antagonisms to produce something like a genuine "general interest" in which all members of society have a stake. In the later writings, the realm of communicative action is a sphere in which such differential property and power relations disappear from view. They no longer produce effects at all in civil society in which the

distinct groups that emerge are neither rooted in opposing and irreconcilable interests, nor forged in struggle against legitimate or illegitimate power. As Habermas has explained, once liberated from the
"Marxist tradition" we are free to dissociate the diverse communities
that make up civil society from the processes of capital accumulation
and class struggle and to understand them as purely "voluntary associations" that have emerged "spontaneously,"[4] that is, in no way determined by relations of domination and subordination. The recognition
that a plurality of spheres has always made up the public sphere
compels us to admit that irrespective of rank, status, or property, and
independently of material differences, there has existed at least from
the dawn of capitalism in Europe a universalism of the human "as
human," even if it was never fully realized as such.

Further, while Habermas initially saw the public sphere as a
"national" phenomenon, both belonging to and helping to define
distinct national cultures, he has followed the argument to its logical
conclusion and posited the existence of an international public sphere,
the global totality not simply of national public spheres, themselves
composed of multiple spheres, but also of transnational public
spheres.[5] Globalization, whatever its challenges, is therefore the bearer
of a genuine universalism that insofar as it is communicative in its
essence transcends the merely material differences between nations.
Indeed, the fall of the Soviet Union has ended the atmosphere of
permanent civil war that characterized international politics for most
of the twentieth century. It no longer makes sense to speak of an
international balance of forces when one of the two contending parties
has ceased to exist and the global realm of communicative action,
governed by the "cognitive content of morality," is said to have finally
escaped the imperatives of material life.[6]

Such an analysis, of course, stands in stark contrast to the pessimism
with which *The Structural Transformation of the Public Sphere* famously
concludes. We may recall that Habermas then argued that civil society,
together with the public sphere that it supported, collapsed under the
weight of its contradictions in the late nineteenth and early twentieth
centuries: first, competition, the means by which market rationality was
realized, was subverted by the concentration of capital and the emergence of trusts and monopolies that fixed prices and upset the equilibrium of the market. Such concentration of wealth necessitated in turn
the organization of workers into unions and labor/socialist parties
whose primary function was to pressure the state into ensuring a greater
diffusion of wealth, thereby expanding its intervention into "free" civil

society. Universal concerns disappeared into the insurmountable social antagonisms of competing interest groups and their particularistic interests: the Rousseauist general interest ceased to exist. Increased state intervention and the degeneration of civil society into monopolies and trusts led to the commodification of news and information, and accordingly transformed the public sphere into a place of passive consumption rather than active critical participation.

In fact, Habermas, from a very different theoretical starting point, arrived at conclusions nearly identical to those of Herbert Marcuse whose *One-Dimensional Man* was published three years later.[7] Unlike Marcuse's text, however, the general argument presented in *The Structural Transformation of the Public Sphere*, which a mere decade ago appeared unlikely to survive the historical moment in which it was conceived, has, in the unique historical conjuncture of the twenty-first century, taken on renewed importance. Interestingly, what in the U.S. today appears most appealing about the work is in many respects utterly opposed to the arguments that captured the philosophical and historical imagination of an earlier generation. The German student movement of the early 1960s found compelling Habermas's critique of the decline of twentieth-century publicity into a culture of passive consumption and supervised, empty leisure. In contrast, his account of a liberal capitalism presided over by a self-denying bourgeoisie so progressive that proletarian politics were at best superfluous and at worst the impulse behind a "refeudalization" of society was greeted with skepticism. Habermas's increasingly strident condemnation of the students' preference for direct action instead of rational–critical debate assured that his text would be seen as an intervention in defense of the politics of social democracy of the Cold War epoch with its acceptance of capitalism as an absolute horizon, its fear of mass movements, its emphasis on legality, and its restriction of the domain of the political to parliament and other elected bodies.

Today, of course, the very themes that earned Habermas the enmity of the German New Left constitute for increasing numbers of U.S. scholars what is most attractive about the work, just as he has himself found signs of hope where there once seemed cause for despair. In place of a society dominated ideologically as well as economically and therefore a society profoundly "one-dimensional," Habermas has borrowed from his critics the notion of a world of innumerable vital public spheres, debating and discussing, unencumbered by what once appeared to be the inescapable constraints of material inequality, a world where communicative agency flourishes in the face of economic and social determinations that only Marxists could imagine matter any longer. To suggest otherwise in the wake of the collapse not simply of the USSR and the East Bloc states but of socialist and communist movements internationally, is to risk appearing like a ghost of time past, just alive enough to die again.[8] So great in fact is the allure of the notion of a public sphere free from the determinations of material life that the relatively few extant critiques of the public sphere have had little effect on the broad reception of the notion in the current American-Anglo context.

The essays that comprise this volume mark an attempt to move beyond the question of whether the public sphere is best understood as fact or as norm, as historical reality or as an ideal always to be realized, to interrogate the ideal itself. To do so it is not enough to note that the public sphere as concept is incompatible with the capitalist market that it both resembles and is founded on, and that therefore Habermas defends as the only possible form of economic organization the very system that makes a genuine public sphere impossible. It is necessary to go further to ask what is the function of the concept of the public sphere today politically, as well as in historical analysis and philosophical reflection. Absolutely central to the notion of the public sphere in all its versions is the opposition between reason and force and between speech and action. The fact that Habermas uses phrases like "communicative action" should in no way be allowed to obscure the fact that these oppositions are constitutive of political reason as he understands it. First the positive thesis: individuals associate and communicate, as we have noted, "spontaneously" and freely; that is, they are unaffected by the determinations of the social, material world and thus can be said to transcend it. Because of this, economic inequality and power differentials are irrelevant; all are able to engage equally in communicative action. Freedom and "agency" are thus liberally bestowed on those most in need of them. This, in turn, implies a second, negative thesis: the public sphere can remain the site of rational communication and deliberation as long as it is the site of communication alone and not action, as long as its participants are content to let reason decide and persuade and never resort to the use of force or even the threat of force. Here, of course, Habermas follows Kant's prescription for enlightenment very closely: "argue but obey."[9] What Habermas calls the "self-limitation of radical-democratic practice"[10] means in essence, argue as much as you like about whatever you like, including the capitalist market and the property and power relations necessary to it, but limit your practice to discursive practice.

Kant, however, was a bit more direct than Habermas about the consequences of practice failing to limit itself to words alone: reason that
does not limit itself will (have to) have limits imposed on it from
without by force, although of course legitimate and, for Habermas,
"constitutional" force.[11] In opposition to Kant, however, it is not simply
the zeal of a reason seeking prematurely to organize the world that
threatens to lead "practice" from disembodied speech to material
action. It is, instead, those "holistic aspirations to a self-organizing
society" that do not know enough to "leave intact the modes of
operation internal to functional systems and other highly organized
spheres of action"[12] (that is, capitalist property relations and the state).
Where are the causes of these "aspirations" or temptations, however, if
not in the contradictions and struggles internal to the systems that
must be "left intact"? To admit that such aspirations are an ever-present
danger to rational social organization is already to have moved beyond
Kant to the pessimism of Hegel, who recognized that the contradictions
of capitalism could only be managed by an ever-expanding police
apparatus. We are thus inescapably led to the conclusion that the
public sphere and even civil society itself can function rationally only
when they rest on a relationship of forces that will guarantee that what
cannot be improved upon will be left "intact."

Of course, yet another feint is involved here: from reading Habermas
one would think that the danger to civilization comes from those fascist
movements at home and those atavistic nationalist or fundamentalist
trends abroad, those dark forces without respect for national constitu-
tions or national and international legality, forces that reject the
adjudicating role of reason altogether and believe that might makes
right. It is a question of defending constitutional order, of universally
agreed upon doctrines of human and civil rights and of defending
them with force, although again legitimate force, if need be. Thus,
reluctantly and with a heavy heart, Habermas was compelled by the
force of his own argument to support the massive prolonged war
against Iraq by what were once called "imperialist" states.[13]

It is not only that such a doctrine renders all those opposed to "the
constitutional order" or the international community indistinguishable,
as if all nationalisms, say German and Kurdish, or White power and
Black power movements are the same, obscuring what was once known
as the distinction between the nationalism of the oppressor and the
nationalism of the oppressed. It is rather that Habermas's work is a
systematic denial and rationalization of the violence and barbarism of
legal and constitutional orders themselves, a violence that is necessary

to preserve the systems that must be maintained "intact." It takes as a kind of second nature or a mere backdrop to social existence over which humans can hope to exert little control or influence, a system of exploitation and coercion that will produce revolt (and thus the violence necessary to contain that revolt) as long as it lasts. We are in danger of forgetting why even the most democratic of the capitalist states could once have been seen as an example of "the dictatorship of the bourgeoisie." The anaesthetizing effects of Habermas's work on our sense of the international dimension are even more serious. We live in an era that threatens to match that in which international law had its origins, that is, the dawn of modernity with its unparalleled genocide and plunder, for the sheer frequency of just wars, legitimate bombardments of cities and legal massacres, all sanctioned by the highest judicial bodies and carried out in strict accordance with the laws of the land, if not those of the earth itself.

We begin Part I, "The Public in Practice," with Crystal Bartolovich's study of exclusionary inventions of London, and of England, in the early modern period. Drawing on John Stowe's 1603 *Survey of London*, Bartolovich asserts that just as Stowe's vertical perspective of seventeenth-century London denied the influence of merchant activity, so too do modern attempts fail to view the public sphere outside transnational influence and exchange. Raúl Villa brings the question of the nation-state back to contemporary Los Angeles as he traces the methods by which Los Angeles's working-class Mexican immigrant population, as well as LA's Mexican-American population, have defended their right to the city. Similarly, concentrating in this case on displaced Chicago residents, Jamie Owen Daniel turns to inner-city Chicago. Consistent with Villa and drawing from the work of Negt and Kluge, she argues that residents of Chicago's public housing projects comprise a counter-public sphere that challenges the spatial, epistemic, and above all legal authority of the official public sphere. Also with Negt and Kluge at hand, Stanley Aronowitz closes Part I of this volume by focusing on organized labor's vanishing public sphere. Chronicling the decline of industrial labor and the recent emergence of the bureaucratic "service model" of union administration, Aronowitz notes the aggravation of rank and the rank and file and the reluctance of labor and socialist movements to foster working-class autonomy.

Part II, "Philosophizing the Public," begins with Etienne Balibar's critical discussion of the seminal work on "the people" in Rousseau and Kant. In this chapter, Balibar analyzes the reciprocal and pathological antagonisms between the individual and the state. Continuing work on the philosophical origins of the public sphere, Warren Montag examines one of its founding features: a necessary opposition to "the street." "The street," the realm in which reason lapses into force, in which the universal is lost to violent particulars, becomes an abyss above which both civil society and the state precariously hover. Discussion of the state, civil society, and collective action take two additional turns in chapters by Ted Stolze and Michael Hardt. Stolze contends that, despite claims to a discursive ethic of intersubjective rational action, Habermas creates a transcendent moral barrier that prevents citizens from exercising their immanent power to change the basic structure of their society. Hardt focuses on Hegel's idea of civil society to explain how the state simulacrum of society excludes or marginalizes social forces foreign to the system. Hardt illustrates how social capital, by appearing to reproduce itself autonomously, emancipates itself from the working class, and labor becomes invisible to the system.

The third and final section of the volume, "Public Knowledge," brings the paradigmatic "practical" concerns of Part I together with Part II's philosophical focus in order to examine the vexed relation between collective agency and the production of knowledge. Two initial chapters, the first by David McInerney, the second by Mike Hill, return to the formative moment of the Enlightenment to examine the specific question of writing. McInerney takes a second look at the theory of "print capitalism" and the origins of nationalism as espoused in Benedict Anderson's seminal work of 1983, *Imagined Communities*. McInerney argues that in this text the disjunction of Marxism and liberalism is elided, allowing non-materialist definitions of capitalism to substitute for critical Marxist concepts. Exploring the legacy of the Scottish Enlightenment in its effect on "Marxist humanism," Mike Hill turns to E.P. Thompson's incomplete reading of Adam Smith's work on moral philosophy. Thompson's account of the eighteenth-century crowd's evolution from rioters to readers tells a tale that looks back to Smith's opposition to "the multitude" as "subjectless" agency, just as it looks forward to contemporary debates within Cultural Studies on the question of agency. You-me Park and Gayle Wald examine how the traditional boundaries of the public sphere, examined by McInerney and Hill in historical terms, are challenged in African American and Asian American women's writing. The volume ends with Henry Giroux's chapter on politics and schooling. Giroux addresses how the attack on both the counter-public sphere and the politics of difference is expressed in continued assaults on public education.

Whether focused historically, or on the philosophical foundations of the Enlightenment, or on contemporary struggles over policy and civil rights, the chapters in this volume seek to throw light on the internal conflicts that have marked the progressive development of the public sphere. Together, these chapters attempt to determine how the public sphere has been realized as a practical object, and to what extent it has not simply been dogged by, but is constituted on the basis of domination and exclusion. There may be a rationality that has escaped Habermas's notice insofar as it is not contained in the anodyne discursive realm where that which cannot be changed is deliberated. This rationality, we hope to suggest, is immanent to the activity of those who can ill afford the luxury of leaving intact the systems that confront them.

Notes

1. Jürgen Habermas, *The Structural Transformation of the Public Sphere* (Cambridge, MA: MIT Press, 1989).
2. *Habermas and the Public Sphere*, ed. Craig Calhoun (Cambridge, MA: MIT Press, 1992), p. viii. Cited hereafter in text as *HPS*.
3. *Habermas and the Public Sphere*, pp. 425–30, and Jürgen Habermas, *Between Facts and Norms* (Cambridge, MA: MIT Press, 1996), pp. 329–87.
4. Habermas, *Facts*, pp. 366–7.
5. On the "peculiar tension" of nationalism and the public sphere, as well as Habermas's search for post-nationalist claims to universal validity, see Habermas, "Remarks on Legitimation Through Human Rights," in *The Modern Schoolman* special issue "Globalization," 75.2 (January 1988): 87–99.
6. On "the cognitive content of morality," see Jürgen Habermas, *The Inclusion of the Other* (Cambridge, MA: MIT Press, 1998), pp. 3 ff.
7. Herbert Marcuse, *One-Dimensional Man: Studies in the Ideology of Advanced Industrial Society* (New York: Farrar, Straus & Giroux, 1964).
8. See Habermas, "Is There a Future for the Nation State?" in *The Inclusion of the Other* (n. 10), pp. 105 ff.
9. *Kant's Political Writings*, ed. H.S. Reiss (Cambridge: Cambridge University Press, 1970), pp. 54–60.
10. Habermas, *Facts*, p. 371.
11. See Habermas, "Kant's Idea of Perpetual Peace," in *The Inclusion of the Other* (n. 10), pp. 165 ff.
12. Both quotes from Habermas, *Facts*, p. 372.
13. Jürgen Habermas, "The Gulf War," in *The Past as Future* (Lincoln: University of Nebraska Press, 1994), pp. 5–31.

Part I

The Public in Practice

2

Inventing London[1]

Crystal Bartolovich

As has now often been pointed out—and, indeed, acknowledged by
Jürgen Habermas himself—the great paradox of the bourgeois "public
sphere"—"a forum in which . . . private people come together to form
a public, [and] read[y] themselves to compel public authority to
legitimate itself before public opinion"[2]—is that this supposed great
vehicle of liberal "inclusion" has actually functioned historically
through social mechanisms of *exclusion*, along lines of "gender, ethnicity, class, [and] popular culture."[3] Nevertheless, in addressing these
criticisms, Habermas insists, however inadequate any actually existing
public sphere may have been (or be), that the quest for such a space
of critical debate and reasoned inquiry remains as necessary as ever for
social justice, and, furthermore, that the public sphere, and the Enlightenment principles that underwrite it, give rise simultaneously to a
means by which various "exclusions" can be identified and overcome:
"the rules that constitute the participants' self-understanding at the
same time provide the resources for a critique of its own selectivity, of
the blind spots and the incompleteness of its own transitional embodi-
ments."[4] To test out Habermas's assertion, I, too, will pursue the
problem of "exclusion" in relation to the public sphere, though along
rather different lines than the critics to whom Habermas has already
responded.[5]

I take as my point of departure certain postcolonial critiques of
much "British" Cultural Studies for *its* exclusions. Raymond Williams's
early work (on which Habermas relies for some of his historical
material on the emergence of the bourgeois public sphere in England)
has been accused, for example, of assuming a coherent (British)
nation-state as a pre-given and, apparently, natural and transparent

unit of analysis, an assumption that has the effect, according to its critics, of problematically distinguishing a "real" British people from interlopers and latecomers (such as the recent diaspora immigrants).[6] In a review of Williams's *Culture and Society* and *The Long Revolution*, C.L.R. James early on took Williams to task along these lines: "Mr Williams has . . . based his devoted and profound work on the purely British experience. But he has fallen into another pit; he has based British socialism and its future purely on the British experience. Hence his great omissions of what the British working class has before it, being part, an integral part, of an international way of life."[7] In this formulation, James points not only to Williams's neglect of what "the British working class" might contribute to that "international way of life," but also—crucially—what it has already gleaned from it, rendering Britain less of an island than it often portrays itself to be. Indeed, as James here asserts, and as later postcolonial critics would emphasize, there is no adequate analysis of any "local" way of life that does not situate it as part of an "international" one—a claim, as I hope to show, that has pressing consequences for how we imagine the "public" of any "locality."

Paul Gilroy, too, has produced a critique of Williams's localism, suggesting that his privileging of communities of (face-to-face) "long experience" has led to blind spots in his work around questions of "race" in particular.[8] Among other problems, these blind spots give rise to claims about cultural purity as well as autonomous development which encourage the (historically insupportable) belief that "England ceaselessly gives birth to itself, seemingly from Britannia's head."[9] Gilroy thus denounces what he sees as Williams's assumptions about the nation-state as a site of independent production: "I am suggesting that even the laudable, radical varieties of English cultural sensibility examined by Williams . . . were not produced spontaneously from their own internal and intrinsic dynamics."[10] Having called into question not only "national" essentialism but also the effectivity of state boundaries in containing "culture," Gilroy goes on to track the multiple tributary streams of culture—not territorially distinct—that (in)form the work of figures usually claimed for an "[African] American" culture, such as W.E.B. DuBois and Richard Wright, as well as contemporary musical artists, and considers how their cultural forms resist enclosure within the boundaries of a U.S. (or any other nation-state) particularism.

Pushing Gilroy to the limit, we can wonder how (and for whom) it came to be that a nation-state and its ideologies, practices, habits; its art, knowledge and institutions; its industries, wealth, markets, and language(s), came to be attributed to "indigenous" forces, and "local[izable]" populations, when they manifestly are not capable of such isolationist enclosure. As Fanon observed long ago: "European opulence is literally scandalous, for it has been founded on slavery, it has been nourished with the blood of slaves and it comes directly from the soil and from the subsoil of that underdeveloped world. The well-being and the progress of Europe have been built up with the sweat and the dead bodies of Negroes, Arabs, Indians, and the yellow races."[11] Indeed, if we take into account the full range of "non-local" labors, peoples, wealth, raw material, ideas, and so on that are *inextricable* from the production of *any* modern state, constitutional or otherwise, the question arises how as to how its communities-of-interest, its "public(s)"—*precisely* as defined by Habermas—can be restricted to merely the "local" peoples inhabiting a particular territory, however "tolerant" of difference *within* those boundaries they might come to be.[12] Such a question encourages postcolonial deconstructions not only of the nation, but also of the state—a gesture that (necessarily) has implications for the "public sphere" as well.[13]

Specifically, such deconstructions suggest that it is not enough to critique the "sovereignty" of the nation-state (as Habermas has done recently); we must also critique statist territoriality (in ways that Habermas has not).[14] In *The Structural Transformation of the Public Sphere*, Habermas suggests that historically a "public" forms itself "within" and in relation to a *particular* "bourgeois constitutional state," whose evident exclusions are not considered absolute by him since (much as Ben Anderson argues in the case of the "nation") theoretically, at least, "everyone [has] an equal chance to meet the criteria for admission."[15] Since he sees it as standing in the way of this abstract equality, Habermas's most recent work rejects the "nation" as the fundamental organizing principle of states, declaring that it has outlived its usefulness, though he retains the (territorial) state form as a fundamental political unit. Nations, he argues, rely on a "prepolitical" understanding of "the people," homogenizing them (by "blood" or "culture"); conversely, the (constitutional) state for Habermas implies *chosen* affiliations (social contracts), independent of either blood or culture. Whereas the nation "falsely projects homogeneity where in fact there is only heterogeneity," the constitutional state provides a space for the recognition and negotiation of differences.[16] So, while he rejects the nation-state, he advocates the formation of "post-national" states with attendant political spheres ("Europe," for example). The post-national state, he argues, would not define membership in terms of "some primordial substrate but rather an intersubjectively shared context of possible mutual understanding."[17] The "public," then, is not to be (indeed cannot be) restricted to ties of blood or descent for Habermas, but rather must emerge from the free affiliation of a "social contract" capable of accommodating difference.[18] Because his focus is on the "rights" of "individuals" and the effects of their "free" association, the terrain of the battle for Habermas, in spite of his fervent rejection of the "nation," remains the *state*, which must be compelled to assure that "equal chances" are respected and protected, that is to say: actually available within a particular territory. Hence, he urges immigration policy reform to make it easier for "economic" migrants as well as skilled technicians and "political" refugees to enter Europe and become citizens.[19] He also envisions a United Nations in which "peoples would be represented as the totality of world citizens not by their governments but by directly elected representatives."[20] In both these cases, while Habermas claims to be subverting the "sovereignty" claims of states (that is, their right to refuse to be compelled to act in accordance with a general—extra-state—popular will), he continues to rely on the organizational structure provided by the territorial boundaries of constitutional states (and "their" peoples). I want to explore further the implications of assuming that this territorial "state-public" (even if "post-national") is the *form* that "the public" has taken—and should take—in the first instance. Among other things, I want to foreground that Habermas's "public sphere" is, of course, a *space*, and that all spaces—as all "publics"—are *produced*.[21]

I take up this problem of the production of the *space* of "the public sphere(s)" to argue that to understand the operation of its logic of inclusion/exclusion, we need to understand what I will call here its "geo-graphy"—the writing of the world on which it depends, a writing in which currently states are viewed not only as the "practical" unit of "international" participation, but also as legitimate in pursuing the interests of that unit. This perspective belies not only the historically multiply-determined formation of states, but also the possibility of a global justice which cannot be predicated on the willingness of the most powerful states and their peoples to "give" aid or "permit" immigration or even offer a "unit" from which democratically elected representatives might be sent to a global assembly, but must be predicated rather on the possibility of all peoples asserting a claim to the global wealth which they have helped to produce, however indirectly, or over long distances of space and time, and, furthermore, on all peoples assuming responsibility for unquestionably "global" problems, such as pollution and dwindling resources, rather than the more powerful states managing to "export" these problems elsewhere.[22] When the world is examined as a "space of flows," rather than of "states," a far more radical definition of "publics" than Habermas envisions becomes possible.[23] When not only a state's "right" to autonomy is called into question, but also its "territory," novel ways of defining "publics" might emerge; this is one of the implications of Gilroy's *Black Atlantic*. Taken in its strongest form (as suggesting a new politics as well as a different way of understanding "culture" and cultural forms), Gilroy's alternative configurations of space (and others that might be imagined) suggest that the descendants of slaves, for example, are *already* interwoven into the history and current material life of numerous states in which they are not physically resident. Why, then, should they be excluded from its public(s)? Such a question can be directed toward any number of groups who have benefited territorial states without ever benefiting themselves. Are not such groups (potential) counter-publics to the already recognized publics of such states?

A re-examination of the politics of "inside" and "outside" in the case of the "public sphere" in particular is called for because even the many critics of Habermas's model (on the grounds of its insufficient attention to "exclusion") tend, at least implicitly, to see "the public(s)" they identify as the public(s) of *a* state, and as spreading out from a European center into a broader system of states over time. Geoff Eley observes, for example, that in *some* instances "public spheres" have been "stimulated from the outside" by an importation of concepts and institutions (the example he gives is of eastern and southern European intellectuals starting up literary societies and debating nationalism after exposure to revolutionary France).[24] However, his insistence on the exceptional and derivative nature of the later cases serves to emphasize that in its originary and paradigmatic (European) instances, public spheres are (as Eley puts it) "the spontaneous outgrowth of indigenous social development" of a given state.[25] Habermas adopts a "diffusionist" model of the nation-state as well, describing its ur-form as the northern and western European territorial states, followed by the "belated states" of Italy, Germany and the states formed by decolonization, as well as, most recently, by the collapse of the Soviet Union.[26] Neither Eley nor Habermas takes into account other flows which disrupt the tidy one-way "diffusionism" they describe, nor considers the possibility that the supposedly originary and autonomous European public spheres may have been "stimulated from outside" as well. My task here will be to indicate that the supposedly pure originary situation cannot be shown to have been either singular or an effect of merely local and internal forces, as Habermas and even many of his critics imply. To make this case I will extend across state boundaries the insights of Nancy Fraser, who has proposed that Habermas's model fails precisely in its insistence that there is a pure, originary moment and space (the bourgeois public sphere) to which all other publics owe their derivation and (may eventually) have their being if its liberatory aspects are properly realized.[27] Fraser proposes instead the simultaneous contentious operation of "subaltern counter-publics" with the bourgeois public (in contrast to assuming that the latter is a single, potentially all-inclusive public in its design if not in its practice).[28] For Fraser it is "external" pressures exerted by such counter-publics, not the efforts of continuous self-interrogation and regulation by the liberal public (as Habermas contends), through which liberatory change is effected. My contention is that it is crucial, given the exigencies of "globalization," to view the interactions of these "counter-publics" *transnationally*, and not simply with respect to the "internal" politics of particular states.[29]

Indeed, it seems to me that one of the great paradoxes (even contradictions) of Habermas's model is that in it an expansive inter-state activity (long-distance trade) gives rise to an apparent *enclosure*, the (single, autonomous) "public sphere" of a single nation-state, in which a distinct and seemingly autonomous "public" develops.[30] And yet it can be amply demonstrated that considerable anxiety was provoked by merchants, whose activities (quite rightly) were viewed as not at all necessarily "national" in scope or interests.[31] For Habermas, however, these unruly boundary transgressors were successfully domesticated, so to speak, and he argues that the emergence of the "bourgeois" or "liberal" public sphere is coincident with the "mercantilist phase of capitalist development," when long-distance trade is articulated with particular nation-states who used mechanisms of taxation, legal protections, military intervention and so on to elicit and support modern "national and territorial economies."[32] In his narrative, the "traffic in commodities and news" on which this merchant capital depended was at first subordinated to intensively localizing feudal institutions, but eventually undermined them as the (national) "market replaced the household" as the fundamental domain of "economy" and news dissemination was rendered "public" with increased circulation of newspapers and journals.[33] Since under such conditions the decisions taken by state officials have a direct bearing on the economic interests not only of merchants, bankers and entrepreneurs, but also of the much larger group of consumers and taxpayers, this larger group begins to form a "public" distinct from the "government," in relation to whom they are ambivalent and "critical." What is crucial about this "public" from Habermas's perspective is its active, reasoning function— its attempt to produce its own understanding of a "common good," whatever officialdom may decree. In contrast with the ostensible passivity and vulnerability to manipulation of modern subjects in media-saturated consumerist welfare states, this "critical" function is progressive for Habermas, however flawed in any actually existing form.

Alternatively, I am interested in what sort of "publics" might be imagined that are neither "national" (here Habermas and I agree), *nor* dependent upon territorial state forms, and I want to consider what the implications of this imagining might be, both for understanding capitalism and for resisting it.[34] How would such "publics," for example, orient themselves in time and space? To begin to answer such a question, I want to return to the preconditions of emergence of the liberal public sphere that intrigued Habermas, and to emphasize some rather different aspects of these preconditions than he does, and suggest different implications for others. I do this with an eye to understanding the "production of space" of "public spheres" and also to considering an alternative space and historical narrative to that which Habermas proposes. Specifically, I will examine one particularly influential chorographical text, John Stow's 1603 *Survey of London*, and the logic of inclusion/exclusion in which it participates.[35] By way of this text, I hope to show not only that the separating out of a territorial "state-public" is predicated upon an (often violent) "exclusion" of the "non-citizen" (a process assumed, but not considered insurmountable, by Habermas's own account), but also that this exclusion requires a remarkable *continuing* disavowal of the constitution of the actual "space" of that "public," which necessarily persists as a site of intermixing and dependence on forces beyond the territorial state, however much the resulting "impurities" and dependencies are decried, disavowed, or ignored.

In at least two senses, this "intermixing" differs from Habermas's appeal to "multiculturalism": first in its timeline and second in its "space." While for Habermas "multiculturalism" and "internal difference" are *new* conditions of existence for many (European) states, I contend that they are not new but rather that there has been a change in the *form* of this "multiculturalism," which was disavowed (rather than nonexistent) in earlier (European) state formations. Anthony Giddens has argued that "globalization," observable in dynamics of "disembedding," which he defines as "the 'lifting out' of social relations from local contexts of interaction and their restructuring across infinite spans of time–space," extends back to the emergence of modernity (which he locates in seventeenth-century Europe).[36] If this is so, a case can be made that territorial borders may not be the best way to configure publics, calling into question not only Habermas's timeline of globalization, but also its space. When we consider the global exclusions from "publics" as well as "local" exclusions (as so many critics have already done), we open up an avenue for considering the complex relation between, say, an eighteenth-century bourgeois European woman relegated to the "private sphere" in France or England, and an African woman sold at "public auction" in the Caribbean of the same period, in ways that recognize that each of these women belongs to different "counter-public(s)" in relation to the states that sanctioned both slavery and the exclusion of women in general from the public sphere. Whereas the eighteenth-century bourgeois European woman is (now) recognized as historically constitutive of a valid "counter-public" in European states in a statist model, the African woman—since the slave is "outside" Europe—is not. Though abolitionism could be (was) part of public discourse and debate in Europe, the slaves themselves—always seemingly situated "elsewhere" in relation to the European states whose merchants benefited from the trade—were not part of a (recognized) "public" in Europe (in spite of the fact that the actions of European states surely impacted on their lives as much as on the life of any "citizen"). There are numerous current analogs of this earlier "disembedding" of social relations, from Third World workers employed by First World corporations to produce the commodities for First World shopping malls, to peoples displaced by wars waged in the interests of oil flows, the vast majority of which go to the First World.

One might object, of course, that, disembedding notwithstanding, modern publics *have*—not least in Third World independence movements—been defined in territorial statist terms. However, the independence movements operated under two assumptions that have not been realized: first, that the movements would result in actual independence (rather than neocolonial subjection) for the states so formed, and, second, that "development" would be possible after the withdrawal of the colonial overlords. But as Samir Amin, among others, has shown, not only do the vast majority of the former colonies continue in relations of dependence in the global economy, but the conditions of development that Europe enjoyed at an earlier time are simply not available to them at the current conjuncture.[37] Given these circumstances, global justice may call for a new understanding of "public spheres" as trans-statist, even though there are long-standing resistances to seeing extra-territorial publics as legitimate, and long-standing habits of legitimating this resistance.[38] An attempt to recognize the "space" of public spheres in terms of flows and disembedding rather than as segmented along state boundaries raises numerous practical questions which I will not be able to solve here. My task is a humbler one: of suggesting problems with the statist model of the public sphere, and tracing these problems to the emergence of "spaces of capital" in the early modern period. For at the very moment that disembedding intensifies in the sixteenth century, we can also detect an emphatic disavowal of its effects, a disavowal, it seems to me, that is continued in the statist model of the public sphere to this moment.

John Stow's *Survey of London* offers an especially attractive example to illustrate this process because it was novel in its moment of emergence and influential as a model of urban description well beyond that moment of emergence. By a particular meshing of a spatial and historical idiom in its content and form, Stow's *Survey* inaugurates a certain "vertical" way of seeing London which invents that city as a space unto itself, in which resident artisan-citizens are the real Londoners, defined by a close weaving of their subjectivities with the space–time of the city, to which the expansive spatial perspective of merchants (much less a perspective which sees the peoples linked by the flows of commodities, ideas, capital and so on to be *socially* interconnected) is alienating and transgressive. Stow's text reminds us that the difficulties of determining the spaces of capital pose challenges long before the emergence of the term "globalization," or the widespread alarm (or celebration) of its effects.[39] Indeed, read as a response to the spatial disruptions of capital, Stow's book on the one hand seems to provide a defensive gesture and make a claim on the space of the city "from below" by its inhabitants against any impositions "from above." On the other hand, however, the book seems to require a fantastical rewriting of the city as spontaneously self-generating in ways that would later be criticized by postcolonial critics in their assessment of cultural studies. By bringing this critique to Stow's *Survey*, I suggest that the sort of public space that it imagines ultimately renders elusive any quest for global social justice, although it is seemingly liberatory—even subversive—in "local" terms, much, I would further suggest, as Habermas's own model.

From this perspective, it is interesting that Stow treats London as a

New World in certain respects, though a New World emphatically populated by peoples with history.[40] By Stow's own account, the *Survey* provides a "*discovery* of London" (I.xcvii, emphasis added). Just over half of the *Survey*'s fifty-four chapters provide a general discussion of the city, including an account of its suburbs, its institutions (such as schools and hospitals), and its governmental structures; the other half of the book is devoted to describing in great detail, from the empirical perspective of an inhabitant walking down its streets, each of the extant London wards, and several of the neighboring areas, in Stow's time. "I will beginne," he announces, "at the East, and so proceede thorough the high and most principall streete of the cittie to the west" (I.117). As he wends his way down these streets, Stow continuously supplies evidence of a buried or otherwise immediately unavailable London. Drawing on his own memories, interviews, records, monuments, and even excavation, Stow locates extant sites of his London temporally as well as spatially: "what London hath been of auncient time men may here see," he assures his readers, "as what it is now every man doth behold" (I.xcviii). It is crucial to understand that, for Stow, these readers are assumed to be *resident* Londoners; he dedicates his book to the then Lord Mayor of London, Robert Lee, and the "comminalty, and Citizens of the same," and, in the course of his "survey," he often produces references to landmarks that presuppose familiarity with the city—indeed, that would be incomprehensible to outsiders (I.xcvii).[41] Why would such a text be necessary for people who already live in London and, thus, presumably, know their way around? To "discover" the city, according to Stow, it is not sufficient to examine the surface only; a proper survey involves a cataloguing of prior dispensations: hence, the horizontal movement of a walk is repeatedly interrupted and marked by the insertion of a "vertical" sounding, a pause and consideration of the genealogy of a particular site.

Nowhere is this "discovery" process more evident than in the *Survey*'s archaeological emphasis. In the course of the perambulations, wherever workmen are to be found digging foundations, or clay or anything else, Stow seems to contrive to be on the scene to see what they turn up. In his survey of Aldgate Warde, for example, he notes that when a certain spot was "digged deepe for Cellerage, there was found right under the sayd Bricke wall an other wall of stone, with a gate arched of stone, and Gates of Timber, to be closed in the midst towards the streete"(I.138). This "other wall" which lies beneath the wall contemporary with Stow and his fellow citizens is testimony to an "other" London, which Stow discusses here and elsewhere in some detail.

Several times he deploys this image of himself as researcher staring into the past from the side of an excavation. In Limestreete Warde he notes the finding of "a harth made of Britain, or rather Roman Tile, every Tile halfe yarde square," during the digging for a water pump. He emphasizes both in a marginal note and in the body of the text that "Cornhill street in some place [is] raysed two fadome higher then of alde time, as appeared by buildings found so deepe" (I.160). In another place, workers collecting clay for brick come across a burial ground, which Stow speculates, from the variety of remains he found there, was used both before and after Roman times. Stow once again places himself at the edge of the excavation and directs the workmen to have objects "reached up to mee" (I.170). Digging in Bredstreete Warde in 1595 revealed, he notes, "at fifteene foote deepe, a fayre pavement like unto that above ground" showing (once again) how much "the grounde of this Cittie in that place [had] beene raysed" (I.345). Likewise, in Farringdon Warde Without, Stow "observed, that when the laborers had broken up the pavement . . . and had digged foure foote deepe, they found one other pavement of hard stone, . . . under which they found in the made ground, pyles of Tymber, driven verie thicke" (II.43). In all of these cases, the text draws the reading subject to imagine London as extending deep into the soil, out of which both he and the current city seem to emerge as present instantiations of an accumulated past.

Most important, in the course of the survey the time of the city and of its citizens become entangled. For example, in Portsoken Ward Stow comes upon the site of one of the numerous suppressed religious houses he mentions in his tour of the city and observes: "Neare adioyning to this Abbey on the South side thereof, was sometime a Farme belonging to the said Nunrie, at the which Farme I my selfe in my youth have fetched many a halfe pennie worth of Milke . . ." (I. 126). His musings on rising prices, altered land-use, and changing customs signal the passing of time and its imbrication of the city and its subjects. Elsewhere he recalls—also in first-person eyewitness accounts—the free-ranging pigs in a marketplace, the former disposition of numerous buildings, the encroachment on his father's garden by a powerful neighbor, and so forth. These are more than charming details (though, of course, they are that and are often noted as such); they additionally signal a paradigm shift in the public representation of the relation of subjects to cities. For Stow, the city's display of its own past, when articulated with the memories of inhabitants, renders the city a temporality in which city dwellers live together—it "spaces" time.

This shared memory-space, I would suggest, enables a *localized* "public" to emerge out of a necessarily territorially ambiguous urban space, made up of a population "freed" from personal service to a lord and attachment to land, or even (though this took longer) guilds. London becomes the city of these unattached persons by way of a certain spatialization of time, in which biography and urbography are intertwined. It provides an attachment lost to peoples for whom the "personal" (which is not to say idyllic!) bonds of feudalism have been severed, and whose spaces are now shot through with ever-increasing pressures from elsewhere via market and other circulations.

Stow generalizes the process of meshing biography and urbography through rhetorical strategies that draw his readers into a certain relation to the spaces he describes. In his description of Aldgate he notes: "the principall street of this warde beginneth at Aldgate, stretching west to some time a fayre Well, where now a pumpe is placed . . . then have ye the Bricklayers Hall and an other Alley called Sprinkle Alley, now made Sugar-loafe Alley" (I.138). It is in the small details such as these even more than in the dramatic post-Reformation shifts the *Survey* describes that we can see the space and time of his extremely localized urban subject emerging. The very casualness of the observations and their banality (in the seventeenth century Thomas Fuller described them as "trifles") renders the *Survey* notable in the history of memorialization.[42] It matters that the well was there, or Sprinkle Alley, not because some remarkable event occurred there, but precisely *because* none did. This is not the itinerary of great acts and great men, but of tiny changes; the stuff of the everyday life of the bricklayers, for example, on the way to their Hall. The well to pump, or Sprinkle to Sugar Loaf, change is significant because it is part of the way in which the lives of the people who pass by it are calibrated, and their identities are formed, which the very form of Stow's text enacts as if in process at the moment of reading, as he draws his readers into the perambulation along with his persona by way of intimating rhetorical ploys such as: "then come you to the Papey" (I.146) or "let us returne to the South side of Cheape Warde" (I.268). The well and the pump matter officially in Stow's book because, in a new sense, the people who are called upon to remember them do. This localized subject can secure "London," and be secured as a Londoner, even in the face of the rapid change and continuous influx and outflow that characterized the living city.

The medieval sources Stow so copiously consults and cites do not engage in this detailed foregrounding of the relation between city and the psyche, history and "personal" memory. Indeed, even though one of the principal sources for Stow's *Survey*, William FitzStephen's twelfth-century *Descriptio*, announces in its preface that FitzStephen saw London "with [his] own eyes," the style of the ensuing description is very different, in no way weaving biography with the fabric of the city.[43] Hence, while many commentators have taken Stow's nostalgia as evidence of his "traditional" sensibilities, it is actually better seen as strikingly modern in its *form*.[44] As the urban theorist Elizabeth Wilson has observed:

> [the] changing nature of cities gives urban dwellers a sense of time that is linear instead of cyclical. "Oh, yes, that's where the old cinema used to be," we say, or "do you remember, that's where those houses were all squatted, before they were pulled down," or sometimes—but less often—"it's wonderful, since they've smartened it up, with that new restaurant looking over the river." Less often, because the urban sense of time and decay is a nostalgic one, and reminds us of our own lives unreeling out behind us like cigarette smoke.[45]

Perhaps no one captured this "modern nostalgia" better than Walter Benjamin, who "played with the idea of setting out the sphere of life—bios—graphically on a map" and recognized, furthermore, that such a map would need to represent depth as well as surface since "he who seeks to approach his own buried past must conduct himself like a man digging." Just so Stow finds his childhood amid the ruins of decayed abbeys and abandoned wells.[46]

The *Survey* encourages a reader's spatial imagination along these lines not only in its preoccupation with excavation and Stow's childhood memories, but in numerous other ways as well. For example, Stow is obsessed with cataloguing grave markers, tracking back the dead for generations, attempting to assure their place in historical memory before weather or the activities of "bad and greedy men of spoyle" can destroy them (I.208). Every churchyard offers him the opportunity to produce an extended list of "monuments" in chronological order. He concerns himself constantly about what has been "discontinued, and therefore forgotten" (I.150) or "grown out of knowledge" (I.151). Indeed, so characteristic of Stow's text is his attention to producing verbal monuments to the outmoded, destroyed or abandoned that in 1662 Thomas Fuller observed that "the citizens of London have erected many fair monuments to perpetuate their memories, but still there wanted a monument to continue the memory of their monuments (subject by time, and otherwise to be defaced) which at last by John Stow was industriously performed."[47] Fuller's observation is especially apt because for Stow, monuments are not restricted to churches and graveyards, but can be discovered anywhere; the whole city becomes to him a monument of its (*and* his) own past; thus Stow details the history of various buildings and sites, explaining as he passes by not just what they now are, but what they used to be. Throughout, the reading subject's relation to the "living" city is continuously mediated by references to this past, which are presented in such a way that the experience of them is seemingly concrete and direct because they are located in buildings and on streets, in the present tense, that the reader contemporary with Stow may well have passed by every day. Stow's emphasis on burial markers, buried London, and "how greatly the ground . . . hath been raysed" draws attention not only to the journey downward required to view it, and the exhumation required to give it continued life, but also to the concrete sites it inhabits with its living population. At the same time, however, it distracts that population's attention from lateral pulls to and from the city: flows of population, commodities, services, knowledges and cultural forms, without which "London" would have ceased to exist as such. These various flows suggest other claims on the "public" space of the city which its territorial integrity attempts to deny.

Indeed, the emphases of Stow's *Survey* again and again locate the forces pertinent to the formation of London as intensely localized: indigenous and self-sustaining. For example, in the course of Stow's perambulation of Queene Hithe Warde he observes: "On the west side of this old Fishstreete hill, is the Bishoppe of Herefordes Inne or lodging, an auncient house and large roomes builded of stone and timber which sometime belonged to the Mounthauntes in Norfolke." After continuing to outline the building's prestigious former inhabitants, Stow notes "the same is greatly ruinated, and is now divided into many small tenementes: the Hall and principall rooms are an house to make Sugar loaves" (II.4). Although in other hands the fate of this house might have become part of a story about the advance of an international industry, for Stow what matters about it—as is typical—is *not* its connection to a global sugar market (sugar not usually being an indigenous commodity), but rather its lineage of inhabitants and uses, a "downward" rather than an "outward" movement: "Radulphus de Maydenstone Bishoppe of Hereford, about 1234 bought it of the Mounthauntes, and gave it to the Bishoppes of Hereford, his successors. *Charles Booth*, Bishoppe of Hereforde and Chauncellour of the Marches, about the year 1517 repayered it, since the which time, the same is greatly ruinated . . ." (II.4). Such a gesture links the identity of contemporary London more immediately with—and against—"its" historical precursors than with and against its geographical coevals, and makes the growth of London appear to be an effect of degeneration from, or improvement upon, this situated past, rather than the tangled web of a globally dispersed present.

The downward, anchoring pull of the past seems all the more powerful in the *Survey* because the text establishes the ostensible bounds of the city so emphatically and meticulously. The description of every ward begins—following a (usually brief) etymological discussion of the ward's name—with a careful tracing of its "bounds." For example, here is part of the opening of the section on "Cheape Warde":

> Next adioyning [Cordwainer Street Ward] is Cheape Warde, and taketh name of the Market there kept, called West Cheping, this warde also beginneth in the East, on the course of Walbrooke, in Buckles Bury, and runneth up on both the sides to the great Conduit in Cheape. Also on the south side of Buckles Berie, a lane turning up by S. Sithes Church, and by S. Pancrates church through Needlers lane, on the north side thereof, and then through a peece of Sopars lane, on both sides uppe to Chepe, be all of Chepe ward. (I.258–9)

Stow goes on to describe the bounds on each compass point in the same detail for this ward, and, in turn, for each of the other wards, so that London seems like nothing so much as a set of boxes set next to each other, each filled, of course, with many noteworthy things which Stow undertakes to explore, all the while remaining within the bounds he so carefully establishes as if—to indulge in a not entirely, or at least not simply, anachronistic metaphor—he were a proto-anthropologist carefully laying out a grid with string.

The ideological work performed by Stow's particular approach to the survey of the city becomes evident when we contrast it with other ways of imagining urban space. For other observers "London's" boundaries were not so very easy—or so desirable—to define. Difficulties with bounding London arise not only because of increases in population in the suburbs, which kept extending the effective reach of the city (a phenomenon which Stow does, grumblingly, acknowledge), but also from the fact (un-noted by Stow) that, as John Lyly put it in 1589, "traffike and travell hath woven the nature of all Nations into ours."[48] Along the same lines a bit later, Henry Fitzgeffrey would satirize the importation of fashion trends from overseas with this recital of the geography of a dandy's outfit:

In Turkie colours carved to the skin,
Mounted Pelonianly untill hee reeles,
That scorns (so much) plaine dealing at his heeles,
His Boote speaks Spanish to his Scottish Spurres,
His Sute cut Frenchly, round bestucke with Burres.
Pure Holland is his shirt, which proudly faire,
Seems to out-face his Doublet everywhere:
His Haire like to your Moor's or Irish Lockes,
His chiefest Dyet Indian minced Dockes.[49]

Thomas Dekker and other ostensible explorers of early modern London's "underworld" typically compared the so-called rogues they described to an alien population, with their own customs, languages and social (dis)order.[50] The "peddler's French" spoken in this other London thus requires wordbooks, similar to those published to acquaint the curious with the speech of New World natives and other so-called "outlandish" people. The nicknames accorded to the areas of the city that underworld figures inhabit ("the Straits" and the "Bermudas," for example, in Ben Jonson's *Bartholomew Fair*) emphasize the "alienness" that infiltrates the very heart of the city, and remind us that the much-critiqued "local" exclusions of the emergent public sphere (along class and gender lines most notably) were bound up with "global" exclusions as well, which become evident only when we take into consideration *all* the peoples impacted by the activities of the early modern states as they traded, fought, and colonized.[51] Stow's focus on a vertical grounding of the city, then, can be seen as at the same time a disavowal of all the many forces tending to subvert the space of London—leading to its imagining as a process of weaving rather than a pure product of (spatially enclosed) time, intact and pure—and a graft of cuttings from numerous "nations" (in the broad understanding of that term) rather than a plant grown from easily identifiable and fully indigenous roots.

Merchants of necessity have a very different view of the city from the one presented in Stow's text—expansive rather than contractive, horizontal rather than vertical. Giovanni Arrighi, following Fernand Braudel, describes the merchant and banking groups of the Renaissance as "cosmopolitan nations"—which is to say detached/detachable from any given territory, though of course capable of making "alliances" with territorial states to achieve short- or long-term interests.[52] The extent to which this was the case is evident from the different emphasis of the texts directed specifically to those merchant elites. Unlike the *Survey*, the maps and views of London that Stow might have seen as he was writing his book, such as the one collected in Braun and Hogenberg (1572) or Wyngaerde's panorama (1543), often are drawn in such a way as to make the Thames appear especially large and imposing; they take pains to fill the river with ships, emphasizing its status as a rising entrepôt, and thus its interconnections with a broader world via trade routes, as do many of the earlier prose (and continental) descriptions. Indeed, a set of directions given by the elder Hakluyt to the Muscovy Company in 1580 emphasizes this aspect of maps: "Take with you the . . . large map of London to make show of your city. And let the river be drawn full of ships of all sorts, to make the more show of your great trade and traffic of merchandise."[53] Lawrence Manley's overview of the "new [urban] topography" of the Renaissance notes that "these works reflect a widespread tendency to organize the world as a transnational grid of urban communities."[54] Accordingly, Braun and Hogenberg's *Civitates Orbis Terrarum* describes London as "a vast commercial town . . . [in which] there is wonderful wealth and abundance of all things and merchandise, which are conveyed here by the River Thames from the whole world." Against such views of London, Stow's localizing emphasis, I have been suggesting, is not accidental, but along with the *Survey*'s formal elements helps to establish a London that seems primarily to give birth to itself, rather than relying on its (irreducible) relations with the rest of "England" and the world in which it is situated and in which it participates.

From the merchant point of view, however, London was, primarily, a *port* city, ruled from the late medieval period largely by a mercantile elite drawn at first from the wool trade with continental Europe, and later from a merchant group with a more diversified commodity portfolio.[55] For these ruling elites, maintaining their position "in" London was crucial, of course, but they did so by initiating and maintaining relations with trading centers elsewhere, extending the reach of the city far beyond its walls. Stow's lifetime spanned a period in which there were significant changes in the bases of operations of major merchant groups. On the one hand "alien" merchants were being displaced by English merchants, who meanwhile were allying themselves more directly and explicitly than ever before with the aristocracy and gentry in England via the new joint stock companies, and were also more likely than ever before to take on a proto-nationalistic discourse, as well as statist claims about their benefit to the realm. Thomas Gresham, for example, merchant and founder of the Royal Exchange, was based in Antwerp until competition among the international merchant groups there, and unrest in that part of the world, made that impossible. Only then did Gresham turn his sights to London, and the building of an alternative bourse. It is important to recall, however, that the scope of Gresham's spatial imagination was by no means altered by this movement from Antwerp to London, though his base of operations was. In Stow's discussion of Gresham's Exchange, however, the only spatial disruption emphasized by him—quite properly given Stow's interests—is a purely local one. He simply notes that the Exchange is "a place for marchants to assemble in," and then spends the two paragraphs devoted to this site in pointing out the considerable destruction of households necessary to build it, and tracing out the trajectory of the progress the Queen made into the city to (re)name it the Royal Exchange (I.192–3). Stow spends over four times as much space discussing the parish church of St Peter's in the same ward (Cornhill), and almost as much discussing the possibility that the devil himself left scratch marks in the stone of its steeple. For Stow, apparently, the Exchange is not where "London" is to be found. For London, Stow looks downward, not to links established beyond the seas.

One way of dealing with the resultant anxiety at the reality of a syncretic London is to attempt to purify the space by defining undesired elements as clearly alien, even if inextricable, as the following passage from a seventeenth-century pamphlet indicates emphatically:

> we have derived to ourselves, with our commerce with foreign Nations, with their wares and commodities, their vices and eveill conditions; as our drunkenness and rudeness from the Germans; our fashions and factions from the French; our insolence from the Spaniards; our Machiavelianism from the Italians; our levity and inconstancie from the Greekes; our usury and extortion from the Jew; our atheism and impiety from the Turks and Moors; and our voluptuousness and luxury from the Persians and Indians.[56]

To trade, of course, means to introduce the "alien" into the local system. As Donald Lupton observes in his "character" of a merchant in 1632: "they are strange politicians, for they bring Turkey and Spaine into London, and carry London thither." Lupton suggests here something of the ambivalence of general attitudes toward merchants, who could consort blithely even with England's worst enemies in the interests of trade, and operated according to a different logic than "politicians" (which is not to say that they would not attempt to manipulate or take advantage of political situations whenever possible).[57] Early modern cultures, as our own, engaged in numerous processes of exchange and circulation in addition to formal trade:

cultural forms, mercenaries, embassies, information, royal spouses, travelers, news, inventions, plants, and so on also all crossed borders; that the material effects of such a process are displaced onto an allegory of moral corruption here should not lead us to ignore the actual intimate entanglements of so-called independent states.

England, for example, imported knowledge of fine clothworking from Italy as well as political theory; religious doctrine came from Germany, with or without "rudeness." Even a book such as Joan Thirsk's *Economic Policy and Projects*, which is anxious to distinguish the specificity of the so-called English "home market" in the early modern period, mentions numerous instances in which that home market depended upon exorbitant knowledges and supplies, such as the importation of "Spanish" feltmaking methods, woad for dye from Portuguese colonies, and wire for pinmaking from the continent.[58] We need to explore these experiences of so-called "corruption" for what they might tell us about the disavowed syncretic formation of the European cultures that supposedly later imposed their pure selves on the rest of the world, and transcoded all manner of local social unrest into vilification of aliens, for which the English were so well known.

Examining, alternatively, the very linkages and alliances unremarked by Stow, Eric Wolf has been prompted to ask the still highly pertinent question: "if there are connections everywhere, why do we persist in turning dynamic, interconnected phenomena [such as 'nation,' 'society,' and 'culture'] into static disconnected things?"[59] In Stow's case, the social rationale for presenting the space of London as he does can be seen as the potentially subversive one of asserting the significance of the ordinary householder over the wealthier and more powerful, albeit smaller, merchant group. Even the way Stow chooses to bring mercantile concerns into the text places them in the space–time of the householder as he is defining it, rather than in terms of the more expansive geo-graphy that the merchant's activity required. Stow repeatedly refers to houses in fashionable areas as having "inhabitants for the most part rich marchantes, and other wealthy Cittizens" (I.211), but he provides almost no detail about the activity through which that wealth was acquired. What attention he does give to discussion of trade is virtually all relegated to the past, much of it following a formula that might be called the domestic displacement of the "forren." He narrates in excruciating detail a distant history of civic extortion from Jews, along with outright confiscation of property and money among other abuses, in addition to a more recent history of riots against, and expulsions of, other resident aliens.[60] For example, when Stow discusses the "Steleyard" in Downegate Warde, he first describes it as "a place for marchants of Almaine, that used to bring hither, as well Wheat, Rie, and other graine, as Cables, Ropes, Masts, Pitch, Tar . . ." —significantly, ship building materials, though Stow makes nothing of this (I.232). After continuing in this vein for over two pages (which pay particular attention to disputes between the local merchants and those from "beyond seas") the account ends abruptly: "In the yere 1551 . . . through complaint of the English marchants, the libertie of the Stilliard Marchants was seised into the kings hands, and so it resteth" (I.234). The merchants from "beyond seas" are thus replaced with "English marchants" (who seem to stay home!). By concentrating on such "localizing" forces, and also by speaking more about trade in the past than in the present, Stow reinforces a sense of the borders of London as intact, and all its fruitful activity as internal to it. This view, of course, is a fiction made possible only by a disavowal not only of the actual history of merchant activity in London, in which "alien" influence had been significant, but also—in the moment of Stow's writing—of what merchants actually do.

It is a fiction whose implications we have to take seriously, because Stow's *Survey* somehow managed to speak to the concerns of a considerable number of contemporaries and successors. Not only did Stow produce two editions of the *Survey* in his lifetime, but between his death in 1605 and the mid-eighteenth century, five additional editions were published, each larger than the last, and a number of spin-off volumes appeared as well, with titles like *Londonopolis* and *Present London, OR Memorials.*[61] All of these texts made much of their continuation of Stow's "method" as they meticulously tracked down burial markers, noted tiny changes in the topography of the city, chronicled changing uses of its space, collected documents and consulted records. In one respect, however, John Strype's 1720 *Survey* deviates dramatically from Stow's practice, and signals an alternative understanding of the city's formation and identity even from within the tradition of Stow's *Survey*. In a chapter devoted to the merchant companies (for which there is no analog in the 1603 Stow), Strype insists that mercantile activity is "that which makes London to be London."[62] Unlike Stow, who situates present "London" virtually entirely in relation to "its" own past, Strype—at least in this chapter—suggests that contemporary London is an effect of *horizontal* relations, which can by no means be restricted to the enclosures of the juridico-political boundaries of the city's wards, however elaborately underwritten by a historical narrative. In the years intervening between Stow and Strype, what had happened?

The London of the eighteenth century is, of course, a very different place from the London of 1603, and this in part, at least, perhaps accounts for Strype's different emphasis. Christopher Hill captures the drama of the changes nicely:

> The England of 1603 was a second-class power; the Great Britain of 1714 was the greatest world power. Under James and Charles English colonisation of America was just beginning; under Anne England held a large empire in America, Asia, and Africa, and the colonial questions were decisive when policy was formulated. The East India company was formed in 1601; a century later it was the most powerful corporation in the country. At the beginning of our period men noted as evidence of the topsy-turviness of the times that some merchants were as rich as peers; before the end, many a noble family had salvaged its fortunes by a judicious marriage in the City.[63]

Hill concludes his observations: "the transformation that took place in the seventeenth century is then far more than merely a constitutional or political revolution, or a revolution in economics, religion, or taste. It embraces the whole of life." He might have added—as C.L.R. James would later instruct Raymond Williams—that this "whole of life" is "international," as well as local.[64] Even in Hill's account the nation-state unit triumphs over the international conditions of its emergence and existence. It is a testimony to the success of texts such as Stow's that the ideology of the nation-state as a unit could be taken for granted within a century, even in the face of numerous, empirically observed, counterforces. Stow himself cannot take this space for granted: he must produce it. For what had *not* yet happened by 1603 was a secure ascendancy of England as a mercantile power, through which the identity of itself and its capital could be affirmed. By 1720, not only had such ascendancy been achieved, but the ideological work of the spatial perspective inculcated by Stow's text had already been successfully performed, so that Strype can both assume that "trade maketh London to be London" *and* that there is a local indigenous "London" which is always already there; Strype discovers it in Stow's text and continues it himself by perambulating the wards just as Stow had done before him. In Stow's time, "London" was less secure in its global identity, and so Stow shores up a local identity. Rather than a merchant's epic, Stow writes a citizen's encomium and weaves the urban walker into the fabric of the city's "vertical" space and time as he imagines it. This "vertical" London anchors the "space" in which a "public sphere" can emerge; in the sixteenth century, it literally had to be invented. At a moment of flux in the merchant groups and

London's place in their spatial politics, Stow brackets this activity and turns his attention to a group whose immediate concerns were seemingly far more localized—artisans—and connects them to the minutiae of the city's space. What he did not take into account is how capital dislocates even contiguous peoples, things, institutions, social practices and cultural forms. In such a context, what Stow's text and others like it manage to do in their particular "invention" of London, however, is to open up a space for a bourgeois public to define themselves within; in the process Stow excludes any possible claims to that "space" that could be made by "outsiders."

This is a remarkable feat, since even at the end of Elizabeth's reign London was already far from an island. Joint stock had already been sold for the Senegal Adventurers, the Russia Company, the Levant Company, the East India Company, among others—and these were simply the upstart crows in a mercantile community long dominated by regulated companies such as the Merchant Adventurers. Among Stow's acquaintances were men who followed these developments closely, along with the early forays into the New World, the circumnavigation of the globe and the colonial resettlement of Ireland: Walter Cope, John Dee and, of course, Richard Hakluyt who by 1603 had already published two editions of the massive collection of travel narratives that Richard Helgerson has described as a merchant epic.[65] Most important, however, Stow, who was trained as a tailor and practiced that art for some time, could hardly have managed to be unacquainted with the impact of the cloth trade on London. During Stow's lifetime, the victualling companies excepted, the cloth-related companies had more members than all other companies combined.[66] The vicissitudes of the cloth market in the sixteenth century had a profound impact on levels of employment and wealth in the city, even with all its diversity of trades, and in turn directed the fate of a network of workers in the countryside.

For those of us interested in teasing out the vast network of incipient capitalism of which London was an effect as much as a cause, it is perhaps more helpful to see "London" as a set of flows and relations—de- and re-territorializations—rather than as an intact topography as Stow attempts to do, and to recall that the space of a "public sphere" can be imagined horizontally as well as vertically. Stow depicts London as "historically" grounded in an attempt to shore up its boundaries at a time when market forces, and other circulations, undermined all possibility of the closure necessary to such ostensible autonomy. The legacy of racialism that attends such bids for purity and enclosure is one of the crucial lessons of recent work in cultural studies such as Paul Gilroy's *Black Atlantic*. Its counter-narrative bids us remember that texts like Stow's, whatever else they may do, help make possible the myth of the territorially intact and pure London—and England—which will inform history, theory and politics for generations to come.[67] Stow's "vertical" anchoring of London helps disavow recognition of the full range of forces on which local "London" relies to be "itself." As a result, Londoners can later cast a (mapping) colonial gaze from their ostensibly pure "countrey" onto numerous distant colonial others, whose own local itineraries go untold by Stow's spatial stories, and whose peoples are never accounted among the constituencies of the states that they have literally helped to build from the "outside."

For this reason, I have my doubts that a critique of the "nation" alone can provide a space in which global inequalities can be addressed—and historical wrongs redressed—adequately. Territorial states must be interrogated as well as "nations," and "publics" must be recognized across state boundaries rather than simply within them. Only in this way can an effective counterforce "from below" to the gaze of global capital "from above" be produced.[68] The historical force of "disembedding" in the development of the modern world argues in favor of a different space of political action than the nation-state provides. If the "Negroes, Arabs, Indians, and the yellow races" on whose behalf Fanon spoke in the passage from *The Wretched of the Earth* I cited earlier are ever to have their share of the "progress of Europe [they] have helped to build up," public spheres must be rethought to include them as part of the counter-publics of that "Europe" (and the rest of the most wealthy and powerful states). Territorial state forms inhibit such possibilities. To give rise to another, more just world, we need, then, to recognize the deceptive certitude of "vertical" localities championed by Stow and his successors, and attempt to see other spaces, and the multiple publics that produce them.

Notes

1. This title emerged at the intersection of insights gleaned from my reading of three books: V. Y. Mudimbe, *The Invention of Africa* (Bloomington: Indiana University Press, 1988), Jose Rabasa, *Inventing A-M-E-R-I-C-A* (Norman: University of Oklahoma Press, 1993) and Eric Hobsbawm and Terence Ranger (eds) *The Invention of Tradition* (Cambridge: Cambridge University Press, 1983). The former two books emphasize the constitutive character of European fantasies of Africa and the "New World" and the work of cultural forms such as atlases, travel narratives and scholarship in underwriting an enduring Eurocentrism. Contributors to *The Invention of Tradition* consider the reliance of nation-building on a "tradition"—constructed rather than simply discovered—in both European

and non-European instances. All three books suggest, as I do here, that geography—as the word itself implies—is an effect of a scripting, a world-writing, which situates subjects in particular ways in (historicized) space and time in order to produce nation-effects (among other things).

2. Jürgen Habermas, *The Structural Transformation of the Public Sphere*, trans. Thomas Burger (Cambridge, MA: MIT Press, 1991), p. 25.

3. Jürgen Habermas, "Concluding Remarks," in *Habermas and the Public Sphere*, ed. Craig Calhoun (Cambridge, MA: MIT Press, 1992), p. 466. The above cited list follows Habermas's admission that: "Empirically, [he had] learned most from the criticisms that point to the exclusionary mechanisms of the public sphere, liberal or post-liberal."

4. Ibid., p. 467.

5. See, for example, Joan Landes, *Women and the Public Sphere in the Age of the French Revolution*, (Ithaca: Cornell University Press, 1988); also "The Public and the Private Sphere," *Feminists Read Habermas*, ed. Johanna Meehan (New York: Routledge, 1995); Mary Ryan, "Gender and Public Access: Women's Politics in Nineteenth Century America" and Geoff Eley, "Nations, Publics, and Political Cultures: Placing Habermas in the Nineteenth Century," *Habermas and the Public Sphere*.

6. Many recent postcolonial critics have taken Williams and early cultural studies in Britain to task along the lines of its implicit ethnocentrism. See, for example, Gauri Vishwanathan, "Raymond Williams and British Colonialism," *Yale Journal of Criticism*, vol. 4, no. 2, 1990–1; also Edward Said's *Culture and Imperialism* (New York: Alfred A. Knopf, 1993), p. 65, which remarks with surprise that Williams pays no attention to imperialism whatsoever in *Culture and Society*; a measured evaluation of Williams's work, examining both its great contributions and its deficits and problematic silences and assumptions— especially those which tend to foster ethnocentrism—appears in Stuart Hall, "Communities, Nation and Culture," *Cultural Studies*, vol. 7, no. 3, 1993. On the whole, it seems to me that Williams has been unfairly scapegoated in the broad critique of British cultural studies, although there are certainly problems with his own formulations of "the nation" in the early work, and in British cultural studies in general on this score. A critique of "British" cultural studies in general has been launched by critics who see it as having assumed a "universalism" of (its own) "culture" (as had imperialism), where none pertains. See, for example, the essays collected in *Relocating Cultural Studies*, eds. Valda Blundell, John Shepherd and Ian Taylor (New York: Routledge, 1993).

7. See C. L. R. James "Marxism and the Intellectuals" in *Spheres of Existence* (Westport: Lawrence Hill & Co., 1980), p. 119.

8. "Williams . . . minimizes the specificities of nationalism and ideologies of national identity and diverts attention from analysis of the political processes by which national and social identities have been aligned. . . . Where racism demands repatriation and pivots on the exclusion of certain groups from the imagined community of the nation, the contradictions around citizenship that Williams dismisses as 'alienated superficialities' remain important constituents of the political field." See Paul Gilroy, *There Ain't No Black in the Union Jack* (Chicago: University of Chicago Press, 1991), p. 50.

9. See Paul Gilroy, *The Black Atlantic* (Cambridge: Harvard University Press, 1993), p. 14.

10. Ibid., p. 11.

11. Frantz Fanon, *The Wretched of the Earth*, trans. Constance Farrington (New York: Grove Press, 1963), p. 96. Eric Williams's *Capitalism and Slavery* (Chapel Hill: University of North Carolina Press, 1944) provides perhaps the strongest account of the formative relation of the slave trade to the industrial revolution in Europe. For a defense of Williams's much-disputed thesis, and a case for the dependence of capitalist ascendancy in Europe on colonialism and the slave trade, see J.M. Blaut, *The Colonizer's Model of the World* (New York: Guilford Press, 1993), pp. 203–6, and also J. M. Blaut, "Colonialism and the Rise of Capitalism," *Science and Society*, 53, 1989, pp. 260–96.

12. See the first sentence of this chapter; the "public," for Habermas, are those people with a stake in coming together to compel "public authority" to heed its opinion. Seeing such publics as limited by state boundaries truncates ahead of time (improperly)

the question of stake, as well as the variety (geographical as well as in interest) of participants.

13. A suggestion made briefly in Homi Bhabha's "DissemiNation," in *Nation and Narration* (New York: Routledge, 1990), p. 304: "The people as a form of address emerge from the abyss of enunciation where the subject splits, the signifier 'fades,' the pedagogical [historical sedimentation] and the performative [cultural identification] are agonistically articulated. The language of national collectivity and cohesiveness is now at stake. Neither can cultural homogeneity, or the nation's horizontal space be authoritively represented within the familiar territory of the *public sphere*. Social causality cannot be adequately understood as a deterministic or overdetermined effect of a 'statist' centre; nor can the rationality of political choice be divided between the polar realms of the private and the public."

14. Jürgen Habermas, *The Inclusion of the Other*, eds. Ciaran Cronin and Pablo De Greiff (Cambridge: MIT Press, 1998).

15. Habermas, *Structural Transformation*, pp. 85, 86. It should be noted that Habermas does, of course, see that in actual practice various groups were indeed excluded from the *bourgeois* public sphere by the vested interests of elites, however fervently they advocated theoretical principles of universalism, and he later also concedes that the exclusion of women before the twentieth century appears to be a somewhat different matter (as feminists have argued) than that of men, since "unlike the exclusion of underprivileged men, the exclusion of women had structuring significance." That is to say, by forming a (male) public against the (feminized) household, or private sphere, women were permanently excluded *by definition* from "the public" in a way that men, who, at least in principle (however rarely in practice), could attain the property and educational requirements for entry, were not. Habermas goes on to suggest, however, that women's agitation for entry into the public nevertheless participates in the very public discourse from which they were ostensibly excluded, preserving the general model of the public sphere, despite the limitation of the bourgeois model, because it contains within itself a capacity for "self-transformation." (Jürgen Habermas, "Further Reflections on the Public Sphere," in *Habermas and the Public Sphere*, pp. 428, 429.) As for Ben Anderson, he argues that all nations "imagine" themselves as "limited"—which is to say "no nation imagines itself as coterminous with mankind." See *Imagined Communities* (revised edition, New York: Verso, 1991), p. 7. Gilroy has vehemently disputed Anderson's claim that this "imagining" is predicated on "print culture" rather than notions of "biology," noting that "Anderson's theory claims that racism is essentially antithetical to nationalism because nations are made possible in and through print languages rather than notions of biological difference and kinship. Thus, he argues that anyone can in theory learn the language of the nation they seek to join and through the process of naturalization become a citizen enjoying the formal equality under its laws. Whatever objections can be made to Anderson's general argument, his privileging of the written word over the spoken word for example, it simply does not apply in the English/British case. The politics of 'race' in this country is fired by conceptions of national belonging and homogeneity which not only blur the distinction between 'race' and nation, but rely on that very ambiguity for their effect." (*There Ain't No Black*, pp. 44–5). Gilroy's critique has implications, I would suggest, for Habermas's model as well, which is both language- and state-based.

16. Habermas, *Inclusion*, p. 161.

17. Ibid., p. 159.

18. Habermas asserts that "citizens must be able to experience the fair value of their rights also in the form of social security and the reciprocal recognition of different cultural forms of life," even if states must be compelled to go along, and at the same time wonders "whether democratic opinion and will formation could ever achieve a binding force that extends beyond the level of the nation-state." Ibid., p. 119, 127.

19. Jürgen Habermas, "Struggles for Recognition in the Democratic Constitutional State," in *Inclusion*, pp. 203–36.

20. Habermas, *Inclusion*, p. 187.

21. Henri Lefebvre, *The Production of Space*, trans. Donald Nicholson-Smith (originally published in French, 1974; Oxford: Blackwell, 1991).

22. David Harvey, *Justice, Nature and the Geography of Difference* (Cambridge: Blackwell, 1996), especially Chapter 13.

23. Manuel Castells, "High Technology, Economic Restructuring, and the Urban–Regional Process in the United States," in *High Technology, Space and Society* (Beverly Hills: Sage, 1985), p. 33. See also Arjun Appadurai, "Disjuncture and Difference in the Global Cultural Economy," in *Modernity at Large* (Minneapolis: University of Minnesota Press, 1996), pp. 27–65.

24. Eley, "Nations," p. 305.

25. Ibid.

26. For a critique of "diffusionist" views of this kind, see Blaut, *The Colonizer's Model*.

27. Nancy Fraser, "Rethinking the Public Sphere: A Contribution to the Critique of Actually Existing Democracy," in *The Phantom Public Sphere*, ed. Bruce Robbins (Minneapolis: University of Minnesota Press, 1993), p. 14: "I contend that, in stratified societies, arrangements that accommodate contestation among a plurality of competing publics better promote the ideal of participatory parity than does a single, comprehensive, overarching public sphere." In the model I am proposing, "world" would be inserted in the place of "societies." Fraser goes on to argue that a "multiple public" arrangement would be preferable even in *non*-stratified "societies" (pp. 16–18).

28. As Fraser puts it: "In stratified societies, subaltern counter-publics have a dual character. On the one hand, they function as spaces of withdrawal and regroupment; on the other hand, they also function as bases and training grounds for agitational activities directed toward wider publics. It is precisely in the dialectic between these two functions that their emancipatory potential resides. This dialectic enables subaltern counterpublics partially to offset, although not wholly to eradicate, the unjust participatory privileges enjoyed by members of dominant social groups in stratified societies." Ibid., p. 15. Earlier, Oskar Negt and Alexander Kluge, too, had proposed the necessity of conceptualizing the proletariat, at least, as a "counter-public," exerting pressures on the bourgeois ("illusory") public sphere which would have to be entirely remade to forge a just society. See their *Public Sphere and Experience*, trans. Peter Labanyi *et al.* (first published in German in 1973; Minneapolis: University of Minnesota Press, 1993), especially p. 79.

29. For an opposing view, see Martin Kohler, "From the National to the Cosmopolitan Public Sphere," *Re-imagining Political Community: Studies in Cosmopolitan Democracy*, eds. Daniele Archibugi, David Held, and Martin Kohler (Cambridge: Polity, 1998).

30. It should be noted that Habermas seems to rely on a "trade" in generated transition to capitalism—a contention which is much disputed. I am more sympathetic to the "trade"/colonialism models myself (which have also been important to World Systems theory and various other Unequal Development theories, and at least take into account the formative force of "external" pressures) than to "internal" development models—though not quite in the ways that they are ordinarily presented (as the argument in this chapter should make clear). For an overview of the theories and debates, see *The Brenner Debate*, eds. T.H. Aston and C.H.E. Philpin (Cambridge, 1985); Blaut, "Colonialism and the Rise of Capitalism"; and also Jorge Larrain, *Theories of Development* (Cambridge: Blackwell, 1989). It should also be noted that Robert Brenner's most recent work seems to accord more determinant force to trade than his earlier work; see his *Merchants and Revolution* (Princeton: Princeton University Press, 1993).

31. For example, tracts were produced with titles such as "The National Merchant" in the England of the eighteenth century, implying of course that merchants were not necessarily "national" in their interests or activities, and that, as one such text argues, it was therefore crucial to take action to "unit[e] the national and mercatorial interests." See John Bennet, *The National Merchant* (London, 1736).

32. Habermas, *Structural Transformation*, p. 17.

33. Ibid. p. 15.

34. My project has its origins in a question posed by Bruce Robbins in his "Introduction" to *The Phantom Public Sphere*, p. xxiii: "Can the notion of the public sphere be

internationalized?" Robbins cites Arjun Appadurai as having suggested as much by naming a "transnational journal," *Public Culture*. Although Robbins asserts that for Appadurai such a transnational public is "only now for the first time coming into being," I am interested in the possibility that such a "public" was always the necessary and occluded "public" of the liberal public sphere outlined by Habermas. See Robbins, "Introduction," p. xxiv.

35. All references to Stow's *Survey* will appear parenthetically in the body of the text and will refer to Charles Lethbridge Kingsford's two-volume edition (Oxford: Clarendon, 1908).

36. Anthony Giddens, *The Consequences of Modernity* (Cambridge: Polity, 1990), p. 21.

37. See Samir Amin, *Capitalism in the Age of Globalization* (London: Zed, 1997), p. 57 in particular, but also throughout. It should be noted that my conclusions differ from Amin's.

38. Some Marxist theorists, such as Tim Brennan—in his impressive *At Home in the World* (Cambridge: Harvard University Press, 1997)—have made a strong case for the subaltern "insurgent state" still offering the best form for the protection of alternative cultures in the face of Western domination. Given levels of global inequality and the irreducible imbrication of economies (as well as, in different ways, societies and cultures), I suggest here that new spaces of resistance may have to be imagined.

39. David Harvey, "Globalization in Question," *Rethinking Marxism*, vol. 8, no. 4, 1995, p. 4, tracks "globalization" as a process to a time long before the widespread use of the term began in the 1980s: "Certainly from 1492 onwards, and even before, the globalization process of capitalism was well under way. And it has never ceased to be of profound importance to capitalism's dynamic. Globalization has, therefore, been integral to capitalist development since its very inception."

40. Indeed, Stow's text can be seen to indirectly participate in producing this divide, as it asserts the very "historicity" which was used to distinguish the European from the New World native.

41. Just to give one example of Stow's typical practice, readily observable in the *Survey*, we need look no further than his discussion of "Portsoken warde," the first he takes up. In establishing the original bounds of the ward he observes that they lay: "from Ealdgate to the place where the bars now are toward the east, on both the sides of the street, and extended it toward bishopsgate in the North, unto the house then of William Presbiter, after of Giffrey Tanner, and then of the heyres of Colver, after that of John Easeby, but since of the Lord Bourchier, & C. . . ." (I.121). He does not provide any other landmark, or even describe this house, so some "local knowledge" would be required about which house belonged to "Lord Bourchier" in order to make any sense of his description. He continuously requires just such a dialectic between presumed local knowledge and the additional account that he provides in order to (re)situate these subjects in a particular relation to London's space and time, as I shall detail below.

42. Thomas Fuller's full comment—in *The History of the Worthies of England* (London, 1662), p. 220—reads: "I have heard him often accused, that . . . he reporteth res in se minutas, toys and trifles, being such a smell-feast that he cannot pass by Guild Hall, but his pen must tast of the good cheer therein." He adds with university-bred superiority: "this must bee indulged to his education [Stow never attended any university] so hard is it for a citizen to write an History, but that the fur of his gown will be felt therein."

43. The "Descriptio" has been translated by Frank Stenton in a volume entitled *Norman London* (New York: Italica Press, 1990).

44. Stephen Mullaney in *The Place of the Stage* (Chicago: University of Chicago Press, 1988), p. 18, for example, associates the text with "tradition": "Stow's *Survey* represents for us, then, a pre-Cartesian or Aristotelian world; a memory theater whose topoi or commonplaces are no less significant than they are substantial; a topological device on the scale of a city, to be compared to the spatial constructs of other traditional societies, Western or not, for whom place and its significance are ritually constituted phenomena."

45. Elizabeth Wilson, "The Rhetoric of Urban Space," *New Left Review*, 209, 1995, pp. 146–60, p. 151.

46. Walter Benjamin, "Berlin Chronicle," in *Reflections*, trans. Edmund Jephcott (New York: Harcourt Brace Jovanovich, 1978), pp. 5, 26.

47. Fuller, *History of the Worthies*, p. 221.

48. John Lyly, "Midas" (prologue), *Works*, vol. III, ed. R. Warwick Bond (Oxford: Clarendon, 1902), p. 115.

49. Henry Fitzgeffrey, "The Third Booke of Humours: Intituled Notes from Black-Friars," extracted in *A Sourcebook in Theatrical History*, ed. A.M. Nagler (New York: Dover, 1952), p. 139.

50. See, for example, the pamphlets collected in A.V. Judges (ed.), *The Elizabethan Underworld* (London: Routledge, 1930).

51. Ben Jonson, *Bartholomew Fair*, in *Drama of the English Renaissance*, vol. II, eds. Russell A. Fraser and Norman Rabkin (New York: Macmillan, 1976), II.vi.80–1.

52. Giovanni Arrighi, *The Long Twentieth Century* (New York: Verso, 1994), pp. 181–2.

53. "Notes given 1580: to Mr. Arther Pet . . . ," in Richard Hakluyt, *Voyages and Discoveries*, ed. Jack Beeching (London: Penguin, 1972), p. 213.

54. Lawrence Manley, *Literature and Culture in Early Modern London* (Cambridge: Cambridge University Press, 1995), p. 136.

55. On the shifting power in merchant groups in the early modern period, see Brenner, *Merchants and Revolution*.

56. Walter Hamond, *A Paradox* (London, 1640), p. 268.

57. Donald Lupton, "London and the Country Carbanadoed," in *The Royal Exchange*, ed. Ann Saunders (London: London Topographical Society, 1997), p. 98.

58. Joan Thirsk, *Economic Policy and Projects* (Oxford: Clarendon, 1978), pp. 12, 22, 81.

59. Eric R. Wolf, *Europe and the People without History* (Berkeley: University of California Press, 1982), p. 4.

60. On the "spoyle" of the Jews, see especially I. 277–81.

61. Kingsford provides a bibliography of various versions in his edition of the *Survey*, p. lxxxv; Manley discusses many of the offshoots in Chapter 3 of *Literature and Culture in Early Modern London*.

62. John Strype, *A Survey* . . ., 2 vols (London, 1720), vol. II, p. 256.

63. Christopher Hill, *The Century of Revolution* (New York: Norton, 1982), p. 2.

64. While many historians have disagreed with Hill's assessment in the *Century of Revolution* of the causes of the changes he describes, as well as certain of his emphases, and especially the significance of regional variation, that there *were* monumental changes over the course of the seventeenth century—locally and globally—is not really in dispute, though these are rarely understood in truly internationalist terms as understood by James. See pp. 14–15 above.

65. Richard Helgerson, *Forms of Nationhood: The Elizabethan Writing of England* (Chicago: University of Chicago Press, 1992), pp. 151–91.

66. According to Steve Rappaport in *Worlds Within Worlds: Structures of Life in Sixteenth Century London* (Cambridge: Cambridge University Press, 1989), p. 93: "Apart from th[e] victualling companies, the many companies associated with London's cloth and clothing industries and trades claimed as members more freemen than all other companies combined: two of every five men sworn citizens from December 1551 to October 1553."

67. Gilroy, in *The Black Atlantic*, p. 15, proposes "in opposition to . . . nationalist or ethnically absolute approaches . . . to develop the suggestion that cultural historians could take the Atlantic as one single, complex unit of analysis in their discussions of the modern world and use it to produce an explicitly transnational and intercultural perspective."

68. Jeremy Brecher and Tim Costello have influentially called this process "globalization from below" in *Global Village or Global Pillage* (Boston: South End Press, 1994).

3

The Right to the City in Los Angeles: Discourse and Practice of a Chicano Alternative Public Sphere

Raúl H. Villa

If in discourse the city serves as a totalizing and almost mythical landmark for socioeconomic and political strategies, urban life increasingly permits the re-emergence of the element that the urbanistic project excluded. The language of power is in itself "urbanizing," but the city is left prey to contradictory movements that counterbalance and combine themselves outside the reach of panoptic power.

—Michel de Certeau[1]

In the celebratory historiography of Los Angeles, the constant restructuring of its built environment is a point of pride and a principal theme. Numerous accounts, both popular and scholarly, narrate the city's cycles of modernization in epic terms, with its great men and great works cast respectively in heroic and monumental auras. As an ideological discourse of "progress," this master narrative of Los Angeles plots an inevitable and glorious evolution of cultural landscapes from that of a sleepy pueblo to one of a super city, as in this typical declaration: "The spectacular transition of a little Mexican pueblo, with its huddle of sun-baked adobes, into one of the world's great cities within so brief a span of time [1850–1950], still entrances the imagination. Hardly less remarkable are the more recent changes."[2]

The city's working-class *mexicano* population[3] has had an ironic place within this historical metamorphosis, being simultaneously in the geographic center *and* the economic margins of the city. Stated differently, their productive labors have always been essential to the city's growth while at the same time their places of reproduction have been in the way of its ceaseless redevelopment. This contradictory location has made Mexican residents of the central city uniquely (if unavoidably) situated to observe the more ignoble consequences of the city's successive physical makeovers. Under these historical conditions they have constantly had to defend their "right to the city"[4] against the disparate impacts of urban growth.

The cultural symbolism of Los Angeles's first "modern" transformation, in the late-1800s, is characterized by Robert Fogelson, who noted that "nowhere in southern California was the new order and new destiny promised by the conquerors in the 1840s more evident than in the emergence of Los Angeles as an American town by the 1880s."[5] Carey McWilliams similarly notes that in this period the "typically Spanish appearance of the Southern California towns changed overnight. With a truly awful swiftness of transition, they became undeniably gringo villages."[6] This aggressive semiosis of the built environment was most evident in the heart of the earlier Mexican pueblo near the Plaza church.

The condition of possibility and the active impetus for Los Angeles's urban metamorphosis was the arrival of transcontinental railroad links in the 1870s and 1880s. In anticipation of the intense real estate speculation that would surely be generated, Los Angeles and other Southern California towns began their first wave of physical makeovers with the plotting of outlying residential subdivisions and, of greatest consequence to emerging barrio social spaces, central urban redevelopment:

> By 1874 the "bubble of expectation" was full-blown. Picturesque cottages were torn down in Santa Barbara, Los Angeles, and San Diego to make way for the new buildings of the cities-to-be. Wharfs, railway terminals, hotels, warehouses, and churches began to spring up in anticipation of the boom that everyone expected.... Old-Town Santa Barbara [the residual Mexican enclave] was "bisected and torn down and almost entirely destroyed." Los Angeles . . . had, by 1876, undergone a similar transformation.[7]

Spanish-language journalists of this era interrogated the symbolism of urban restructuring in this initial Anglo-urban transformation. In 1877, an indignant editorial by José Rodríguez protested the disregard of the city council for the Mexican residents of the city. His critique of downtown urban designs made particular reference to the destruction of Mexican historical place-memory sited in the Plaza district, objecting to the planned demolition of Pio Pico's house. Rodríguez noted its significance as a cultural landmark, since Pico—the last Mexican governor of the region—had used it as his seat of governance. That same year, the editors of *La Cronica* objected to the "inferior roads and public services" in the Mexican residential district adjoining the Plaza: "Why . . . don't they give us the same services that the others have?"[8] Clearly interrogating the two-tiered social structure of urban amenities, editors Pastor de Celis, Mariano J. Varela, and S. A. Cardona laid the blame squarely on the "discriminatory neglect of public officials."[9] In this, and similar editorial interventions by the Spanish-language press, the purposeful activity of civic leaders in the initial thrust of Los Angeles's Anglo-urbanization was put up to public scrutiny.

Such critical interventions were compelled by the repressive apparatuses of the dominant culture—most notably in the work of metropolitan growth coalitions, the allied police-judicial system, and the mainstream media—which were effectively marginalizing Mexicanos from social power. Albert Camarillo notes that this social marginalization was explicitly spatialized in the late nineteenth and early twentieth centuries, as the subordinating apparatuses combined to produce "a new reality . . . [in] the *barroization* of the Mexican population—the formation of residentially and socially segregated Chicano barrios or neighborhoods" (original emphasis).[10]

However, barroization was not imposed without significant response by Mexicanos, as they acted to buffer and resist the externally compelled assault on their social spaces within the emerging "landscape of power."[11] The resistive public agency of the earliest barrio residents was aptly figured by the previously cited editors of *La Cronica* in a poignant proclamation on 16 May 1877: "We still have a voice, tenacity and rights; we have not yet retired to the land of the dead."[12] While there is clearly a self-reference to the "voice" of the editors themselves, and of the Spanish-language press generally, the expression of place-rights and cultural presence by "*la raza*" (as Mexicanos were increasingly identifying themselves in collective solidarity) assumed other forms as well.

The practical and symbolic activities of organizations promoting Raza consciousness through public cultural spectacle entered into the textual contents of the Raza press, producing a symbiosis of discursive and enacted group self-consciousness. Identifying this conjunction, Richard Griswold del Castillo notes that the community press gave regular and extensive coverage to Mexican patriotic celebrations, with editors essaying on the significance of nationalist symbolism and consciousness.[13] Similarly, a variety of barrio voluntary associations, cultural societies and self-help organizations were formed between 1850 and 1900, including various political and labor organizations, musical associations, fraternal orders, and a patriotic junta (which organized the Mexican national holiday celebrations).

On occasion, these groups engaged in symbolic spatial practices, as in the organization of *días patrias* (patriotic holiday celebrations) and related cultural events, most commonly in the Plaza area. Although with reference to the early-twentieth-century barrio of Sacramento, Ernesto Galarza described the symbolic function of such events as publicly affirming community performance. His observations would certainly hold true for the ritual psychological effects of similar events in the nascent Los Angeles barrio. In a social context wherein the barrio had no individuals "who had official titles or who were otherwise recognized by everyone as important people .. [and where] everything ... was decided at City Hall or the County Court House," Galarza notes that

> [t]he one institution we had that gave the colonia some kind of image was the Comisión Honorífica ... [which organized] the celebration of the Cinco de Mayo and the Sixteenth of September, the anniversaries of the battle of Puebla and the beginning of our War of Independence. These were the two events that stirred everyone in the barrio, for what we were celebrating was not only the heroes of Mexico but also the feeling that we were still Mexicans ourselves.[14]

These nationalistic celebrations were cherished occasions in which *mexicanismo*, mediated through expressive cultural practices (music, dance, food, oratory, costuming . . .), was momentarily projected into and against a broader Anglo-metropolitan social space, overlaying a strong public persona upon the enforced anonymity that was ever more obscuring the civic identity of La Raza in the larger public sphere.

In the early twentieth century, the downtown residential core radiating out from the Plaza area was heterogeneously comprised of immigrant workers, most notably southern and eastern Europeans (Italians being the most numerous), Chinese, Japanese, African Americans, Russian Molokans, Jews and a smattering of other ethnic and national-origin groups. The labor needs fueled by the tremendous urban expansion of Los Angeles in this period[15] drew great numbers of workers to the city. The Plaza area served as the principal point of entry, recruitment and dispersal for workers to all the compass points of the growing metropolis. A bifurcated immigration pattern, with affluent Anglo-Americans settling in the suburbs and working-class and poor "ethnic" laborers in the central city, made class difference the most rigid socio-spatial demarcator of the city at large.[16] The various ethnic-national immigrant communities in the downtown core lived in relative, sometimes immediate, proximity to each other, producing conditions for cross-cultural contact and influence without, however, melting away their culturally distinct ethnic traditions and orientations.

As the largest of the central city groups, most Mexicanos were still clustered in their own barrios, but these were spreading in every direction out from, and including, the original Plaza and Sonora Town barrio area, moving increasingly east and northeast across the Los Angeles River during and after the 1920s. While American religious missionaries (mostly Protestant) and social workers (religious and secular) were a fixture in the central urban area since the turn of the century, their impact on the daily round of activities of barrio residents was relatively benign. In relation to the city at large, Mexicanos were largely left alone to organize their everyday practices as they saw fit. As with other workers, so long as their rent was paid, they were left alone in their residential spaces of reproduction, where they could be called upon as a convenient pool of reserve labor.

In the case of Mexican workers particularly, it was commonly understood by the "good citizens" of Los Angeles that they were driven by an unerring "homing instinct." This made it even less important to interfere with them, since they were considered laboring wayfarers who would return to their motherland after satisfying whatever transient economic goal they had come to fulfill. But when it became apparent that Mexicanos were not just gathering a few dollars and returning to Mexico, the first stirrings of a "Mexican problem" entered the imagination of social reformers and civic leaders. Consequently, the relative live-and-let-live attitude would be significantly altered in the 1920s by the large-scale proselytizing activities of "Americanization" campaigns. However, prior to this period, in one of the regular "spatial fixes"[17] which urbanizing capital requires for its continued growth, Mexicanos living in the downtown core would be reminded that their residential milieu was a vulnerable commodity within the dominant organization of urban space.

In a 1906 visit, Jacob Riis, the most recognized national figure in the progressive reform movement, observed that he had seen slum conditions "of greater area, but never any which were worse than those in Los Angeles."[18] In a precursory exercise of eminent domain, a Housing Commission was immediately formed and empowered to erase this social stain on the golden image of Los Angeles so carefully crafted by its boosters. While the commission lost no time in razing over 450 units of slum housing, "better housing was not provided. So, Mexicans watched their barrios destroyed as they confronted the pain of total displacement."[19] The evacuated land was quickly put to use in expanding the commercial and government district downtown. Whether this was a consciously racist exercise, as implied in the characterization of it by Rios-Bustamante and Castillo as "Mexican removal," or whether it was a purely objective planning decision, the end result of the commission's actions made it very clear that "Los Angeles' urban planners gave priority to large economic interests and led government officials away from improving living conditions"[20] in the central city. According to Albert Camarillo this "encroachment/displacement phenomenon would determine the course of barrioization for Los Angeles Chicanos for the next two decades and more."[21]

Responding to Los Angeles's early-twentieth-century growth pains—characterized by tremendous population increases, unchecked physical expansion, social disorientation and erratic variances in property values—civic leaders felt they needed to intervene and bring order to the perceived chaos of the city. Zoning emerged as the principal institutional apparatus for realizing their vision of a comprehensively organized metropolitan region. Revealing the influence of progressive-era ideology, urban elites believed they could apply scientific method to city planning. As Christine Boyer notes of this period mentality:

> Knowledge, which [was] neutral, objective, technical, and scientific, beyond the domain of special group and class interests, became the ideal motivator for social change. . . . Planners, public elites, rational men were to be the overseers of this new positivity, the neutral theoreticians of the planning mentality in a nation of cities.[22]

It was thus felt that through a precise evaluation of urban needs, a map of segregated urban functions (residential, commercial, industrial, recreational) could be laid out on the disorderly space of the city. Like a well-constructed machine, the city would then operate predictably for the benefit of all its citizens.

As "pioneers in the city zoning movement in the United States,"[23] Los Angeles municipal planners proceeded experimentally through a series of amended and increasingly variegated zoning ordinances beginning in 1908 and culminating in a comprehensive ordinance in 1925. This emergent form of government spatial regulation purported to reform the early American township's founding relationship of influence between private enterprise and public authority in urban development. In practice, however, the temerity of city planners, who "considered it essential to secure the support of the developers,"[24] assured that capital interests would remain the driving force in shaping the metropolis. With the countless exemptions routinely granted to developers, the exercise of public zoning authority "sanctioned the patterns already imposed by private enterprise far more often than they shaped the cast of future development."[25] In this way, early Los Angeles public planning revealed the practical contradictions (if not a more insidious intent) of progressive era ideology in which the "ideal of a public interest embodied in a comprehensive plan ... conflicted with the reality that private interests directly influenced public policy for-mation and that political decision making operated on fragmented choices, not integrated wholes."[26] This coalescence of civic well-being with entrepreneurial benefit was the precursor to subsequent formulas for urban redevelopment, both locally and nationally, as the public sector good was always tempered, if not directed, by the private sector bottom line. The status of barrio residents and their urban interests under these modernizing conditions was clear. As poor people, rather than well-connected place entrepreneurs, Mexicanos were "not in a position to effectively claim that their neighborhoods, *as used by them,* ... [were] useful for attracting capital" (original emphasis).[27] The slowly growing home-owner class of the Mexicano community, much less the majority rentier population, could thus expect little recourse to defend their needs against the public-good determinations of the allied urban planners, city officials and private developers.

Los Angeles's metamorphosis in the early twentieth century was dramatically signed in space by the new Civic Center complex of government and commercial buildings due south of the Plaza district. The premier signifier of the city's modernist refashioning was the new City Hall building, completed in 1928, whose rotunda declared: "THE CITY CAME INTO BEING TO PRESERVE LIFE, IT EXISTS FOR THE GOOD LIFE." While prosperity was being promised 150 feet above ground, the Raza living on the ground near the city's first skyscraper found the places of their "good life," such as they were able to constitute it, squeezed out to accommodate the new landscape of the self-proclaimed "wonder city". Thousands of Mexicanos were forced to abandon the remaining barrios adjacent to the Plaza and relocate to the next ring of inner-city housing. This exodus seeded the ground of several new barrios immediately north, east, and west of downtown, most notably in Lincoln Heights, Chávez Ravine, Boyle Heights and Bunker Hill. The instrumen-tal practice of community removal, under the guise of urban renewal, was thus first fully exercised upon the residential places of working-class immigrants in the central city. However, even within such shape-shifting, community-displacing parameters, Mexicanos in the early twentieth century exercised a variety of countervailing tactics to preserve the form and character of their distinct urban cultural milieu.

Evincing the continued importance of Raza discursive activity, and fueled by the increasing size of the community, the number of Raza publications grew steadily in number and variety through the 1920s. Given the demographic majority of immigrants in the community, news and commentary about the civil conflict in Mexico were regular features. Tied to this homeland orientation was Raza press coverage of various issues and debates pertinent to Mexican nationalist sentiment as expressed within the United States (should Mexicans become U.S. citizens?, how to combat Anglo stereotypes and increase the Mexican public image in the larger civic sphere, etc.).[28] Also, considering the substantial proletarianization of the Mexican community, many publications gave significant coverage and editorial support to labor activism and anti-capitalist agitation, most notably in *Regeneración*, published by Ricardo and Flores Magón. Even with its strong internationalist orientation, *Regeneración* gave critical attention to local problems of barrio community residents, such as continuing racial violence, job discrimination, and judicial system abuses. Similarly, a content analysis of *La Opinion*, the major Raza journal in this period (and still today), shows that significant attention was also given to issues of "colonia solidarity," a category which treated matters of local concern,[29] ranging from civic festivals to organizational politics and urban development.

Perhaps the major development issue treated under this rubric was the contentious 1927 battle over the possible municipal incorporation of Belvedere. Under county jurisdiction just east of the city limits, Belvedere was emerging as the major area of Mexican home ownership, with a rate of 44.8 percent compared to the rate of 18.6 percent for Mexicanos within city limits.[30] Neighborhood residents, who fought off several incorporation attempts by the city of Los Angeles, were informed in their actions by a clear consciousness of external threat, drawing on their knowledge—for many, from direct experience—of previous community displacements in the central city barrios. Belvedere residents saw the incorporation plans as a thinly masked ploy by the city council, acting in concert with private developers, to pressure them out and redevelop the annexed area. The failure of this early growth coalition to take over Belvedere proved the will of this growing working-class community to develop and sustain its place in the greater urban map.

The public debate fueled by this and other community issues treated in the Raza press was a significant element in the constitution of a Mexican "alternative public sphere."[31] In fact, the very means by which Raza press materials were disseminated and the interpersonal dynamics through which their contents were discussed were important manifestations of urban spatial praxis.

> In downtown's Main Street area, from First Street to the Plaza, people gathered informally to read local newspapers and argue perspectives. There were several bookstores in the area, and most of them offered a selection of Mexican as well as U.S. Spanish-language publications. Magazines and newspapers were usually distributed by people pushing carts along Main Street and throughout the Plaza area. . . . Often, workers would meet in poolhalls and billiard parlors spread along the northern sections of Main Street. It was there that they would read newspapers aloud and discuss points of interest.[32]

In the same time and place, popular commercial media also contributed to the vitality of Raza public culture. Music record producer and distributor Mauricio Calderón would regularly play the latest *corridos* (ballads) through a loudspeaker facing out from his store on Main Street, attracting groups of attentive listeners who would discuss among themselves the merits and contents of the latest recordings.[33] In some cases, the *corrido* texts available on disc or broadside in Calderón's store were self-reflexive meditations on the vibrant street milieu in which they were being disseminated. Such is the case of the strange fatalistic verses—probably inspired by the conjunction of economic decline, millenarian proselytizing, and Mexican deportation in the Depression era, all of which would have been especially manifest in the Plaza area—in the text of "El fin del mundo–musica de la casita":

Y a los de saco rajado	And those of split-tailed coat
y del pelo embadurnado	And of oiled hair
tambien se los lleva el tren.	The train will also take them.
Ya se acabo el palo blanco,	The pale blonde is out of the picture,
ya no se les oira el tranco	No longer will they hear
por las calles de la Main.	The life on Main Street.
[. . .]	[. . .]
Y a los cuates papeleros	And the pals, newsies
ese atajo de arguenderos	That bunch of noise makers
que nos gritan en la Main	That shout to us on Main Street
Con todo sus papelotes	With all their big papers
y sus raspados ganotes,	And their scraped throats
tambien se los lleva el tren.	Will also go to wreck.[34]

The active street culture intimated here was largely male-centered, since most of the residents, job-seekers and other habitués of the Plaza/Main Street corridor were single men. Single women, married couples and families were increasingly concentrating in the growing Eastside barrios, such as Belvedere, where home ownership was a more viable option. However, the Plaza zone was not exclusively a male enclave. Even while there was a slowly growing concentration of small business enterprises emerging on the Eastside, the business corridor running north and south of the Plaza remained the major enclave of mercantile, entertainment and civic festival activity for all Raza, young and old, male and female, immigrant and native-born, until the 1940s.[35] Residential dispersal of the community away from the central business district did not diminish its connections to the historic heart of the Mexican city around the Plaza. The recently extended electric railway connections to the Eastside, and the concentration of industrial, construction and service employment in the central area kept otherwise scattered barrio dwellers connected in a network tied to the traditional urban core.[36] Furthermore, the Plaza district did offer urban benefits to women who transgressed the patriarchal boundaries which otherwise kept them from the area, except in the sanctioned contexts of commercial or festival occasions.[37] But this was exactly the attraction of the area for many Mexicanas, as noted by historian George Sánchez:

> "Here no one pays attention to how one goes about, how one lives," declared Elenita Arce, pleased at the greater freedoms allowed unmarried women. . . . Knowledge and use of effective birth control, for example, seemed concentrated in a small group of Mexican women living in these downtown communities.[38]

The Main Street commercial and entertainment corridor, running through the Plaza, was the key zone of Mexicano public cultural identity within the larger Anglo metropolis. In the context of a growing ersatz "Spanish" cultural landscape—marked by such signal phenomena as "Mission Revival" design in architecture and home furnishings, the rash of civic "fiestas" and "Mission Day" celebrations, and the fabrication of a pseudo-Mexican tourist market on Olvera Street adjacent to the Plaza—the real places of Raza marketplace practices were sites of authentic cultural expression and reproduction.

While the popular marketplace culture of the Plaza and Main Street environs was, for the moment, largely unnoticed and unimpeded by the larger Anglo society, other uses of public space in the area provoked acute responses from urban elites. The regular use of the

Plaza for political gatherings—such as the efforts by radical Partido Liberal Mexicano organizers to rally support for the Magón brothers and other PLM leaders during their 1911 federal trial for violating United States neutrality laws—struck a nerve among the city's public and private leadership which was equally troubled by the class and racial alterity of the Raza in its midst. Related to progressive-era concerns about the corrupting influences of urban mass culture among its eager consumers in the growing ethnic immigrant communities of the urban centers was a corollary fear of the political mob lurking within that "Other half." Much of the founding impulse for late-nineteenth-century urban moral reform, whose discourses and practices underlay early-twentieth-century progressivism, was a conscious reaction against this perceived threat of mass uprising and political anarchism. The many spectacular public manifestations of working-class unrest in the late nineteenth and early twentieth centuries impressed the image of unruly crowds in public congregation as a great urban evil in the collective consciousness of the urban bourgeoisie and their increasingly suburban, middle-class functionaries.[39]

A noteworthy enactment of Mexican political congregation in the Plaza, and an equally telling police retaliation, occurred on Christmas Day, 1913. On that day the International Workers of the World organized a peaceful rally, principally attended by Mexicanos, to protest unemployment in the city. Police officers attempted to halt the event under the pretense that the organizers had not secured the necessary permit. Refusing to disperse the crowd, the organizers brought the wrath of the waiting officers upon it and a riot ensued between police and citizens. When the Plaza was finally emptied, police carried out retributions in various Mexican public leisure spaces, invading restaurants, pool halls, and movie houses in search of suspected rioters.[40] In spite of multiple witnesses attesting to the initial police provocation, many public officials called for measures to prevent "rabble-rousers" from instigating future unrest. Most fervent among these "leading" voices was Chief of Police Charles Sebastian. His call for legislative restriction of the right to free speech in public gathering places,[41] while not limited to the Plaza or its environs, was clearly meant to disable this political–cultural space in particular.

The growing expressions of a collective Mexican political and marketplace culture were echoed in other organizational activities. The latter comprised a range of ideologically diverse, community-directed institutions following in the historical trajectory of late-nineteenth-century voluntary associations. Now, however, the self-help impulse was increasingly exercised within greater *American* institutional culture, in the areas of educational reform, electoral politics and legal defense of civil rights.[42] Among the more notable organizations emerging in the 1920s and 1930s were the civil-rights-oriented Congreso de Pueblos que Hablan Español, the more accommodationist League of United Latin American Citizens, and the education-oriented Mexican American Movement. The efficacy of Raza public cultural and civic manifestations/expressions was still circumscribed by the community's continuing second-tier social status within the Anglo-dominant urban and national order. Nonetheless, the sense of growing participation or membership in the larger American polity and the perception of achievable economic security fueled a slowly growing optimism and sense of civic entitlement among Raza, who might now be more appropriately identified (and would increasingly self-identify) as Mexican American or Chicano in their cultural–national orientation.

While Mexican Americans were consolidating their sense of cultural citizenship and place identity through labor activism, institutional structures and everyday practices, the Anglo-American leadership of Los Angeles was coordinating the apparatuses to discursively represent and materially locate this emerging community in a rebuilt landscape of power. During the 1930s, the increasingly nativist scrutiny of the "Mexican problem" in academic and mass media discourses gained a virulent momentum. On this discursive count, Rodolfo Acuña notes that "Anglo-American educators and social scientists . . . blame[d] the Mexican[s] for their failure to Americanize and progress in the utopia known as 'America.' "[43] The consequences of these supposedly objective discourses would prove brutally repressive to the Eastside Chicano community, particularly its youth. The conjoined forces of educational tracking, police antagonism, judiciary prejudice, and even vigilante violence were increasingly employed to curb or root out perceived Mexican maladjustment. While these actions were directed particularly at youth, their cumulative effect, particularly via sensationalized mediation in the mainstream press, produced a generalized vilification of the Mexican American community. Social scientific and pseudo-scientific discourses of Mexican cultural pathology were used to prove the necessity of urban renewal as a social panacea for the "infected" barrios. These discourses were supported by a cottage industry of committee reports and academic investigations, couched in the positivist rhetoric of clinical evaluation, and made public spectacle in the press. This broad discursive-cum-institutional degradation of the growing Eastside Chicano community, not to mention the long prior history of working-

class Mexicanos' maligned otherness to Anglo-Angelino society, underlay the racialized assault they would be spectacularly subjected to from
the 1940s on.

In June 1943, the violent transgressions of Mexican social spaces during
the misnamed "Zoot Suit Riots" gave dramatic public notice to Chicanos of their place in the dominant urban order. On the hunt for
"pachucos," U.S. servicemen invaded public and private places of
Chicano congregation—including principal streets and boulevards,
movie theaters, streetcars, homes, and restaurants—to harass, beat,
and strip young men of their sartorial and "un-American" zoot suits.
These assaults were often conducted with the help or tacit approval of
local police agencies. Several major newspapers exhorted patriotic
Angelenos to attack this perceived threat to civic well-being and the
greater war effort, thus making the young Chicanos into folk devils
against whom the good citizens exorcised their own wartime anxieties.[44]
In like fashion, although not to the same extent, Chicanos engaged in
their own defensive guerrilla strategies to protect themselves and their
barrios, setting out ambushes for unwitting servicemen who wandered
into their turf. Barrio popular history documents numerous accounts
of such retaliatory efforts by young men, and it has been a theme in
literary and autobiographical narratives of growing up Chicano in this
period.

Ideologically related to the aggressions of press, police, and vigilante
servicemen against Chicanos and their community spaces, were the
aggressions of 1940s urban planning discourses. Advocating highway
construction, "slum clearance" and "higher use" redevelopment of
prime central city land, planning campaigns "took on the spirit of wartime propaganda, particularly aerial bombings," suggesting the urgent
need for scorched-earth policies to raze the diseased central-city neighborhoods as a check against their spreading to the better areas of the
city.[45] The specter of urban blight, in discursive currency both locally
and nationally since the late-nineteenth-century reformist "discovery"
of the immigrant slums, returned with magnified intensity during the
1940s. For the next quarter-century, "blight" became a mantra of
professional planners who saw themselves as "surgeon generals"[46] bat-
tling for the physical, economic, and moral health of the metropolitan
body.

The repressive police and discursive exercises enacted against Chicano social spaces in the 1940s were a prelude to much larger-scale
violations of the community's residential milieus that followed, as the

Eastside, and other compass points in the immediate circumference of downtown Los Angeles were aggressively altered by monumental urban highway construction and urban renewal projects throughout the 1950s and 1960s. The two most spectacular instances of spatial violation against Chicanos and other poor people in the central city were the displacement of the barrios in Chávez Ravine, immediately north of downtown, for the construction of Dodger Stadium, and the bisection of Eastside barrios to make way for the East LA freeway interchange and the several highways that radiated out from it. The latter alone consumed 12 percent of the residential land in East Los Angeles.

These signal developments of the 1950s and 1960s materially facilitated Los Angeles's next transformation—into the nation's super-city—and symbolically represented this image to the outside world. In the process of their realization, the arguments of barrio residents for how best to use the land that their neighborhoods occupied were dismissed as parochial, if not wholly regressive, by the urban elites spearheading the city's latest mutation in the built environment.[47] Mayor Norris Poulson voiced the modernizing credo with imperious bravado. In a public radio address to the city in 1959, he chastised the critics of his administration's growth plans: "if you want Los Angeles to revert to pueblo status, if you want nothing changed . . . then my best advice to you is to prepare to settle elsewhere, because whatever you may do . . . [you] cannot stop the momentum which is thundering this city to greatness."[48] The worn but familiar environs of the Chávez Ravine and Boyle Heights neighborhoods provided an essential range of social, cultural, and economic resources for their residents, but these could not measure up against the higher and better uses projected for these areas by the city's growth machinery.

While a nearly unrestrained engine of central-city redevelopment was thus set in motion, barrio residents expressed concerted opposition to the plans of the downtown ruling elites. In the early 1950s, Eastside residents were mobilizing to defend their neighborhood turf-base and use-values. The "battle against the bulldozers" of urban development and highway construction in the Eastside and central city was the principal rallying cry of Chicano community defensive spatial mobilizations in the 1950s and 1960s.[49] For example, in 1953, while the planners and developers were celebrating the much-heralded opening of the downtown interchange of the Hollywood and Pasadena freeways—the first four-level freeway exchange in the country—there were mass community rallies in Boyle Heights to protest the bisection of their community space.

In this period, city council member Edward Roybal proved himself to be a major advocate for Eastsiders' place rights. Elected in 1949 by a major grassroots effort of Eastside Chicanos, Roybal was a committed public servant and organic intellectual for the community which rallied to put him in office. Often as a lone voice on the council, Roybal raised regular objections to the disparate impacts of unchecked urban development in his district. In this capacity, he regularly clashed with the growth machinery, particularly "the *Los Angeles Times*, not only over the issues of rent control, the scapegoating of Mexican youth and police brutality, but also over freeway construction, urban renewal and public housing."[50] In a corollary effect, the fresh wounds of the multiple spatial assaults upon the barrios were engraved as implicit social knowledge in the popular imagination of Los Angeles Chicanos.

On the journalistic front, repeated allusions to community place-violations appeared in the critical editorial and reportorial interventions of the weekly *Eastside Sun*. In the 1950s, this critical posture was most often voiced in editorials by its crusading publisher Joseph Eli Kovner. Kovner was a Jewish-American liberal whose persistent advocacy for Eastsider place-rights both recalled the once-significant Jewish presence in Boyle Heights and signaled his strong, if "somewhat paternalistic and flamboyant," identification with the eventual Chicano majority in the area.[51] In the 1960s and early 1970s columnist Arturo Montoya replaced Kovner as the most consistent critic of downtown public and private development interests. Similar positions were evident in the reporting of community place-struggles by Mario Hernández and Eddie Pardo, in various letters to the editor from neighborhood residents, and in the published articles and interviews with Chicano professionals involved in urban planning issues. Examples of these texts show how broad social critique and insider community analysis were variously used by Eastsiders to interpret their spatial structuration and argue for their urban place-needs and rights.

In a published copy of a letter addressed to Sargent Shriver, then Federal Director of the Office of Economic Opportunity's Community Action Program, Isabel Medrano and N. Sterlink complain that

> in cities such as Los Angeles, elements in power and influence begin looking for land that can become available in single tracts and at negligible prices . . . from low-income minority areas, and it is these areas that suffer the most serious land expropriations. Those expropriations, of course, eventually lead to the so called "asphalt jungles" and to continually more crowded living conditions that in turn induce, augment and perpetuate many of the evils associated with poverty.[52]

While Medrano and Sterlink deconstructed the purposeful and disabling impacts of *external* growth interests, community planner Raúl Escobedo focused *internally* to identify the sustaining, if vulnerable, place-bound mechanisms of community life. In "Life Style Within the Boyle Heights Community," he offered his observations on the use-value orientations and culturally defining practices of Eastside residents. Relatedly, in the rhetorically titled "Is Boyle Heights Worth Saving?" Escobedo noted the symbiosis of economic necessity and affective links to local place that made Boyle Heights a valuable social resource for its low-income residents: "It has many characteristics of neighborhood cohesiveness and many residents are socially, emotionally and historically tied to the area. To a great majority of the residents—long-term residents, recent arrivals, young couples, senior citizens, homeowners and renters alike—this area is their only economic alternative."[53] Escobedo goes on to intimate the Chicano community's felt legacy of spatial expropriations, noting that the "emotional scars of Bunker Hill and Chavez Ravine are not easily erased. And the social disruption and physical displacement caused by four major freeways is still considered recent history by many long term community residents."[54]

With unflagging persistence, and often colored by rhetorical bursts of indignation, the various contributors to the *Eastside Sun* collectively narrated and interpreted the continuing saga of urban land grabs in the Eastside. The private-cum-public benefits driving urban renewal and the complicity of key public officials in the process were regularly interrogated. Unfortunately, many of the more substantial community mobilizations reported and supported by the *Eastside Sun* were limited or defeated in their efforts to repel the spatial assaults. While Eastsiders gained scattered concessions, they failed to stop the major displacements and social disruptions of urban renewal and freeway construction. Ironically, after protesting the coming of the freeways, Eastsiders subsequently had to rally to have freeway exits *put into* their neighborhoods. The bias of the planners was revealed in this neglect of local access to the Eastside, which would have been cut off from the greater metropolitan mobility promised to suburban commuters. If the *Eastside Sun* largely documents the circumscribed political power of barrio residents, it nevertheless offers a testimonial record of their individual and collective efforts to defend the integrity of their places in the city.

Just as the various spatial assaults upon the Eastside in the 1950s were a flashpoint of community protest and defensive mobilizations, so they were again in the late 1960s and early 1970s. During this next period of the battle against the bulldozers, coincident with the urban Chicano civil rights movement, the lessons learned or transmitted about earlier community turf battles helped some barrio residents in defending their place-rights. Don Parson notes, for example, that "Chicano grassroots actions in the early '70s stopped, froze or limited urban renewal plans in Latino areas: Temple-Beaudry project, clearance plans for Lincoln and Monterey Hills were recast to do housing rehabilitation only."[55] An important actor in these defensive mobilizations was Rosalío Muñoz, working with the East/Northeast Committee to Stop Home Destruction, based in the Lincoln Heights area of Los Angeles, and the United Neighbors of Temple-Beaudry, in the barrios just west of downtown. Published in the *Eastside Sun, La Gente* and the *Community Defender* newspapers, Muñoz's documentary and deconstructive journalism brought to light the community-disabling effects of dominant urban planning. His 1973 essay "Our Moving Barrio: Why?" is exemplary. Responding to drafts of the new city and county Master Plans (they were made final in 1974), he took aim at the likely effects in Chicano barrios of a new wave of urban renewal.

In the Master Plan rhetoric which called for "recycling the inner city," Muñoz saw a thinly veiled effort by the "political economic elite" to forestall the "imminence of Chicano political strength and domination in the heart of one of the largest metropolitan areas of the world."[56] Linking past effects to present circumstances, he argued that "this is at least the third effort to carry out the strategy of removing the Mexican population. The first two were relatively successful. The first was around the turn of the century when Los Angeles was changing from a village town to a small city. [. . .] The second wave came during the forties and fifties. . . ."[57] In the full text, Muñoz describes the upheavals of initial Civic Center development, downtown industrial expansion, Union Station and additional railroad yard construction, freeway building, and Federal Urban Renewal and Housing projects (most significantly the notorious battle over Chávez Ravine); in other words, many of the signal or trophy constructions of Los Angeles's twentieth-century odyssey from boom town to wonder city and into its supercity future. In his periodization, the 1960s and early 1970s were the "third phase" in which he found himself writing and acting. This phase was monumentally enacted in space by the "Bunker Hill Urban Renewal Project which destroyed the last barrios immediately next to downtown,"[58] replacing them with the new Music Center complex, the headquarters building of the Department of Water and Power, and the first generation of trophy-building skyscrapers and upscale residential complexes of the recentered financial district.[59] Muñoz's critique of hegemonic urban planning "brushes history against the grain"[60] by situating contemporary urban restructuring within a recurring cycle of Chicano neighborhood displacements. In the process, he offers clear detail and incentive to fuel the present and future struggles of barrio residents against the assaults of Los Angeles's ceaseless growth machinery.

In both his organizational activism and his critical reportage Muñoz re-enacts an impulse which, consciously or unconsciously, underlies all the representative expressive practices discussed in this chapter. The common impulse is an "old chant of the urban condition: the transformation of the space of exclusion into the space of freedom," in which the marginalized milieu can serve the "community as the material basis of social organization, cultural identity, and political power."[61] As we have seen, the positive outcomes of this transformative impulse are never secure, since the compelling forces of capitalist urbanization continuously threaten the vulnerable social space of the barrio. In this protracted turf war, barrio residents continuously find ways of "establishing a kind of reliability within the situations imposed on . . . [them], of making it possible to live in them by reintroducing into them the plural mobility of goals and desires."[62] Manifesting alternative needs and interests from those of the dominant public sphere, the expressive practices of barrio community reproduction—from the mundane exercises of daily round and leisure activities to the formal articulation of community defensive goals in organizational forums and discursive media—reveal multiple possibilities for re-creating and re-imagining dominant urban space as community-enabling place.

Notes

1. Michel de Certeau, *The Practice of Everyday Life* (Berkeley: University of California Press, 1984), p. 95.

2. Arnold Hylen, *Los Angeles Before the Freeways, 1850–1950: Images of an Era* (Los Angeles: Dawson's Book Shop, 1981), p. 1.

3. Several terms of ethnic group reference—Mexicano, Raza, Mexican American, Chicano—will be used in this chapter to refer to persons of Mexican descent. These terms are not precisely synonymous. Each one has connotations that tie its use to distinct historical periods or to different modes of ethnic subjectivity in relation to a dominant Anglo-American society. I am not using them to designate official categories of national citizenship. They are *cultural* terms of group self-reference that have been used in varying personal and historical contexts by members of the general Mexican-descent population in Los Angeles.

4. Henri Lefebvre, "Right to the City," *Writings on Cities*, trans. and ed. Eleonore Kafman and Elizabeth Lebas (originally published as *Le Droit à la ville*, Anthropos, 1968) (Cambridge, MA: Blackwell, 1996), p. 63.

5. Robert M. Fogelson, *The Fragmented Metropolis: Los Angeles, 1850–1930* [1967] (Berkeley: University of California Press, 1993), p. 23.

6. Carey McWilliams, *Southern California: An Island on the Land* [1949] (reprinted New York: Peregrine Smith, 1976), pp. 64–5.

7. Ibid., p. 116.

8. Richard Griswold del Castillo, *The Los Angeles Barrio, 1850–1890: A Social History* (Berkeley: University of California Press, 1979), p. 128.

9. Ibid.

10. Albert Camarillo, *Chicanos in a Changing Society: From Mexican Pueblos to American Barrios in Santa Barbara and Southern California, 1848–1930* (Cambridge, MA: Harvard University Press, 1979), p. 53.

11. Sharon Zukin, *Landscapes of Power: From Detroit to Disney World* (Berkeley: University of California Press, 1991).

12. Griswold del Castillo, *The Los Angeles Barrio*, pp. 128–9.

13. Ibid., p. 131.

14. Ernesto Galarza, *Barrio Boy* (Notre Dame, IN: University of Notre Dame Press, 1971), pp. 201–2.

15. Total population figures for the city of Los Angeles show a dramatic increase from 102,479 in 1900 to 1,238,048 in 1930. The low to high population estimates for Mexicanos in this period range from between 3,000 and 5,000 in 1900, to between 97,000 and 190,000 in 1930 (Camarillo, *Changing Society*, p. 200).

16. George J. Sánchez, *Becoming Mexican American: Ethnicity, Culture and Identity in Chicano Los Angeles, 1900–1945* (New York: Oxford University Press, 1993), p. 77.

17. David Harvey, *The Condition of Postmodernity* (London: Blackwell, 1993).

18. Camarillo, *Changing Society*, pp. 202–3.

19. Antonio Ríos-Bustamante and Pedro Castillo, *An Illustrated History of Mexican Los Angeles* (Los Angeles: University of California Chicano Studies Research Center, 1986), p. 113.

20. Sánchez, *Becoming Mexican American*, p. 82.

21. Camarillo, *Changing Society*, p. 203.

22. M. Christine Boyer, *Dreaming the Rational City: The Myth of American City Planning* (Cambridge, MA: MIT Press, 1983), p. 272.

23. Robert M. Glendinning, "Zoning: Past, Present and Future," in *Los Angeles: Preface to a Master Plan*, ed. George W. Robbins and L. Deming Tilton (Los Angeles: Pacific Southwest Academy, 1941), p. 181.

24. Fogelson, *The Fragmented Metropolis*, p. 254.

25. Ibid., p. 271.

26. Boyer, *Dreaming the Rational City*, p. 285.

27. John R. Logan and Harvey Molotch, *Urban Fortunes: The Political Economy of Place* (Berkeley: University of California Press, 1987), p. 135.

28. Francine Medeiros, "*La Opinión*, A Mexican Exile Newspaper: A Content Analysis of Its First Years, 1926–1929," *Aztlán: International Journal of Chicano Studies Research*, 6 (1975): pp. 43–67.

29. Ibid.

30. Sánchez, *Becoming Mexican American*, p. 198.

31. Oskar Negt and Alexander Kluge, "The Public Sphere and Experience: Selections," trans. Peter Labanyi, *October*, 46 (Summer 1988): pp. 60–82.

32. Ríos-Bustamante and Castillo, *Illustrated History of Mexican Los Angeles*, pp. 118–19.

33. Nellie Foster, "The *Corrido*: A Mexican Culture Trait Persisting in Southern California," Master's thesis, University of Southern California, 1939.

34. Ibid., pp. 122–3.

35. Sánchez, *Becoming Mexican American*, p. 181.

36. Ríos-Bustamante and Castillo, *Illustrated History of Mexican Los Angeles*, p. 129.

37. With an emerging Mexican marketplace culture east of the LA River, specific sites of commercial activity catering to and run by women provided less culturally (patriarchally) transgressive, but still empowering, public spaces for female

congregation and women-centered discourses of daily life. For example, Vicki Ruiz describes the appearance of Eastside barrio beauty parlors in the early twentieth century as an epiphenomenon of the expanded commodification and promotion, via Hollywood imagery and print advertising, of personal grooming and style (Vicki L. Ruiz, "'Star Struck': Acculturation, Adolescence and the Mexican American Woman, 1920–1950," in *Building with Our Hands: New Directions in Chicana Studies*, ed. Adela de la Torre and Beatriz M. Pesquera [Berkeley: University of California Press, 1993]). She claims that "neighborhood beauty shops reinforced women's networks and became places where they could relax, exchange *chisme* (gossip), and enjoy the company of other women" (p. 117). Such public commercial women's spaces were specifically outside the purview and control of husbands, fathers, brothers and other male figures of domestic patriarchal influence.

38. Sánchez, *Becoming Mexican American*, p. 138.

39. Paul Boyer, *Urban Masses and Moral Order in America, 1820–1920* (Cambridge, MA: Harvard University Press, 1978); Robert Weibe, *The Search for Order, 1877–1920* (New York: Hill and Wang, 1973).

40. Edward J. Escobar, "Chicano Protest and the Law: Law Enforcement Responses to Chicano Activism, 1850–1936," Dissertation, University of California, Riverside, 1983, pp. 213–16.

41. Ibid., pp. 216–17.

42. Rodolfo F. Acuña, *Occupied America: A History of Chicanos* (third edition, New York: Harper and Row, 1988), p. 235.

43. Ibid.

44. Mauricio Mazón, *The Zoot Suit Riots* (Austin: University of Texas Press, 1984).

45. Norman M. Klein, "The Sunshine Strategy: Buying and Selling the Fantasy of Los Angeles," in *Twentieth-century Los Angeles: Power, Promotion, and Social Conflict*, ed. Norman M. Klein and Martin J. Schiesl (Claremont, CA: Regina Books, 1990), p. 13.

46. Robert Goodman, *After the Planners* (New York: Touchstone, 1971), p. 67.

47. Don Parson, "'This Modern Marvel': Bunker Hill, Chavez Ravine, and the Politics of Modernism in Los Angeles," *Southern California Quarterly*, 75/3–4 (Fall–Winter 1993): pp. 333–50.

48. Joseph Eli Kovner, "East Welfare Planning Council is Tool of Mayor's Urban Renewal Committee, as is West LA Group!" Editorial, *Eastside Sun*, 8 January 1959: 1.

49. Rodolfo F. Acuña, *A Community under Siege* (Los Angeles: Chicano Studies Research Center, UCLA, Monograph No. 11), p. 48; Ricardo Romo, *East Los Angeles: History of a Barrio* (Austin: University of Texas Press, 1983), p. 169.

50. Rodolfo F. Acuña, *Anything But Mexican: Chicanos in Contemporary Los Angeles* (New York: Verso, 1996), p. 45.

51. Acuña, *A Community under Siege*, p. 274.

52. Isabel Medrano and N. Sterlink, letter, *Eastside Sun*, 13 May 1965 (no page number given).

53. Raúl Escobedo, "Is Boyle Heights Worth Saving?", interview, *Eastside Sun*, 8 August 1974: p. A-10.

54. Ibid.

55. Don Parson, "The Development of Redevelopment: Public Housing and Urban Renewal in Los Angeles," *International Journal of Urban and Regional Research*, 6/7 (September 1982): p. 408.

56. Rosalio Muñoz, "Our Moving Barrio: Why?" *La Gente*, 5 April 1973: p. 5.

57. Ibid.

58. Ibid.

59. For a concise account of the historical morphology of Bunker Hill, from its late-nineteenth-century status as an exclusive residential enclave through its transformation into the densest working-class neighborhood in the city, and up to its wholesale erasure and postmodern refashioning after the 1960s, see Anastasia Loukaitou-Sideris and Gail Sansbury, "Lost Streets of Bunker Hill," *California Quarterly*, 74/4 (Winter 1996): pp. 304–407.

60. Walter Benjamin, "Theses on the Philosophy of History," *Illuminations*, trans. Harry Zohn, ed. Hannah Arendt (New York: Harcourt, Brace & World, 1968), p. 259.

61. Manuel Castells, *The City and the Grassroots; A Cross Cultural Theory of Urban Social Movements* (Berkeley: University of California Press, 1983), p. 67.

62. Michel de Certeau, *The Practice of Everyday Life* (Berkeley: University of California Press, 1984), p. xxii.

4

Rituals of Disqualification: Competing Publics and Public Housing in Contemporary Chicago

Jamie Owen Daniel

Millennial capitalism is . . . not remarkable, but a symptomatic moment in the history of a logic; at the same time, the changes that it induces can be read at all levels of the social.

—Paul Smith[1]

What some writers are calling "the coming welfare wars" will be largely wars about, even against, women. . . . Moreover, the welfare wars will not be limited to the tenure of Reagan or even of Reaganism. On the contrary, they will be protracted, both in time and space.

—Nancy Fraser[2]

Throughout the fall and early winter of 1998, the *Chicago Tribune* ran a series of articles on the difficulties encountered by the Chicago Housing Authority (CHA) as it undertook to relocate the first of the more than 42,000 residents who are being forced out of the city's public housing. In conjunction with new laws enacted to allow the Federal Government to, as it were, wash its hands of public housing "as we know it" (to use the ubiquitous phrase), people all over the United States who have grown up and themselves raised families in public housing are now being evicted, relocated, and otherwise displaced in unprecedented numbers. Because of the extent to which the CHA and other authorities consistently mismanaged and neglected this housing, and because in September 1995 the U.S. Congress repealed a 1937 law that had required that every unit of public housing that was torn down be replaced, four times as much public housing will be demolished in Chicago as anywhere else.[3]

Among the housing already being demolished at the time of this writing are what one local writer termed "some of the most demonized addresses in recent Chicago history,"[4] including the Cabrini-Green projects north of the Loop that are currently home to 6,000 people, the Henry Horner complex on the near West Side, and the Robert Taylor Homes. With its corridor of twenty-eight identical concrete high-rises that stretched for several miles along south State Street, the Robert Taylor Homes project was one of the largest and most densely populated such complexes in the U.S. Built hurriedly and inexpensively between 1960 and 1962 along a narrow track of land squeezed between railroad lines and the Dan Ryan Expressway, its original 4,415 units once provided homes to "some 27,000 residents (20,000 of them children), all poor and virtually all black."[5] And it remained the most completely segregated complex in a public housing system that had been quite intentionally and ruthlessly segregated by successive city administrations acting on behalf of private interests. Of the 11,000 people still living there in late 1998, 99 percent were black, and just 2 percent were white.[6] The great majority of the residents were women with children; seven out of ten were under 21. Only 4 percent were employed, with the annual income averaging just under $6,000.[7] Ironically, the project's namesake, who was CHA chairman from 1943 to 1950, had advocated unsuccessfully for locating public housing in racially and economically mixed neighborhoods. By the time this chapter is in print, most of the Robert Taylor Homes will have been razed to the ground.

The third installment of the *Chicago Tribune*'s "Odyssey: Resettling the City's Poor" series appeared in October 1998 and was entitled "Tenants No One Wants."[8] It began with a brief portrait of a woman who was clearly meant to personify just this sort of tenant, Robert Taylor Homes resident-in-transit Katie Sistrunk. Sistrunk is described as "a tough-edged 45-year-old mother of 13"; the 5×7-inch color photo on the paper's front page, showing her against a background of coiled razor-wire as she leaves the Cook County Jail where one of her sons is incarcerated, allows the author to avoid identifying her in print as African American. The article itself elaborates in some detail the various factors that have made it so hard for the CHA to "place" her in a new apartment,[9] the first and foremost of these being her extended family's reputation for trouble. "When she tried to move from the Robert Taylor Homes, Katie Sistrunk's name preceded her," the article begins. "Just say 'Sistrunk' to area police: 'I've sent several to prison,' said Officer Andre Cureton. 'They're a story by themselves, the Sistrunk family.'" That story includes, we are told, one son in college, but another convicted of murder; "five of her children have been shot and wounded. A brother was shot and killed. A sister died in police custody."[10] In addition, two of her younger children had just been accused of attacking police as they were arresting the older brother she is shown visiting in the county jail.

This article is both remarkable and typical of how the displacement of CHA residents has been covered by Chicago's news media. For it is most often the CHA itself, the administrative authority, rather than the 42,000 residents, that is portrayed as the "suffering victim" of the new public housing policies. Here, Katie Sistrunk and the volatile behaviors she and her family supposedly exemplify are invoked so as to give readers "a glimpse of the daunting challenge facing the CHA as 19,000 units of public housing are demolished": "CHA workers have already labored for months to find homes for dozens of families that have proved difficult to place."[11] If the impact of the forced displacement of CHA residents on those residents is alluded to at all, it is linked to histories of spontaneous anti-social and/or criminal behavior, making it necessary for CHA workers to "labor for months" to find landlords willing to accept them as tenants.[12] Katie Sistrunk's *name*, her family's notoriety with Chicago's police and social service agencies, is meant to intimidate a reader who, it must be assumed, will sympathize with the problem she represents to a public agency trying to implement efficiently new policies enacted for "the public good," rather than empathizing with her. She is figured as a volatile threat to that "public good," rather than as a member of "the public." In addition, the article grants her no space in which to represent herself, or to speak of the difficulties she and her family are experiencing as they are forced to leave the Robert Taylor Homes and find alternative housing. She is not allowed to name herself, to comment on how her name has been circulated, or to offer any information that might give readers a sense of why she has had to develop such "tough edges."

If Katie Sistrunk is being displaced, both literally and discursively, in the name of a greater "public good," who, we must ask, is the public? And who is she, if not a member of it? Why is the *Chicago Tribune* authorized to use her name in this way, while she is not authorized to speak about or for herself? I want to dwell here on the discourses used to position her as a "problem" for the CHA, to figure her as the "tough-edged" originating instance at the center of a kind of maelstrom of pathological behaviors that need to be controlled (in the way a riot is controlled) by means of disbursement accomplished through displacement, because the genealogy of this positioning provides brutal evidence of the extent to which certain fundamental shifts in public discourse and public policy in the U.S. have conformed to equally fundamental shifts in the logic of millennial capitalism. Subsequently, there has also been a subtle but important shift in just who is being disqualified from inclusion in the public sphere and thus from the "rights and privileges" of citizenship. This is everywhere apparent in the forced displacement of Chicago's public housing residents, who are overwhelmingly desperately poor black women and children.

Let me begin by acknowledging that the positioning of women like Katie Sistrunk as threats to the common good is hardly anything new. Indeed, such positioning has become so commonplace that it might seem reasonable to read the *Chicago Tribune* article as simply the continuation of a tradition of negative characterizations of underclass women who have had to rely on some form of public assistance. In an unflinching analysis of the discourses and practices that combined to produce the stereotype of the "welfare mother" who had, by 1989, become both "the principal subject of the welfare state"[13] and the principal target of legislators seeking to dismantle it, feminist philosopher Nancy Fraser describes how the U.S. public assistance system as it was then functioning worked through two parallel, gender-specific "subsystems." These subsystems positioned men and women differently, albeit in both instances passively, as "cases" who could only "qualify" for financial and other assistance by allowing the system to, as she puts it, translate their "experienced situations and life problems . . . into administrable needs." While men had to check in regularly and prove they were "willing to work" to collect unemployment benefits and what little job training was available, women with children had to agree to become "dependent clients" and allow themselves to be treated as if they were incapable of meeting or even of *defining* their own needs or those of their children without the constant intervention and supervision of caseworkers, therapists, counselors, and other social service workers. In this "feminine" subsystem, women had to allow themselves to be stigmatized as "deviant," so that "service provision [had] the character of normalization."[14] Subsequently, the circumstances that led these women to submit to what might be termed the "rituals of qualification"[15] involved in requesting public assistance were reduced to a supposed *individual* inability or unwillingness on their parts to be proper or "normal" mothers, regardless of contributing *systemic* factors such as social tolerance of chronic domestic violence, or the lack of living-wage jobs and adequate and affordable day-care services.[16] This is still the case; even the name of the new welfare legislation that coincides with the radical restructuring of public housing shifts responsibility both for their poverty and for finding a way out of it from the collective social body to individual poor women themselves: the Personal Responsibility and Work Opportunity Reconciliation Act of 1996 that has replaced Aid to Families with Dependent Children.

Of course, the public rhetoric that has created an image of women with children in desperate circumstances as incompetent and irresponsible has not been generated solely by the public assistance system that Fraser refers to, following Althusser, as the "juridical-administrative–therapeutic state apparatus."[17] In describing her own experiences as a "welfare mother" and food stamp recipient, Theresa Funicello recalls a policy commonly practiced by stores in New York throughout the 1970s. Whenever women bought food with food stamps, the stores gave them "store change" in the form of aluminum tokens or paper receipts instead of actual currency. The policy made lots of unearned extra money for the stores, since the tokens or slips of paper were often lost or not used for other reasons, but they justified it by claiming that this was the only way to ensure that women using food stamps could use them only for food. Because of the conventional portrayals of the mothers "as inferior, ignorant, deviant, mentally and/or morally deficient, an inappropriate and wasteful policy enriched the grocery stores while children went hungry. This fundamental fallacy permeated the welfare system directly, the social welfare agencies that received huge government contracts . . ., the policy-making bodies that concocted the rules, and the media."[18] The extent to which Chicago's media have legitimated the displacement of public housing residents by systematically representing them as threats to the social body rather than as a part of it is evident in the *Chicago Tribune*'s selective use of data in its portrayal of Katie Sistrunk. The information provided in "Tenants No One Wants" would seem to suggest that she is precisely the embodiment of the welfare mother unable to parent responsibly; with one adult son in prison, another in jail, and two teens attacking the police, we are clearly meant to assume that she either can't or won't control her children.

But in spite of her notoriety among Chicago's social service agencies, Katie Sistrunk, 45-year-old mother of thirteen and grandmother to twenty-eight, has actually relied very little on welfare, although we would never know this from reading her profile in the *Chicago Tribune*. All odds to the contrary, she and her husband, who passed away only recently and whose ashes Sistrunk carefully carried to the new apartment she finally landed on Chicago's north side, raised their thirteen children together in the Robert Taylor Homes during their twenty-seven-year marriage. Many of these were spent in the cluster of buildings that came to be known as "the Hole" because of chronic gang shootings and drug dealing. Sistrunk's oldest son Henry has a tattoo of "the Hole" across his back. Pam Belluck told a quite different version of the "Sistrunk story" in an article that appeared in the *New York Times* a full six weeks before the *Chicago Tribune*'s "Tenants No One Wants." According to Belluck, the Sistrunks lived mostly on Mr Sistrunk's earnings, only occasionally relying on welfare. Yes, five of the Sistrunks' adult children have police records, but there are also three who have attended college, and one is about to graduate with a degree in architecture. And, importantly, Katie Sistrunk is revealed as a "passionate advocate for herself" and the family she has managed to hold together. Rather than simply allow the CHA to determine where her grown children would live, she "lobbied housing officials until [they] got rent-subsidized apartments" with hard-to-get Section 8 vouchers. She likewise advocated for housing for herself and her two younger children, rejecting one "scattered-site" apartment and phoning CHA officials when she was denied others she wanted because authorities had confused her with a sister involved in drug dealing. When she found herself still without a place to go two days before her building in the Robert Taylor Homes was to be emptied, "she rounded up other tenants and threatened not to leave."[19]

This is hardly a woman who is passive, incompetent, or unable to control her family. Indeed, it seems more likely that her "name" is as well known as it is among Chicago's social service authorities precisely *because* she is so active, so competent, and so willing to advocate for her family and herself when these authorities would rather she not do so. In its rush to dismiss Katie Sistrunk as an incorrigible impediment to the smooth operating of the CHA, the *Chicago Tribune* is willing simply to ignore the questions it could have asked about her, or rather asked her about herself—how did a mother living in what were arguably the most dangerous buildings in the city's most isolated projects manage to keep a family of thirteen together? How did they survive "the Hole"? How did she get those three children through college? And why does her experience not qualify her for anything when she looks for new housing? Why doesn't it at least qualify her for the respect of her fellow Chicagoans? Instead, her complex and considerable experience is reduced conveniently to a pre-existing "deviant" stereotype in an article that both silences her and encourages readers to hope she isn't eventually placed in their neighborhood.

This slotting of Katie Sistrunk into a pre-existing deviant category represents, then, a particularly blatant example of the recent shift in the public rhetoric around recipients of public assistance generally that Lauren Berlant, relying appropriately on the language of "ethnic cleansing," has characterized as

> a particularly brutal mode of what we might call *hygienic governmentality* . . . the ruling bloc solicits mass support for such "governing" by using abjected populations as exemplary of all obstacles to national life; by wielding images and narratives of a threatened "good life" that a putative "we" have known; . . . the nation must at all costs protect this image of a way of life, even against the happiness of some of its own citizens.[20]

I want to push this a bit further by arguing in what follows that Chicago's solution to the "problem" of public housing suggests that it is willing to sacrifice not only the happiness of these abjected citizens, but also finally their status as *citizens* and even as *people* as a way of justifying their compulsory disenfranchisement and displacement. The disqualification of Katie Sistrunk's experience lays bare certain assumptions about whose experience counts and whose doesn't in public discourse and policy, and about who is authorized to self-represent within the official public sphere. Before returning to how these assumptions are impacting on Chicago's public housing residents as they are just now, it will be useful to re-examine three recent models for how public and counter-public spheres are formed and how they function in relation to each other, because it is within this relationship that the fates of Katie Sistrunk and people like her are being determined.

The first major and certainly the most thoroughly discussed elaboration of the concept of "the public sphere" is Jürgen Habermas's *Structural Transformation of the Public Sphere*. Because it has, deservedly, received so much critical attention, I will refer here only very briefly to those points that will help me eventually to answer the questions raised above. Habermas argues that the classical bourgeois public sphere as postulated by Kant and taken up by the emergent bourgeoisie of the Enlightenment was understood as a formal structure that would enable them to wrench intellectual and political exchange away from private authorities and allow them instead to use it to impact actively on, and thus control, public life. Access to this public sphere was, "in principle," open to "anyone who understood how to use his reason in public," the only prerequisite being that potential discussants be willing to "emerge from the confines of their private spheres."[21] The "public sphere" was thus intended as a forum within which informed and reasoning subjects could come together as equals to discuss and reach democratic consensus on issues important to their community.

But even Habermas realizes that this was not how it worked. The public sphere was only theoretically open to "*anyone* who understood how to use his reason in public" since, in practice, "only *property-owning people* were admitted to a public engaged in critical political debate." The justification for this restriction was the assumption that the reasoning capacities of property owners were somehow less likely to be burdened with special interests and agendas than those of propertyless wage-earners because the former were "their own masters" in a way that the latter were not. Habermas explains Kant's logic:

> Only *property-owning private people* were admitted to a public engaged in critical political debate, for their autonomy was rooted in the sphere of commodity exchange.... [W]hile the wage laborers were forced to exchange their labor power as their sole commodity, the property-owning private people related to each other as owners of commodities through an exchange of goods. Only the latter were their own masters; only they should be enfranchised to vote—admitted to the public use of reason.[22]

The assumption is that propertyless people couldn't be trusted to take part in a democratic process of forming rational consensus because they were in competition with one another for buyers of "their sole commodity," their labor power, while property owners could "relate" to each other as owners of property and other commodities. Property was thus the "authorization" required to participate properly as a citizen in the public sphere.

> Consequently the propertyless were excluded from the public of private people engaged in critical political debate.... In this sense, they were not citizens at all, but persons who with *talent, industry and luck* might someday be able to attain that status; until then they merely had the same claim to protection under the law as others, without being allowed to participate in legislation themselves. (emphases added)[23]

In this way, as Oskar Negt and Alexander Kluge would subsequently argue, the criteria for political enfranchisement "exclude from politics and the public sphere all those sections of the population that do not participate in bourgeois politics because they cannot afford to."[24] The bourgeois public sphere is thus from the onset a "mechanism of exclusion"[25] that presents itself as precisely the opposite, a mechanism for democratic inclusion.[26]

In her influential response to Habermas, Nancy Fraser takes him to task for underplaying the extent to which the "official public sphere rested on—indeed, was importantly constituted by, a number of significant exclusions."[27] Habermas does initially mention, albeit with considerable understatement, that his analysis "leaves aside the *plebeian* public sphere as a variant that was in a sense suppressed in the historical process";[28] he also admits that the bourgeois public sphere made universalizing claims for the "basic rights of man" even as it was taking steps to institutionalize their "de facto restriction to a certain class of men."[29] But, Fraser argues, Habermas "never explicitly problematizes some dubious assumptions that underlie the bourgeois model," tending instead to idealize it as having made possible a "specific kind of [interest-free] discursive interaction."[30] He does this, I would add, so as to be able to compare the "pure" classical bourgeois model positively to the contemporary public sphere, which he argues has been contaminated both by the media and by competing economic (that is, class) interest groups.

Fraser then turns her attention to what she terms the "plurality of competing publics" that Habermas overlooks, alternative publics that have always existed alongside the official public sphere and challenged its authority at the level of its "styles of political behavior" and "norms of public speech."[31] She calls these "subaltern counterpublics," as she says, "in order to signal that they are parallel discursive arenas"; as a contemporary example of such an arena, she points to "the U.S. feminist subaltern counterpublic, with its variegated array of journals, bookstores, publishing companies, film and video distribution centers, academic programs, conferences, conventions, festivals, and local meeting places."[32] In an argument structured so that she can conclude with a projected model of how these parallel public spheres might be able to speak constructively to each other in a "non-stratified" (by which I must assume she means classless) society, she focuses not on blatant criteria for exclusion such as property ownership that have been used historically by the bourgeois public sphere, but on what she calls "informal impediments to participatory parity that can persist even after everyone is formally and legally licensed to participate."[33] These impediments are the "expressive norms"[34] that distinguish one public constituency from another and can be used to legitimate or delegitimate their public authority. She uses the example of a faculty meeting in which contributions to the discussion by women are more often interrupted, dismissed, or outright ignored than those by men. But she implies that similar criteria for dismissal can and have been used to deauthorize contributions to the public sphere by other parallel but marginalized groups, such as people of color, gay men and lesbians, and the working class.

Certainly, Fraser comes much closer here than does Habermas to recognizing explicitly how counterpublics made up of "unequally empowered social groups [that] tend to develop unequally valued cultural styles"[35] are often informally disqualified from sharing public authority in spite of laws guaranteeing equality. And it would be tempting to conclude that Katie Sistrunk and the particular "subaltern counterpublic" of poor black public housing residents to which she belongs have been denied "participatory parity" simply on the basis of that group's decidedly non-bourgeois cultural styles. But Fraser's analysis comes up short on several counts. First, it is clear from her examples of what she considers already existing subaltern counterpublics that she herself ignores or at least brackets the extent to which the economic or *class* differences (and, therefore, interests) that separate some counterpublics from the bourgeois public sphere play a more decisive role in their marginalization than do differences in "cultural style." The most striking example of this is her assessment of the "U.S. feminist subaltern counterpublic," with its apparatus of cultural capital as well as the actual capital needed to finance bookstores, conferences, publishing houses, etc. This is clearly a subcategory or, to use Habermas's term, a variant *within* the bourgeois public sphere; while it has functioned as a valuable corrective for bourgeois women, it is hardly an alternative to it. Likewise, the women faculty members whose comments are ignored by their colleagues are still well educated (that is, "well qualified" in terms of a particular mode of articulation), and, compared to most working women, well paid. Whether or not their remarks are snickered at, these women's everyday situations are quite different from those of women who are not now, and will most likely never be, "formally and legally licensed to participate" in political decision-making.

In addition, although Fraser expands on Habermas's model by insisting on the inclusion of counterpublics previously excluded, her assumption that these can simply coexist peacefully *parallel* to the official public sphere is finally as idealistic as his in that it does not adequately account for the rhetorical violence currently being utilized to willfully misrepresent and thereby delegitimate the counterpublic of public housing residents. By turning now to an earlier but much more aggressively contestatory response to Habermas, I want to suggest that women like Katie Sistrunk aren't being excluded from the hegemonic bourgeois public sphere primarily because of cultural differences, but because they constitute a counterpublic sphere that, rather than existing parallel to the official bourgeois/national public sphere as a competitive alternative, challenges it at *every level* of its cultural, legal, financial, spatial, and epistemic authority. The official public sphere does not, therefore, seek merely to delegitimate Katie Sistrunk at the level of discourse, but rather to disqualify her experience and that of the counterpublic to which she belongs as meaningful; in Wahneema Lubiano's words, it uses "narrative means" to wage "ideological war" against it.[36] This in turn makes it possible to represent that counterpublic as a contaminating impediment to "public" interests.

The response of Oskar Negt and Alexander Kluge to Habermas in *Public Sphere and Experience* (originally published in 1972) argues that there is and always has been more than one public sphere and that the category is not the exclusive property of the bourgeoisie. Like Fraser, they contend rather that there are at any one time a range of public spheres that exist simultaneously, formed by different and often competing constituencies and often manifesting themselves in contexts that are not officially recognized as public spheres. Such officially unrecognized public spheres exist and operate outside the usual parameters of institutional legitimation, responding to the contingent needs of all of those groups whose self-expression and self-representation are excluded or, as Negt and Kluge put it more contentiously, "blocked" from the usual arenas of public discourse.

In their discussion of how the official bourgeois public sphere blocks access to it for some people as well as blocking the legitimation of other, counterpublic spheres, Negt and Kluge contend that this blocking is accomplished surreptitiously through, for example, the requirement that those attempting to gain access first adapt their mode of self-expression to conform to bourgeois "standards" for self-presentation. "All bourgeois forms of the public sphere presuppose special training, both linguistic and mimetic. In public court proceedings, in dealings with officials, it is expected of all parties involved that they be concise and present their interests within forms of expression fitting to the official context."[37] Importantly, the standardized forms of expression considered proper in official contexts require more than conforming to rules for proper grammar and spelling. They also require "economy of thought" and "an abstract flexibility" that result in precision and "the ability to talk abstractly about all situations"[38]—in other words, the ability to assume a stance of objective "universal subjectivity" from which to express oneself impersonally about matters that may in fact be very personal.[39] Conversely, modes of expression such as anecdotes, which are grounded in the concrete specificity of experience explicitly marked as personal, are dismissed as improper, excessive, and merely subjective. Lauren Berlant has written persuasively about this function of the official public sphere, noting that it "protects and privileges" those subjects able to "appear to be disembodied and abstract while retaining cultural authority"; indeed, "the power to suppress [the] body, to cover its tracks and traces, is the sign of real authority."[40] Cultural authority is granted only to those who can appear to be disembodied (and therefore disinterested), and supposedly thus able to speak for everyone in general but no one in particular. This performance of disembodied cultural authority is what Negt and Kluge refer to, following Horkheimer and Adorno's genealogy of its development, as the bourgeois "character mask, the personification of capital";[41] it is a mask of universality that allows the (white and male) bourgeois subject to control the terms of public discussion of his interests without ever having to acknowledge them *as* interests.

Negt and Kluge's discussion of "forms of expression" here focuses on what is required of working-class people trying to enter into public discourse as it is carried out in public school systems or the media. But their analysis just as accurately helps to explain how members of what might be called "the counterpublic sphere of the propertyless underclass" are discursively and politically disenfranchised. As we have seen, rather than being positioned first as "a citizen" or even "a person," Katie Sistrunk is immediately identified as the "45-year-old mother of thirteen," a description so specific that it not only makes it impossible to think of her as a "disembodied universal subject," but also reduces her precisely to her body and its gendered reproductive behavior. She is thus the opposite of the non-gendered, non-racialized bourgeois character mask. Because she is, as it were, doubly embodied (as a black woman *and* as a mother), she is disempowered and deauthorized in the official public sphere.[42] This identification denies her not only cultural authority, but also epistemic authority; because she isn't allowed to self-represent, she can be ruthlessly (mis-)represented, as in the *Chicago Tribune* article, as an out-of-control body. And since the social meaning of that sort of body has already been well established discursively in the print and visual media, this representation functions to evoke the whole range of pathologized behaviors and experiences specific to the counterpublic of the propertyless underclass.

But while this explains *how* Katie Sistrunk is systematically disqualified from participating in the official public sphere, it still does not get to the heart of *why* she and people like her are being so aggressively pathologized and disenfranchised just now. In order to answer this more difficult question, we must look at what Negt and Kluge understand as the distinct advantages, but also the distinct limitations, of the counterpublic they examine. In contrasting a legitimated bourgeois public sphere with the marginalized proletarian public sphere[43] as one example of a counterpublic grounded in differing behaviors and experiences, they clearly understand the term "public sphere" to refer to far more than either Habermas's or Fraser's public forum model, wherein people respecting each other as equals form consensus. In a 1988 interview, Kluge explained that an organic public sphere such as the one they refer to as "proletarian" is something "filled with experience"; it is a "substantive" context for living that "has a conscience."[44] This is an important expansion of the meaning of the term; as Bruce Robbins has noted, "to speak of a working-class public sphere, as Negt and Kluge do ... is to stress a *site of interaction and continuing self-formation* rather than a given or self-sufficient body of ideas and practices distinguishing one group from others."[45] And rather than imitate the conventions of the official public sphere, this "fuller" public sphere operates in its own vernacular (whether gestural, verbal, etc.) in accordance with the needs and experiences of its constituents. This definition proceeds from a radically different set of assumptions to that of Habermas. His is derived from the emergence of the middle class which emphasized a separation of its supposedly separable public and private spheres; theirs rejects the notion that public and private interests have ever been really split like this in the first place, especially for working people. This is the case, of course, for public housing residents and other recipients of social services, who must expect that any and every aspect of their private lives will be submitted arbitrarily to public scrutiny and comment if they are to continue to "qualify" for services.

While Negt and Kluge are adamant that the proletarian and other experientially full counterpublic spheres can and do exist, they are equally adamant in examining the contradictions in late capitalist societies that prevent, and, as they argue it, *must for their very survival continue to prevent*, these counterpublic spheres from developing the autonomy and thus the power they would need to be meaningfully "equal" to the official one. The proletarian public sphere may be outside of the dominant bourgeois public sphere, but it is not independent of it; the difference in its perspective lies not in its characteristic "cultural styles" but rather in its relationship to production, the key category whose importance the bourgeois public sphere masks even to itself. Negt and Kluge in their analysis of co-existing and competing public spheres explicitly emphasize that none of the counterpublic spheres will ever supersede or overcome (or, to refer back to Fraser's "parallel public spheres" model, be allowed to coexist legitimately alongside) the dominant one as long as they do not have access to the means of production and thus to economic and political power. Rather, the relationship between the two will remain antagonistic.[46]

A similarly structured oppositional relationship exists between the official bourgeois public sphere (which is overwhelmingly white) and the counterpublic of the propertyless underclass (which is overwhelming black). In this case, the line of demarcation and contestation between the two is not their relationship to production, given the extent to which postindustrial capitalism has made it increasingly impossible for underclass people to form such a relationship, but rather their relationship to *property* and its role in economic and political power. In his stunning critique of millennial capitalism and its rhetoric of globalization, Paul Smith has pointed to "the use of consumption as a form of social regulation and the reproduction of appropriate social subjects for capital's relation to and transformation of labor";[47] he describes this as a process by which the "normative human subject" (the same bourgeois subject to which Habermas refers as "freely self-actualizing"[48]) becomes what is now better termed "the subject of value." Rather than understanding itself in Enlightenment terms as an inherently valuable "Individual," this millennial subject defines itself and others in terms of relationships to consumption and property. Smith describes the social consequences of this transformation unequivocally:

> The most important aspect . . . of the subject of value is its acceptance of the system of private property. . . . Thus it is property rights (rather than, say, human rights or rights to economic justice) that constitute the basis of the legal frameworks of the Northern democracies. The law protects precisely the accumulation of capital in private hands, and in doing so fixes subjects into juridical relations to one another and defines their obedience to the law as *an acceptance of the rights of private property*. It is to this complex and circular logic that the subject of value must adhere.[49]

Unfortunately for people like Katie Sistrunk, the subject of value defines itself not only in terms of self-identification with property, but also by contrasting itself to those whose relationship to property is less congenial:

> [F]or this totalizing vision of capitalism to be realized, there must exist . . . a series of others, temporally and spatially displaced, of course, but also discriminated against. . . . Subjects who choose not to, or are not in a position to, sign the contractual forms which guarantee equality, under this system are by definition disenfranchised.[50]

And, I would add, pathologized, if, like Chicago's public housing residents, they are understood as *incapable* of maintaining a "proper" relationship with property. Just as the rhetorical conventions of the 1980s and early 1990s created and demonized the irresponsible "welfare mother," so those of the late 1990s have created a pathologized image of a propertyless underclass that either fails to give proper respect to the property provided it by the state, or willfully destroys property that belongs "rightfully" to subjects of value. And just as that earlier rhetoric was divided into parallel but gendered subsystems that figured men as potential workers and women as dependent clients, so we now find two subcategories within the pathologized counterpublic of the propertyless. Women with dependent children are still portrayed as incompetent mothers and inept housekeepers, but this stereotype has been negatively expanded into that of the "welfare queen," the black parasite[51] who, although she could and should be working, doesn't work, choosing instead to "live off the system" and, as the often-circulated myth has it, even having more children so as to be able to collect more benefits. This myth has been so powerful that "workfare" was introduced to, in effect, force such women to "earn" the little aid they and their children still receive. The women being displaced from public housing in Chicago must now submit to a new "ritual of qualification," not to collect benefits, but to be eligible for adequate replacement housing. This ritual of qualification tests not for whether they are good mothers, but whether they are sufficiently respectful of property to deserve a new place to live. Pam Belluck describes how one of Katie Sistrunk's fellow Robert Taylor Homes residents-in-transit lost an apartment she wanted for herself, her sister and her three children because she failed the "housekeeping inspector's" evaluation of her soon-to-be-demolished CHA unit; there were roaches on the walls, and the family was using plastic milk crates and an old hairdryer bonnet for kitchen chairs. Because she couldn't personally control the roaches in a building that most likely has been infested with them since it was built, and because she couldn't afford "proper" furniture, Angela Smith failed the inspection "just weeks before her building was to be emptied."[52] Since women with children are the fastest-growing segment of the homeless population (which has been estimated in Chicago to include already up to 80,000 people), it is not unreasonable to assume that she and her children might soon be joining them.

While women in these circumstances increasingly are reduced discursively to the level of parasites on the social body, their male counterparts are likewise reduced to another non-human metaphor. No longer under- or unemployed workers, they are now "predators" waiting to attack that body's weakened defenses. Car-jackings have been the form of assault on property most often linked to disenfranchised black men of late; incapable of becoming subjects of value themselves, these men are portrayed as threats to the vital linkage of consumption, property, and citizenship upon which the subject of value depends for his cultural and political authorization. These men are no longer figured as potential subjects, but rather as potential "*objects* of value"; as was confirmed by a 1997 article in *Business Week* jubilantly entitled "Go Directly to Jail: Wackenhut is Scoring in the Prison Biz," the private prison industry is one of the nation's most successful growth industries.[53] That this growth has been made possible by skyrocketing incarcerations of black men is no secret: in 1970, the entire U.S. prison population was 200,000; by 1999 it had topped 2 million, and that population is disproportionately made up of black men. Many of these have been imprisoned for drug-related offenses; "in the last decade the number of whites imprisoned for drug crimes rose by 306%, the number of blacks by 707%."[54] As Paulette Olson and Dell Champlin have noted, the same behaviors that are almost obsessively linked to black men in the media and in political rhetoric, such as alcoholism, drug dependency, and neglect of children, are also rampant among corporate executives whose livelihoods depend on "corporate welfare," but the latter remain for the most part invisible because theirs are assumed to be private rather than social problems.[55] Such behaviors are certainly not used to pathologize corporate executives as a "deviant population."

Because such rhetoric has been so successful in disqualifying public housing residents as citizens and even as people, it has also succeeded in disqualifying public housing as a "context of living" in the sense of Negt and Kluge, as the site of community and family stability. For example, the accumulated experience of Katie Sistrunk's twenty-seven years in the Robert Taylor Homes, the networks of family members and friends she must have built up to deal with childcare emergencies, getting to and from jobs, and the endless trips she had to make back and forth to social service agencies to keep herself and her family "qualified," are simply dismissed. Like the housing she finally had to accept in north Chicago, far from the South Side Robert Taylor corridor, these networks are being forcibly dispersed and "scattered" throughout the city.[56]

Now that the land under them has been recognized by Chicago's property developers and city government as more valuable without their presence than with it,[57] and now that it is more profitable to house black men in prisons than to house them in public housing, or to provide them with job skills and a place to earn a living, women like Katie Sistrunk will increasingly be denied not just adequate housing but the contexts of living that have helped make it possible for them and their children to survive against considerable odds. Jürgen Habermas noted of the propertyless people excluded from Kant's ideal bourgeois public sphere that "they were not citizens at all, but persons who with talent, industry and luck might someday be able to attain that status." As I hope to have shown through this example of the experiential consequences of late millennial capitalism for Chicago's displaced public housing residents, it seems unlikely that even these options will remain available to them much longer.

Notes

This chapter is greatly indebted to discussions that took place in and around a graduate seminar on "Public Cultures, Public Spheres, and the Poetics of Citizenship" that I taught at the University of Illinois at Chicago in the fall of 1998. I would like to thank the members of that seminar for their engagement with the sorts of questions I discuss here: Joe Alter, Daniel Blaney-Koen, John Breedlove, Duriel Harris, Annie Knepler, Jean Petrolle, Jermaine Singleton, Bridget Harris Tsemo, Susan Vervaet, and Vershawn Ashanti Young.

1. Paul Smith, *Millennial Dreams: Conteporary Culture and Capital in the North* (London and New York: Verso, 1997), p. 22.

2. Nancy Fraser, *Unruly Practices: Power, Discourse and Gender in Contemporary Social Theory* (Minneapolis: University of Minnesota Press, 1989), p. 144.

3. The sequence of new legislation that facilitated the dismantling of public housing and other components of the social safety net is elaborated in Harold Henderson, "There Goes Their Neighborhood," *Chicago Reader*, 27:34 (May 29, 1998). Public housing legislation and mandates from 1940 to 1960 are discussed in Arnold R. Hirsch, *Making the Second Ghetto: Race and Housing in Chicago, 1940–1960* (Chicago: University of Chicago Press, 1998), especially pp. 212ff.

4. Henderson, "There Goes Their Neighborhood," p. 20.

5. Hirsch, *Making the Second Ghetto*, pp. 262–3.

6. Of the city's 67,000 families in public housing, 97 percent are black, according to Pam Belluck, "Razing the Slums to Rescue the Residents," *New York Times* (September 6, 1998): 4.

7. Ibid., p. 8.

8. The entire "Odyssey" series can be read on the *Chicago Tribune* web site beginning from the initial address, www.chicagotribune.com/go/cha.

9. Three "options" are given to CHA residents whose units are scheduled for demolition. They can request to be placed in a rehabbed CHA unit (of which there will be very few); they can ask the CHA to find them a so-called "scattered site" apartment; or they can apply for a Section 8 voucher that will allow them to find an apartment for which they can afford to pay 30 percent of the rent. In the latter case, the federal U.S. Department of Housing Development (HUD), which oversees all local public housing authorities, must pick up the remainder. As numerous studies have shown, there are not nearly enough such housing alternatives available in Chicago's already-overburdened rental market for the number of former or soon-to-be former residents who will need them; see especially "The Plan to Voucher Out Public Housing: An Analysis of the Chicago Experience and a Case Study of the Proposal to Redevelop the Cabrini Green Public Housing Area. The Nathalie M. Voorhees Center for Neighborhood and Community Improvement Report," Publication V-155 of the Voorhees Center of the University of Illinois at Chicago (1997).

The CHA has responded to this situation not by postponing demolition until sufficient replacement housing is available, or by lobbying for more rehabbing of existing units, but by increasing the numbers of resident evictions from buildings scheduled for "redevelopment—a move that reduces the number of public housing tenants the agency must provide with replacement housing" (Brian J. Rogal, "Transforming Public Housing: CHA Tenant Evictions Jump as Buildings Fall," *StreetWise* (January 5–18, 1999): 1). Once a tenant has been evicted, which usually occurs because they have fallen behind in rent payments, the CHA is no longer obliged to help them find replacement housing. Eviction rates in CHA buildings scheduled for demolition or for "revitalization" as "mixed-income communities" are nearly triple those in the ten projects not so scheduled (ibid.).

10. Linnet Myers, "Tenants No One Wants," *Chicago Tribune* (October 15, 1998): 1.

11. Ibid.

12. A later installment of the "Odyssey" series suggests that CHA workers are under duress not so much because of recalcitrant tenants as because too few workers have been assigned to help the daunting number of tenants being relocated. For example, only two were assigned to all of the tenants needing such help at the Henry Horner Homes. See Faith McRoberts, "Move From CHA High Rise Can Involve a Leap of Faith," *Chicago Tribune* (September 2, 1998).

13. Fraser, *Unruly Practices*, p. 147.

14. Ibid., p. 155.

15. As Theresa Funicello points out, the "qualification requirements" to which anyone requesting public assistance is subjected include "endless demands" to supply both paper documentation and "evidence of 'proper behavior'"; see her *Tyranny of Kindness: Dismantling the Welfare System to End Poverty in America* (New York: Atlantic Monthly Press, 1993), p. 57. I would add to this evidence of willingness to have one's personal morality subjected to scrutiny; in my own experience, one of the first questions asked routinely of a single woman with a child applying for basic food-stamp assistance was not "Do you receive any help from your child's father?" but "Do you know who the father is?"—a question that is remarkably straightforward in its assumptions.

16. For statistics on the connection between domestic violence and women with children requesting public assistance or becoming homeless, see Laura Butterbaugh, "Homelessness: Women Search for Answers," *Off Our Backs*, 28:7 (July 1998): 12–14; Elizabeth W. Lindsey, "The Impact of Homelessness and Shelter Life on Family Relationships," *Family Relations*, 47:3 (July 1998): 243–52; and especially Valerie Polakow, Peggy Kahn, and Nora Martin, "Struggling to Survive: The Lives of Women and Children Under the New Welfare Law," *Journal for a Just and Caring Education*, 4:4 (October 1998): 374–92.

17. Fraser, *Unruly Practices*, p. 154.

18. Funicello, *Tyranny of Kindness*, p. 55.

19. Belluck, "Razing the Slums," p. 8.

20. Lauren Berlant, *The Queen of America Goes to Washington City: Essays on Sex and Citizenship* (Durham and London: Duke University Press, 1997), p. 175.

21. Jürgen Habermas, *The Structural Transformation of the Public Sphere: An Inquiry into a Category of Bourgeois Knowledge*, trans. Thomas Burger (Cambridge, MA: MIT Press, 1991), p. 105.

22. Ibid., pp. 109–10.

23. Ibid., p. 111.

24. Oskar Negt and Alexander Kluge, *Public Sphere and Experience: Toward an Analysis of the Bourgeois and Proletarian Public Sphere*, trans. Peter Labanyi, Jamie Owen Daniel, and Assenka Oksiloff (Minneapolis: University of Minnesota Press, 1993), p. 10.

25. Ibid., p. 11.

26. My summary of Habermas and then of Negt and Kluge here relies somewhat on wording in my essay, "Virtual Communities?: Public Spheres and Public Intellectuals on the Internet," *Electronic Book Review*, 2 (Spring 1996): http://www.altx.com/ebr/ebr2.daniel.html.

27. Nancy Fraser, "Rethinking the Public Sphere: A Contribution to the Critique of Actual Existing Democracy," in *Habermas and the Public Sphere*, ed. Craig Calhoun (Cambridge, MA: MIT Press, 1992), p. 113.

28. Habermas, *Structural Transformation*, p. xviii.

29. Ibid., p. xii.

30. Fraser, "Rethinking the Public Sphere," p. 116. Habermas responds to Fraser and his other U.S. critics in his "Further Reflections on the Public Sphere," in *Habermas and the Public Sphere*, pp. 421–61.

31. Fraser, "Rethinking the Public Sphere," p. 116.

32. Ibid., p. 123.

33. Ibid., p. 119.

34. Ibid., p. 126.

35. Ibid., p. 120.

36. According to Lubiano, such narratives "work as a form of shorthand, functioning effectively even when their content . . . is not explicitly spelled out." Wahneema Lubiano, "Black Ladies, Welfare Queens, and State Minstrels: Ideological War by Narrative Means," *Race-ing Justice, En-gendering Power: Essays on Anita Hill, Clarence Thomas, and the Construction of Social Reality*, ed. Toni Morrison (New York: Pantheon, 1992), p. 331.

37. Negt and Kluge, *Public Sphere and Experience*, pp. 45–6.

38. Ibid., p. 48.

39. As they put it succinctly, "Having 'experience' within this public sphere means to have dominant knowledge. . . . This knowledge includes the capacity to cloak the immediate fractionalized interests of capital in the form of an imagined sovereignty, a feigned collective will." Ibid., p. 11.

40. Berlant, *The Queen of America*, p. 176.

41. Negt and Kluge, *Public Sphere and Experience*, p. 54. Horkheimer and Adorno discuss the "prototype of the bourgeois individual" (p. 43) in their celebrated chapter on "Odysseus, or Myth and Enlightenment" in *Dialectic of Enlightenment*, trans. John Cumming (New York: Continuum, 1972); Negt and Kluge provide a brilliant homage to the Odysseus chapter in their discussion of Odysseus's inability to consider a collective solution to the problem of the Sirens; see their footnote 42, pp. 24–5. *Public Sphere and Experience* was dedicated to the memory of Adorno, who died in 1969; this dedication was inexplicably deleted from the English translation.

42. In an essay on Douglas Sirk's film *Imitation of Life*, Lauren Berlant argues similarly that a black woman in the U.S. is a "twice-biologized and delegitimated public subject—a 'woman' and a 'Negro'": "National Brands/National Body: *Imitation of Life*," in *The Phantom Public Sphere*, ed. Bruce Robbins (Minneapolis: University of Minnesota Press, 1993), p. 175.

43. While I have been alternating here between "working-class" and "proletarian," Negt and Kluge intentionally use "proletarian" instead of Habermas's "plebeian" precisely because they believe that "what is at issue here is not a variant of the bourgeois public sphere, but rather an entirely separate conceptualization of the overall social context . . . rooted in the production process" (Negt and Kluge, *Public Sphere and Experience*, p. xliv) which results in an oppositional counterpublic, an opposition the term "working-class" doesn't necessarily suggest. For another argument for the term, see Raymond Williams, "Working-Class, Proletarian, Socialist: Problems in Some Welsh Novels," in *The Socialist Novel in Britain*, ed. H. Gustav Klaus (Brighton: Harvester, 1982), pp. 110–21.

44. Stuart Liebman, "On New German Cinema: Art, Enlightenment, and the Public Sphere. An Interview with Alexander Kluge," *October*, 46 (Fall 1988): 41.

45. Robbins, ed., *The Phantom Public Sphere*, p. xvii.

46. Contra Fraser, Negt and Kluge argue that: "The boundary between the bourgeois and proletarian public spheres, between the bourgeois and proletarian articulations of the circumstances of everyday life, does not exist as a spatial, temporal, logical or concrete threshold . . . the proletarian public sphere negates the bourgeois one because it dissolves, partially destroys, and partially assimilates the latter's elements. In serving its opposing interests, the bourgeois public sphere does the same to every form of the proletarian which is not supported by the powers opposing it and thus cannot protect itself from attack. *A coexistence is impossible.*" Negt and Kluge, *Public Sphere and Experience*, p. 35, (emphasis added).

47. Smith, *Millennial Dreams*, pp. 47–8.

48. Habermas, *Structural Transformation*, p. 13.

49. Smith, *Millennial Dreams*, p. 83.

50. Ibid., pp. 83–4.

51. As Lubiano notes, "the welfare queen [is] always black" ("Welfare Queens, Black Ladies," p. 340).

52. Belluck, "Razing the Slums," p. 4.

53. G. DeGeorge and J. Flynn, "Go Directly to Jail: Wackenhut Is Scoring in the Prison Biz," *Business Week*, 3357 (December 15, 1997): 139.

54. For an excellent analysis of the relationship between such disproportionate representation and the "deep structural entrenchment of contemporary racism," see Angela Y. Davis, "Race and Criminalization: Black Americans and the Punishment Industry," in *The Angela Y. Davis Reader*, ed. Joy James (Malden, MA, and Oxford: Blackwell Press, 1998), pp. 61–74.

55. Paulette Olson and Dell Champlin, "Ending Corporate Welfare as We Know It: An Institutional Analysis of the Dual Structure of Welfare," *Journal of Economic Issues*, 32:3 (September 1998): 759–71. This article is invaluable both for its statistics on amounts spent annually by the federal government on corporate "subsidies" and on public welfare programs, and for its analysis of the "dual structure of welfare policy" that allows such corporations to mask the extent to which they are parasitically dependent on such government welfare, while subjecting human recipients of public assistance to constant public scrutiny and criticism.

56. Nancy Fraser discusses the informally organized networks that facilitate the structuring of community through the exchange of "prepared meals, food stamps, cooking, shopping, groceries, furniture, sleeping space, cash . . . transportation, clothing, child care, even children. They span several physically distinct households and so *transcend* the principal administrative category that organizes relief programs" which, following the bourgeois model for a "proper" household, focus only on individual households. See *Unruly Practices*, p. 153 (emphasis added). For evidence that Chicago public housing has functioned for many of its residents in just this way as a positive "context of living", see Andrew Fegelmann, "To Many, Public Housing is Still Home Sweet Home," *Chicago Tribune* (January 26, 1997): 1; Henderson, "There Goes Their Neighborhood"; and especially Sudhir Alladi Ventakesh, "An Invisible Community: Inside Chicago's Public Housing," *The American Prospect*, 34 (September/October 1997): 35–40.

57. For background on how Chicago's displacement of its public housing residents

confirms Mike Davis's claim that "middle-class demand for increased spatial and social insulation" has led to "de facto disinvestment in traditional public space and recreation" which in turn has "supported the shift of fiscal resources to corporate-defined redevelopment priorities" (*City of Quartz: Excavating the Future in Los Angeles* [New York: Vintage, 1992], p. 227) such as those currently fighting over the prime real estate upon which Cabrini-Green was built, see Andrew Fegelmann's series of brief articles in the *Chicago Tribune*: "Daley's Cabrini Proposal Ready for Sale" (February 14, 1997): 1; "Cabrini Residents Waiting to be Invited to Unveiling" (February 15, 1997): 5; "Fifteen High Rises in Cabrini Left Out of Big Plan" (February 21, 1997): 1. See also Jeffrey Manier, "Cabrini Plan Profits Told," *Chicago Tribune* (May 28, 1998): 3; Dan Peterson, "Stealing Cabrini Green. A Great Chicago Land Grab" (1997) at http://student-www.uchicago.edu/users/jkw3/ink3cg.html, as well as the Voorhees Center Report (1997) already cited.

5

Unions as Counter-Public Spheres

Stanley Aronowitz

Since the end of World War Two, United States trade unions and their leaders have come under heavy fire from two quarters. From the right came the criticism that unionized workers had become "too greedy." For most of the period ending about 1975, as productivity stagnated, they accuse unions of driving up wages to the detriment of economic growth. Conservatives have blamed labor for the loss of well-paid factory jobs in the most developed capitalist societies since 1973. In their view, higher wages combined with lackluster productivity gains caused major inflationary trends in the 1970s and, even worse, drove investors to seek other outlets.[1] Attracted by the plentiful low-wage labor supply offered by developing countries in Latin America and Asia, capital has accelerated offshore investment.

Signaled by the energy crisis of 1973–75, capital found the wedge to drive down real wages to overcome pressure on profits produced by the world economic stagflation. Unable to counter charges of ruining the U.S. economy, by the early 1980s unions had been put on the defensive. Leading industrial unions granted concessions to corporations which claimed that they would pull up stakes and go overseas unless American workers made themselves competitive both by relaxing work rules to permit speedup and by renouncing wage and benefits gains. Facing budget cuts and consequent threatened layoffs, unions in the public sector abandoned their militancy and chose instead to cooperate with local and state governments to reduce costs in order to save jobs. Between 1973 and 1995 real wages declined by 25 percent but concessions bargaining mostly failed to stem the tide of capital flight not only to offshore locations but also to the U.S. South and Southwest where, after World War Two, unions had failed to establish strong beachheads.

The left has weighed in on several levels. While refuting neo-liberal accusations that labor is largely responsible for the worldwide economic crisis that has afflicted most countries since the mid-1970s, the left has accused unions of being timid in the face of capital's assaults on wages and working conditions—and if not that, then of being outright guilty of ruling-class collaboration. In the United States, the left has criticized unions for becoming, at best, service organizations in the model of insurance companies, rather than remaining social movements; and at worst, it is said that unions are merely sitting on the heads of a restive rank and file, in the process of implementing soft bargaining and other policies. Taken together, these criticisms amount to the charge of accommodation to the globalization of capital.[2] More particularly, the left holds union leaderships responsible for going along with capital's program to transfer the burden of the world economic crisis to working people in the form of a long-term reduction in real wages, cuts in the social wage, and, increasingly, tendencies toward the creation of a two-tier wage system in many production and service industries.

Consequently, on a dual program of union democracy and revived militancy to reverse labor's free fall in membership and in economic and political power, in the 1980s and 1990s the left has helped organize rank-and-file movements to oppose established leaderships, notably in the corruption-ridden Teamsters, in the formally democratic but hierarchical United Auto Workers, and at the local level in unions such as the once-progressive New York Municipal Employees District Council 37, teachers' unions, and the blue-collar-dominated Transport Workers. In the main, these efforts have been narrowly focused on the pressing economic problems faced by many groups who have suffered deteriorating living standards and increasingly onerous working conditions, and upon violations of the democratic rights of dissidents.

By 1995 some sections of organized labor's top leadership began to smell the coffee. In October 1995 in the first contested election in the forty-year history of the AFL-CIO, John Sweeney, president of the million-member Service Employees, became federation president, and since 1996 he has undertaken some major initiatives to reverse organized labor's apparent free fall in membership. He has openly advocated that affiliated unions adopt an "organizing model," according to which the emphasis of "service" yields to "organizing." (In the service model the union member is transformed into a client and the union bureaucracy occupies itself with addressing her multitude of needs from grievances on the job to education and legal counseling.) This shift would be reflected in the allocation of union resources, in expanded rank-and-file mobilization which would play an important role in organizing, and in a call for more activism on political and legislative issues of concern to organized labor.

Make no mistake. Sweeney is no radical democrat, if by that phrase is signified adopting a "social movement model" in which members' sovereignty is not confined to choosing leadership in union elections and to votes for or against contract approvals, and union issues are no longer narrowly construed. In the social movement model, the rank and file runs the union from top to bottom, both at the level of decision-making and in administration.[3] The labor movement allies itself with movements of feminists and racialized minorities, and movements for sexual freedom. But together with top leaders in a number of key unions, the AFL-CIO president seems genuinely concerned lest complacency send the labor movement into obscurity. Since 1996 he and his associates have taken genuine steps to reverse the decline of labor's membership and influence. By 1999, for the first time in two decades, unions had recruited more new members than they lost; at the same time, the density of unionized workers to the labor force continued to decline. Job growth outpaced organizing by a narrow margin.

On the whole, rank-and-file trade union movements have experienced mixed results. But the most successful of them, Teamsters for a Democratic Union (TDU), has recently also suffered setbacks after entering a coalition with a traditional although militant leader of a local union of United Parcel drivers, Ron Carey, who in 1991 went on to win the union's presidency. In 1997, after his reelection for a second term, Carey led the most successful national strike in recent memory aimed at reducing gaps in United Parcel Service's two-tier wage system. But two years after his successful reelection bid, Carey was forced out of office after charges were brought that he had used members' dues to finance his campaign. Although TDU disavowed Carey, its candidate to replace him went down to defeat at the hands of James P. Hoffa, son of the famous Teamsters president, in 1999.

There are encouraging beginnings at the local level. It was a rank-and-file leader in the Municipal Employees District Council 37, a New York Parks Department truck driver named Mark Rosenthal, who blew the whistle on union corruption at the highest levels, including leaders of DC 37's largest locals. Quickly a number of dissident local union presidents, mostly of smaller groups, gathered together to form a Committee for Real Change. They exposed corruption, and equally important, made union democracy the cornerstone of their program for union reform. More to the point, they have tried to establish a link between this and the leadership's accommodationist collective bargaining policies (it negotiated a five-year contract with no raises for the first two years and perpetrated contracts with similarly paltry increases over a twenty-five-year period). Soon, a New York rank-and-file municipal workers' coalition emerged and won the affiliation of about a dozen rank-and-file groups whose unions bargain with city government, all of whom were fighting for the twin objectives of democracy and renewed militancy.

Yet, none of the leading forces behind union renewal—either on the left or among progressives—have addressed one of the underlying issues in labor's decline: the virtual disappearance of a labor public sphere. While there is a large labor press—indeed, every major national union publishes a newspaper which appears at least monthly, and some unions have used the internet to post web sites that offer organizing information and news—labor opinion is neither a staple of the airwaves, nor is there a national labor newspaper. Moreover, the extant labor press is little more than a public relations vehicle for the established leadership. Photos of union presidents and other officers regularly adorn the pages of these publications. In only a few instances do they print dissenting or alternative opinions, mostly in the letters column. In New York, with the sole exception of the Transport Workers' New Directions caucus, the insurgent caucuses have not offered the membership a means by which to communicate with each other over the heads of the leaders. New Directions has published an impressive tabloid which appears regularly. But most of the other rank-and-file groups content themselves with newsletters and periodic letters and leaflets to convey their message. And the once-ubiquitous union hall, where members congregate, socialize, and discuss union and political issues, is all but a relic, as the union "office" offers little space for conviviality.

Raymond Williams has insisted that trade unions are sites of working-class culture as well as instruments of struggle and collective bargaining agents. He insists that their character as bureaucratic organizations does not exhaust their cultural importance. Williams's declaration probably derived, in part, from his long experience as a workers' education teacher, but also from his boyhood experience in Wales, the site of the most militant miners' movement in recent memory. Williams's father was a railroad worker, albeit in a rural setting. Still, as he relates his father's experience, it is clear that in this predominantly farming community, despite their minority status, "the political leaders of the village were the railwaymen."[4] The social ties of these union men translated into public activity, and in early-twentieth-century Britain, such instances were by no means a rarity, even in rural precincts. For in the most industrial of European societies, the workers had a cohesive tradition of struggle and cultural solidarity that dated from the enclosures and the corn laws that drove millions from agriculture to the sixteenth- and seventeenth-century cities.

Similarly, in the United States in the nineteenth century when the country made its turn from agriculture to industrial production, the craft unions of the American Federation of Labor frequently built "labor temples"—in smaller communities as much as in big cities. These locations housed the offices of affiliates to the local trades council and provided space, not only for routine union meetings, but also for public lectures and discussion groups. During the great industrial union upsurge of the 1930s and 1940s, unions of semi-skilled as well as skilled workers in mass production established their own union halls. The Auto Workers, the Electrical Workers, Textile Workers, and the older needle trades unions' halls, among others, were sites of public and social life for hundreds of thousands of workers. Needle trades unions prepared their members for citizenship by teaching English and conducted their education program by using labor and radical texts as well as literature. In New York, local 65, a manufacturing, retail, and wholesale union that organized small shops and large department stores, had a restaurant and bar, as well as a large hall that featured concerts, dances, and other cultural activities such as art exhibits, and made its membership meetings occasions for political education.

"65" built the union and sustained considerable rank-and-file activism by maintaining close contact with its members. For decades after World War Two, when most unions had resorted to the automatic check-off method of collecting dues, in which dues were, like taxes, deducted from wages, 65 maintained the archaic practice of collecting dues "by hand." Every member in good standing appeared at the union hall at least once a month to pay dues, grab a snack or a full meal, and attend a local union meeting, which was mandatory. On occasion they could attend a lecture or an art exhibit, and on Saturdays they might take classes in painting and drawing, creative writing, photography, and crafts. During its fifty-year existence, 65 sporadically offered its members a children's program as well. But in 1989, under a cloud of corruption and membership erosion, the union dissolved into a series of local unions of the Auto Workers to which 65 had previously affiliated. Thus one of the more striking instances of a working-class public sphere is now nearly forgotten, except by mostly retired members who were among its beneficiaries.

There is a scene in Orson Welles's film *Lady From Shanghai* depicting a hall similar to many maintained by the Seafarers and National Maritime Unions in the 1940s and 1950s. Since the contract obliged employers to fill jobs by using a union hiring hall, as did that of 65, the hall in Welles's film had a dispatcher who sent workers out on jobs. The time waiting was spent by members playing cards and shooting the bull. In many industries such as the maritime, construction, music and other arts, and urban retail and wholesaling, where the workforce was otherwise widely dispersed, the hiring hall was the glue that held the membership together. It was both a culture in the highly specific sense of bringing people together on the basis of their common occupational and work experiences and a public sphere to the extent that the hiring halls were sites of conversation about politics and personal lives and, most important, related to but relatively independent of the marketplace, the state and the family. Their demise may be attributed to many influences having to do with the differential restructuring of U.S. capitalism, but the consequences for working-class movements were epochal.

As Miriam Hansen has argued, Jürgen Habermas's important contribution to the discussion of the public sphere consists, principally, in two points: his insistence on its *historicity* and its autonomous character as a "fourth sphere" distinct from the state, marketplace and family.[5] The public sphere is a site established by the bourgeoisie within which it addresses its own problems apart from commercial interests or state policy and, perhaps equally important, exercises its ideological "dictatorship"[6] or, in Gramsci's terms, its hegemony over society.[7] The public sphere is the space of the press or, in contemporary terms, the media, public conversations in cafés, the streets, organizations of civil society, including the trade unions, business groups, religious institutions, social clubs and so forth. These are sites of "the marketplace of ideas"— they use values rather than exchange values, yet are crucial for the bourgeoisie's project of social rule.

The determination that these sites were genuine public spheres, but were historical rather than contemporary, is signaled by the passing of the classical bourgeoisie and its culture and their replacement by a "post-bourgeois" sphere. Note well that, while calling attention to the public sphere as an ideal type, Habermas argued forcefully that even at its apex, the bourgeoisie undermined the public sphere, fearing that it might spin out of control.[8] In the current conjuncture, capital has penetrated the means of communication, which have become primarily exchange values, sources of investment from which (at least) the average rate of profit must be extracted. The media are a domain of capital accumulation and, from the perspective of the marketplace, the means of communication are increasingly owned by oligopolistic corporations. That, as Oskar Negt and Alexander Kluge acknowledge, that "decayed" elements of the bourgeois public sphere survive barely disguises the fact that ideas have become commodified and the space of public discussion becomes ever more narrow.[9]

Negt and Kluge argue for the possibility of a "proletarian" public sphere but warn that the working class cannot hope to take over the "bourgeois world." This illusion has pervaded the labor and social-democratic movements and, in the reading of Negt and Kluge, has been a leading theme in these movements' downfall. In the twentieth century the emergence of electorally successful labor and social parties drew a significant portion of the working class into the decayed bourgeois sphere where, even when they attain a certain influence, their participation tends to strengthen social and ideological integration rather than working-class independence. Negt and Kluge attempt to explain why the working class and its institutions have succumbed to the illusion that they can participate as players in the bourgeois public sphere:

> Evidently this stems from the contradictory relation between *totally socialized context*—which is governed by the manifold forms of the division of labor, interdependence, and cooperation—and the private *forms of appropriation and of life.* The libidinal economy of individuals is not completely exhausted in the everyday oppression of isolated existence and the labor process. There develops in the masses a surplus interest that enables these groups that associate power with the public sphere to repeatedly reactivate (especially when the existing power relations are endangered) symbols of community and of general welfare, confirmations of their own reality.[10]

Without the emergence of a counter-public—which Negt and Kluge propose as the "proletarian" public sphere—the decayed bourgeois public sphere produces ideologies that still engage the libidinal economy of individuals and groups. The key element in the formation of the proletarian public sphere is the construction of "autonomous structures of [working-class] communication." Mass meetings, a labor press, education, face-to-face interaction among small, decentralized groups that, nonetheless, are linked by bonds of class solidarity and of political organization are only a few of the necessary components of this "model." The model is drawn from the experience of the English working class of the first thirty years of the nineteenth century, the years of mass struggle for suffrage, for wage increases and for a national labor movement. The strength of the proletarian public sphere derives from these efforts and one more: even as the globalization of capital forges ahead, capital remains frustrated by its inability to globalize politics. Its political hegemony at the national level is dependent on its capacity to draw the subaltern classes and groups into its sphere as dependent participants. This contradiction between capital's internationalization and the fact that it still must be valorized politically as well as economically at the national level constitutes the space for the counterpublic.

Needless to say, the development of electronically mediated communications in the twentieth century presented enormous problems for the project of autonomous communications in which the working class can share its own experiences without the mediation of institutions that constitute hegemony. The model of the proletarian public sphere, derived from the era of competitive capitalism, may already have been surpassed, not merely by the relatively iron grip of corporate capitalist media or by the emergence of the ersatz public life provided by shopping malls, but by the reluctance of the labor and socialist movements to foster working-class autonomy. In the twentieth century Western Communism no less than social democracy displaced this sphere by *bureaucratic publicity*, and the unions they control followed suit.

As a result, when workers engage in the autonomous sharing of experience, it takes the form of a cultural sphere rather than a public sphere. The working-class cultural sphere may become a site of resistance both to what Lefebvre calls the bureaucratic society of controlled consumption and to the decayed bourgeois public sphere; in the United States it becomes a *counter-public* in the form of union reform movements for radical democracy, or the temporary but powerful wildcat (unauthorized) strikes that periodically dot the industrial canvas. What is missing in these scenarios is the kind of unfragmented activity of which the nineteenth-century British Chartist movement was made or, for that matter, the Minority Shop Stewards movement in the 1920s and 1930s within British trade unions.

*

If you take a ride south on New Jersey's route number 1 past Elizabeth and into the city of Linden, within minutes you will notice, on your right, a modest sign, "Linden Assemblers." There is an oddly shaped parking lot and two buildings: the credit union and the union hall of local 595, United Auto Workers. As you enter the union hall your olfactory organs are assaulted by a distinctive musty, slightly alcoholic, smell. The fragrance is that of a poorly ventilated tavern, and for good reason. The union offices sit on a slightly elevated street floor. Walk a little further down the corridor and you cannot miss the meeting room, which, cheek to jowl, can hold about two hundred people, maybe one hundred and fifty comfortably. The room is used for the local's regular monthly meetings, larger meetings such as that of the shop committee (the smaller meetings are usually held in one of the offices), the monthly retirees' meeting, and the occasional social event or conference.

The basement is the real center of the local union. On the right side is a long bar that is usually full during the hour and a half after the two shift changes. On the left is a large space where, after meetings, several members of the union and their families cater a Southern dinner of ribs and chicken and the usual fixins. On ordinary occasions people take their meals in this room, mainly because of the proximity of the bar. During a conference I helped organize, the relatively large attendance made the upstairs space more feasible.

What goes on here is talk: people watch sports on TV and have the usual arguments about teams and leading figures in the game; since almost every union election is contested three or four months before the vote, people debate the relative merits of the candidates; and because this is a relatively active union, national and state politics is often on the informal agenda. The retirees are forever discussing their health problems, sometimes relating to anyone who would listen the usual healthcare atrocities. During the Social Security scare of the late 1990s, retirees debated issues such as whether there was a real crisis (most were skeptical of the politicians' claims). But like most everyday-life communication, most of the talk is personal. The working members of the local average about 47 years old and some are starting to have grandchildren. Their children are getting married or graduating from college, and many are sweating over the problem their non-college kids are having getting good jobs. In New Jersey, high school graduates or dropouts are having a tough time even in the midst of the so-called "prosperity."

This sixty-year-old General Motors (GM) plant once employed some 6,800 workers. In 1999, employment barely reached 2,600 because the company then introduced "lean production," and a vehicle design that combines parts in order to save labor. Lean production means parts are delivered to the assembly line "just in time." There is virtually no inventory. The result is that hordes of off-line jobs such as welding fenders, bending sheet metal, and producing small parts once done in the plant are now "outsourced," sometimes to domestic and foreign non-union plants that pay a fraction of the basic auto wage of almost $20 an hour. As a result, save a few hundred temporary workers who were offered permanent jobs at the end of 1998, there has been no appreciable hiring since 1982. This accounts for the middle age of most of the workers. In March 1999, some of the talk at the bar turned to rumors that the plant, which assembles Chevrolet's main sports utility vehicle, might eventually shut down if they do not get another "product." By that time, hopefully, a considerable fraction of the labor force will be eligible for the thirty-and-out provision of the union contract, which enables workers at age 55 who have thirty years on the job to retire at $2,000 a month. Those who choose to work or are ineligible for retirement would be offered jobs in other GM plants, a right guaranteed by the contract. In fact, some recently entered the plant when the company shut down the Tarrytown, NY, and the Trenton, NJ, facilities.

In any case, there is strong evidence that if the Linden GM plant survives, like similar assembly plants in the industry it will produce vehicles by means of a relatively new technology called "modular production." In this technology, parts are preassembled and delivered to a nearby shop which "stuffs" them inside a module, a method that copies "containerization," the automated process of longshoring introduced on the waterfront in 1970. The whole car assembly would entail putting four modules together, and the plant's workforce might be thus reduced by half. At least that is what some local unionists believe. The union hall and the shop floor are sites of similar rumor and speculation. Contrary to newspaper reports of a booming economy and a bright economic future, most plant workers here agree with one assessment that, whatever the outcome of the fight for new product, they are "doomed." Their kids are not finding jobs that pay as well as those they held in 1969—which brought an average of $65,000 to $70,000 a year, more for skilled trades—and their own prospects over the intermediate run are uncertain, to say the least. In fact, many are hoping to hang on long enough to qualify for the thirty-and-out provision of the UAW–GM contract. Although the contract also guarantees relocation rights to laid-off workers, many fear that there simply will not be enough jobs in the company, even if they are willing to move to faraway places such as Texas or Oklahoma.

Local 595's hall is one of the premier remaining, but rapidly disappearing, working-class cultural spheres. Of course, it is not a space of cultural development as some radicals and progressive labor educators might wish it to be. Nor is it a place where the discourse of common ground is articulated among competent speakers, in the middle-class sense. What goes on is a lot of informal talk, mostly routine union and retirees' meetings and some political and trade union education—hardly enough to qualify as a working-class public sphere by standards that prevailed until the 1940s, when many single-plant or neighborhood-based industrial union locals maintained lively halls that offered a variety of educational and social activities, as well as the staple of a meeting hall and a bar.

Since World War Two when the auto, steel, electrical, and textile corporations abandoned the cities and moved to suburban locations, the old labor temple or craft-based hall, in which hiring was done as well as union business and socializing, has given way to the union hall of a large local representing workers in a single or a fairly small number of large industrial plants. Many union halls were built next to the plants on the highways. Today, since many workers travel as much as a 100-mile round trip to get to and from the job, for most the connection between home and work is irretrievably broken. Still for many, as employees of large enterprises, the union hall and bar provided a major site in which to forge friendships, enjoy a sense of community not available elsewhere, watch the ball games, or relax with a game of darts, pool, or shuffleboard.

As goods production increasingly employs fewer workers, plants are scattered and smaller, and as there are fewer of them, the industrial union halls are closing. In steel, for example, when once a typical mill had thousands of workers, the newest-technology, so-called "mini-mills," which now account for half of U.S. steel output, often employ fewer than three hundred workers and are typically located in anti-union areas. Now, under the impact of similar technologies, many union plants across industry are closed or have been reduced to hundreds rather than thousands of workers. Short of money to support their large headquarters, local unions tend to sell their valuable property to real estate developers and move their operations to suburban office buildings where, along with other locals, they become administrators of the contracts and little else.

In short, many of the older industrial unions have been hollowed out by the transformations that have afflicted the manufacturing sector. And yet, after a prolonged period during which unions were the track upon which the corporate locomotive traveled, with few stops in recent years, some workers have regained their taste for industrial combat. Strikes in auto and trucking have increased over the issue of capital flight—coded as "outsourcing" to lower-wage non-union plants—as well as the perpetuation of the two-tier wage system. But with diminished power at the bargaining table has come another loss: the disappearance of a specifically labor and class culture. As workers have become riven by consumerism—which drives many to seek as much overtime as they can get—separated by the chasm between workplace and living space, and estranged from their unions by pervasive bureaucratic practices, some emanating from their leaderships and others dictated by collective bargaining and by the law, the bonds of solidarity have gradually loosened. Under these conditions there is dramatically reduced time for conviviality with fellow workers.

The underlying motifs of the disappearance of working-class spheres are the rearrangement of space by the dispersal of physical capital and the narrowing of time available for anything but paid labor. The failure, even refusal of unions to address the issues of hours, industrial location, capital flight, and, ultimately, the configuration of everyday working-class existence has had enormous consequences for the workers' own survival and for the ability of labor to have a voice in reshaping its own future. Since 1975, membership of industrial unions has fallen off by more than half, and this statistic does not tell the whole story. The decline would have been greater if many of the unions had not organized in the public and service sectors. For example, membership in the Auto Workers is down by nearly 50 percent from its apex of 1.4 million, even though in the last twenty years it has gained some 100,000 members in such occupations as clerical workers, graduate assistants, healthcare employees, plus thousands who were members of the defunct district 65, which pioneered in the unionization of university clerical employees.

The last thirty years of the twentieth century were marked by a decisive shift in the social composition of trade union membership. In broad strokes this period was marked by the emergence of public employees' unionism and by the growth of unionism in the private services sector. Today, these unions constitute more than half of labor's diminished legions, which highlights the steep decline of labor's industrial backbone—"backbone" because the giant industrial unions were once the core of what there was of an autonomous labor public, the place where, on the basis of shop-floor and union-hall communal life, organized workers once flexed the political and economic muscle that forced a dramatic rise in living standards for large chunks of the population and played a vital role in the communities within which they lived and worked.

Public and service unionism has introduced new traditions into the labor movement. Even if not always faithfully followed, the older craft and industrial unions were built around the concept that the union was of and by, as well as for, the members; this led to the formation of fairly large cadres of rank-and-file union activists who, it might be said, constituted the labor public sphere. The newer unions, however, are constructed on a "service" model. Except for the teachers' union, which was built on the industrial union model of aggressive bargaining and membership sovereignty, in the liberal democratic model emphasizing bureaucratic administration rather than rank-and-file control over everyday union affairs, many of the largest units of public and service unions regard their members as clients to be served by a staff of professional representatives, lawyers, teachers, and counselors.

Take New York's Municipal Employees' DC 37 for an example. With 120,000 members in fifty-six locals representing employees in almost every branch of city government except the uniformed services, in the 1970s and 1980s the union became one of the more potent urban political machines in the United States. According to a former executive director, it was the "best service organization in the labor movement."[11] Its membership—predominantly black and Latino—works mostly in a wide variety of low-salaried jobs as cafeteria workers, crossing guards, nursing aides, housekeeping and dietary employees in hospitals, clerical workers in nearly every city agency, and blue-collar public parks workers. Another substantial group—case workers in public welfare agencies, professional categories such as engineers, librarians, professional nursing and technicians in municipal hospitals and public health centers—is, in the wake of sharp cuts in relatively well-paid blue-collar and clerical jobs, a fast-growing section of the union, representing some one-third of the membership.

Since the 1970s, the union has offered a wide array of services to individual members. Its legal department handles a myriad civil cases associated with typical problems faced by low-income people: tenant–landlord relations, especially evictions and rent increases; disciplinary issues of members' children who attend public schools; matrimonial disputes; and problems associated with bank loans and time-payments on various consumer goods. Like many other unions in the not-for-

profit sectors, DC 37 has taken a great interest in providing its members
with credentials since these are often requisite for achieving higher pay
and a rung up on the promotion ladder. The union maintains on its
premises a branch of the College of New Rochelle, a regional Catholic
college, and through arrangements with other local colleges and
universities it sponsors a number of short-term training programs. The
union, rather than the employer, is the administrator of the benefits
programs, which obliges many members to consult with the appropriate
program administrator to obtain reimbursements and deal with their
retirement plans.

DC 37 is a leader in the transformation of many unions into a
private welfare state. Like the public agencies that deal with the
unemployed, the union tends to view its members as clients rather than
acknowledge their sovereign power in the organization. Its mode of
operation is marked by relationships that are closer to those of the old
urban political machine than to a democratic public sphere, let alone
anything to do with the concept of counter-publics. Outside its attendance to the highly formalized grievance procedure of which its
members must avail themselves in order to get a measure of job justice,
the everyday life of this form of unionism may be characterized by the
seriality typical of banks and insurance companies. There are numerous
interactions, but they are largely confined to those between professional servants and the clients whom they dispense benefits to and
represent on the job. The shop chair or steward, the staple shopfloor
leader of a union, is relegated to agent or reporter of problems, rather
than problem-solver. During the twenty-five years during which this
regime has been in force, the idea of the union headquarters as a
counter-public sphere, either in the industrial union or labor temple
model, was unthinkable for two reasons.

The first has to do with the specific history of the New York public
and service sector unions. The key organizers who generally became
the key leaders of these unions were not rooted in the occupations and
work sites that make up the membership. Many were imported from
political groups with ideological and power perspectives: whether of
the social-democratic or communist variety, they were "sent in" either
as staff members, or as rank-and-file workers, for the purpose of
building and then leading the union. The second has to do with the
legal framework of public employees' bargaining, which places severe
constraints on a compliant union leadership.

Perhaps the most famously militant among them, local 1199 of the
New York-based, 100,000-member hospital workers' union illustrates

the folly of deriving unwarranted conclusions from ideological premises. The New York City Hospital's patient, dietary, and housekeeping
services are performed largely by low-wage black and Latino workers.
But the union was organized by a small, 3,000-member local of phar-
macy workers, comprising professional pharmacists and retail clerks.
Organized and led since the early 1930s by communists who were
indigenous to the occupations within large drugstores, in the mid-
1950s 1199's leadership became persuaded by one of its own, pharma-
cist Elliot Godoff, to tackle the unionization of New York's non-profit
voluntary hospitals. With hefty appropriations from the union's treas-
ury, volunteer organizers' contributions by members, and substantial
financial and staff support of its sister union, district 65, Godoff
assembled a small organizing staff supplemented by the volunteer rank-
and-file organizers. Brandishing the banners not only of economic
justice but also of the civil rights movement and its icon Martin Luther
King, and with strong support from the Central Labor Council and its
president Harry Van Arsdale, the union wisely chose to disregard legal
avenues to gaining union recognition and instead mounted a series of
demonstrations, job actions, and strikes against the key hospitals in the
vast medical empire of New York: Mount Sinai, Montefiore, and
Maimonides, as well as others such as Beth Israel and Flower-Fifth
Avenue. The strategy of combining direct action with the symbolic
language of social liberation and of wage justice to recruit thousands
of workers, and with adroit political maneuvering among the city's
Establishment institutions and politicians, paid off handsomely. Within
a decade, 1199 had driven a wide wedge in the once-impenetrable wall
of hospital management, and thus began to organize the non-Jewish
voluntaries such as Lenox Hill and Columbia-Presbyterian (which
proved far more difficult). By the 1970s, the union widened its purview
to New Jersey, Pennsylvania, Massachusetts, and Connecticut.

For two decades after its initial victories, the hospital workers were
led mainly by those who had organized the union, white leftists. By
1975, these leaders had forged a solid trade union mass base and
created a new language and culture of militant unionism which was
reminiscent of, but not identical to, labor's strategies in the era before
the Cold War. Race, nationality, and the traditional leftist vocabularies
of class exploitation were represented both visually in murals and other
art works and in the rhetoric of liberation, rather than the leaders
merely invoking the promises of business unions to deliver only wages
and better benefits. What was missing was a new generation of black
and Puerto Rican hospital-floor leaders.

But by the early 1970s the turbulence of the organizing phase was over. While maintaining the rhetoric of social change, the union adopted some of the business-union practices of the old AFL: reliance on full-time business representatives to handle small and large grievances and, in tandem with management, to act as a disciplinary agent over the workers. Like DC 37, but with far more panache, 1199 members were transformed into clients and the leadership was transformed into a service bureaucracy whose main task was to administer the contract and to serve members. By the mid-1970s, black staff were chafing under the benevolent, but nonetheless paternalistic, leadership of the white progressives who ran the union. They began to demand a succession plan since the union's leader, Leon Davis, was already well into his seventies.

Like 65, whose social composition was similar to that of 1199, the leadership did little to anticipate the inevitable transfer of power and the equally probable turmoil that might accompany it. There was no real education program either for rank-and-file leaders or for the members. Most key staff were hired from other unions, from its large professional membership of social workers and technical categories, or from a coterie of eager college graduates. Within a few years of consolidation, the union staff was a professional cadre similar to that of any social service agency. They were poorly paid, at least by general union standards, but despite being treated as employees rather than as a part of the movement, many organizers and staff stayed as long as the work was exciting. 1199 never ceased to organize and did not hesitate to "mobilize" its members around contract issues and political questions such as the Vietnam War and civil rights. In 1999 it brought out its members to protest the murder by New York City police of Amade Diallo, an unarmed peddler of West African origin.

At 1199, the union's organizing and mobilizing model was not enough to prevent a searing conflict when Leon Davis announced his retirement in 1986. His hand-picked successor, a black woman, Doris Turner, a union vice-president, moved rapidly to distance herself from the union's mostly white and Latino inner circle. Within a few years, the union was embroiled in a raging internecine struggle between the two factions. Davis's coterie backed Dennis Rivera to run against Turner, and he won a relatively narrow victory. Although charismatic and politically sophisticated, Rivera has maintained the service model alongside an organizing model. After the defeat of President Bill Clinton's National Health Care plan in 1993, when an austere cost-cutting program was implemented by the hospitals together with a regime of managed care, the union found itself unprepared to deal effectively with the changes.

Anticipating thousands of layoffs, new affiliation agreements and massive changes in job titles and descriptions, 1199's solution was to demand early retirements and a large-scale training program for displaced members; it engaged in its familiar tactic of political mobilization to force the city and state administrations to pour money into the hospitals. Absent from the union's response was a concerted attempt to rebuild union culture and finally to build a base of rank-and-file leadership.

The prevailing service model of unionism has been particularly strong in the public sector. While the fact that many of these unions are dominated by professional staff may be due to specific histories, among the elements that have fostered this form of unionism are the historical circumstances that framed public labor relations law. While the organizing phase of state and local public unionization occurred before legislation to enable these unions to enjoy recognition for the purposes of collective bargaining, in many instances the most rapid growth of unionization followed passage of these laws. Many state legislatures restricted or banned the right of public employees to strike and, eager to obtain bargaining rights, many union officials accepted this constraint. But beyond collective bargaining, some struck a Faustian bargain with lawmakers. In return for accepting arbitration to settle contract and grievance impasses, the legislation provided the unions with control over part or all of the social wage package: health and pension benefits; funds for legal services to members; training and education funds, and with them, the choice of training and educational institutions to provide these services.

While public sector unionism is marked deeply with legalism, the public sector unions took a page from the book of industrial unions that grew up in the shadow of the New Deal. Recall, rank-and-file insurgents were successful in three general strikes in 1934. It may be argued that the National Labor Relations Act, one of the crucial "achievements" of the New Deal of Franklin D. Roosevelt, was intended to regulate what his administration considered a runaway radical movement. Organized labor gained from the procedural democratic provisions of the Act. Workers could now vote for unions of their own choosing rather than relying on the strike weapon to achieve union recognition. But the new contract unionism successfully replaced direct action with a bureaucratic grievance procedure and thereby relegated the strike to an occasional tool, used only within legally restricted limits. As a result, direct action at the workplace and in union bargaining went underground.

Thus, the bureaucratic organization of public employees and many private sector unions that adopted a similar model followed from the tacit decision to put members to sleep, except on relatively rare occasions when mobilization was deemed necessary to win expanded wages and benefits or legislation, but also from the legal or implied agreement to forgo the use of the weapons of direct action, only some of them connected with strikes. Needless to say, in recent years the union bureaucracies have been under increasing pressures from rank-and-file organizations and from widespread member discontent with their performances at the bargaining table and in the legislative arenas.

In effect, if not intentionally, the emergence of the rank and file as a potent economic and political force is producing the simultaneous development of labor counter-publics. To be sure, much of the counter-public is the result of sustained protest against the leadership's accommodationism in this era of crisis, rather than seeing itself as an alternative to the current world-view of the prevailing bureaucracy. But there are exceptions to the rule. Movements like Teamsters for a Democratic Union (TDU) and the Transport Workers' New Directions caucuses exhibit some of the characteristics of a new type of counter-public within the labor movement. Neither has forged itself entirely out of protest but instead has tried to put forward an alternative vision and has provided an autonomous space for the labor movement. Although the leading figures in both movements have socialist origins, their rhetoric and program are thoroughly trade unionist in the American sense: advocating the broad social welfare state and opposing racism and sexism. At the heart of their conception is simple class solidarity combined with a fervent commitment to what I have called radical, as opposed to procedural, democracy.

In what sense are the rank-and-file union movements and those local union leaders affiliated with them a counter-public? I submit it is their participatory or radical democratic practice, which inevitably opposes the bureaucratic, clientist conception of the liberal labor movement, that constitutes and explains their successes. While they have occasionally been co-opted by the liberal yet militant labor leadership, some like the TDU have survived setbacks, built a membership organization, and continued to fight for a new unionism. Whether most of the others born of protest are able to emulate this persistence remains to be seen. What is evident, however, is that the new insurgency means to change the face of labor and bring it back to the future – back in the sense that the movement involved large sections of rank-and-file workers prior to the New Deal.

Notes

1. From 1979, when the Federal government and the United Auto Workers agreed, by equal measures, to bail out Chrysler Corp. by contributing $800 million, half from workers' wages, the business and daily press ran dozens of articles accusing unions of wrecking the economy. By 1986 some industrial relations experts, especially Thomas Kochan, Harry Katz, and Robert McKersie, concluded that union labor's historic role to drive wages had been reversed and the non-union sector was now dominant in wage determination. See Kochan, Katz, and McKersie, *The Transformation of American Industrial Relations* (New York: Basic Books, 1986).

2. See Stanley Aronowitz, *From the Ashes of the Old American Labor and America's Future* (Boston: Houghton Mifflin, 1998), Chapter One; Mike Davis, *Prisoners of the American Dream* (London: Verso, 1984).

3. Aronowitz, *From the Ashes*.

4. Raymond Williams, *Politics and Letters* (London: New Left Books, 1979), p. 24.

5. Miriam Hansen, "Foreword," to Oskar Negt and Alexander Kluge, *Public Sphere and Experience: Toward an Analysis of the Bourgeois and Proletarian Public Sphere*, trans. Peter Labanyi, Jamie Owen Daniel, and Assenka Oksiloff (Minneapolis: University of Minnesota Press, 1993).

6. Ibid.

7. Antonio Gramsci, "On Intellectuals," *Prison Notebooks* (New York: International Publishers, 1971).

8. Jürgen Habermas, *The Structural Transformation of the Public Sphere: An Inquiry into a Category of Bourgeois Society*, trans. Thomas Burger (Cambridge, MA: MIT Press, 1989).

9. Negt and Kluge, *Public Sphere and Experience*.

10. Ibid., p. 75.

11. Victor Gotbaum, in a personal conversation with the author.

Part II

Philosophizing the Public

6

What Makes a People a People?
Rousseau and Kant

Etienne Balibar

Translated by Erin Post

Modern philosophy has revolved around a theoretically revolutionary statement: "Before, therefore, we consider the act by which a People chooses their king, it were well if we considered the act by which a People is constituted as such. For it necessarily precedes the other, and is the true foundation on which all Societies rest."[1] Thirty years after these words were written, political revolution provided Rousseau with the missing referent. The evidence he acquired, as well as its aporias, have resulted in a transformation of political philosophy into a philosophy of history and, more profoundly, in the inscription of the question of the (political, juridical, transcendental) subject in the theoretical space circumscribed by the two categories *historical subject* (subject *in* history and constituted by it) and *subject of history* (the constituting subject of which history would be the process of realization). I will propose here a sketch of this genealogy, limiting my discussion to the transition which, from Rousseau, leads us to the premises of Kant.

Rousseau's Question: What Is a Citizen?

Rousseau begins by showing that all the foundations of a social order based on the principle of subjection are intrinsically contradictory. He is therefore driven to oppose the notion of "aggregation" (a multitude subjected by a master) to that of "association" (that which must be a people). This last notion simultaneously challenges the individualist and corporatist representations of civil society. Indeed, in both these representations, the distinction between *private* and *public*, without which there are no such concepts as right or State, becomes unintelligible. And in both instances, men are politically passive—meaning that there is no notion of citizen. A true association can be neither the juxtaposition of individualities, nor their mystical fusion, nor a pure multiplicity, nor the emanation of the One. Hence the question: what is the *act* by which an association constitutes itself, by which "a people is a people"?[2]

The word "act" must be taken, simultaneously, in the sense of institution and in the sense of permanent activity, of "production." The pact or contract in which a public person finds him/herself instantaneously constituted by a "total alienation of each associate with all his rights belonging to the entire community" concentrates all sovereignty. However, because this person is nothing other than the unity of citizens, it is not synonymous with subjugation to a master. On the contrary, it actually institutes liberty and equality—as though each person, "contracted only with himself" and "giving himself to everyone," gives himself to "no one." Total alienation is a total conversion of private individuality to social, that is, political individuality.

What are the consequences of this conception? The general will, which expresses itself through law, that is, by decisions both universal and imperative, is necessarily immanent in each of the decisions made by society as long as it keeps in mind the common interest alone. Thus emerges an inter-individual "common *self*" (*moi commun*), with its own life, that confers on a people its identity. This results in a particularly exacting definition of citizenship: absolutely sovereign, the citizen has at its disposal the unlimited collective power "to make law" and to transform it. However, in return, each citizen taken individually owes absolute obedience to the law. For the *subject of the prince*, subjected to a permanent arbitrariness, is substituted a *subject of the law*, who is subjected to a rational necessity. Such is the real meaning of autonomy: to decide himself, *generally*, in an absolutely free manner, the legislation which he *in particular* will obey absolutely. Aristotle's citizen was at times in a position of command (*archôn*) and at other times in a position of obedience (*archomenos*).[3] That of Rousseau is *at once* one and the other: the citizen is immediately subject, and vice versa.

It is clear however that this remarkable unity of contraries is suspended on a very strict and perhaps very unrealistic hypothesis: that no gap is ever introduced between the body of the citizen and the body of the subject, in either composition or behavior, until it always appears to be exactly the same body. And yet difficulties begin to manifest themselves in the text of the *Social Contract* itself.

The first is the logical circle inherent in the notion of general will. By definition (precisely because it does not confuse itself with the "will of all"), it would not exist as long as the "collective moral body" was not constituted; in other words, it would exist before the *act* which concludes the social pact. Nevertheless, how would this same act be possible if it did not emanate from a conscious or unconscious will, from a "self"? This difficulty is linked to another, practically more formidable one. The general will is "indivisible": it is an essential condition ensuring that the law which it institutes does not express the interest of an individual or group. This general will must "come from everyone to apply to everyone." But what will be its reality? Rousseau sees the risk of a considerable gap emerging between an *ideal people* and a *real people* (which never ceases to resolve into "private" individuals who are not guaranteed to favor the community over their particular interests).[4]

He therefore finds it necessary to assume that a *general interest*, superior to particular interests, or more capable of integrating and subordinating them, is at the basis of the existence of general will. Here lies the heart of Rousseauian politics: the government's task is to preserve the general interest and allow it to prevail over particular interests. But, for this politics to succeed, the particular interests must be actually compatible. In Rousseau's eyes, the condition is such that differences in fortune would be contained within very narrow limits so that these differences would not produce antagonistic "little societies" in the heart of the social body and, thus, result in factions and parties. Here is yet another circle: except under miraculous historical conditions, only egalitarian legislation can authorize the government's permanent action against the development of class inequalities. Yet this very legislation presupposes a will, thus an interest, and an egalitarian society! Rousseau is perfectly conscious of this. He undoubtedly takes the point of view of the law (*droit*), not of fact. However, he seeks to describe what might be, provided that certain conditions are met. This is why the *Social Contract* ends with a chapter devoted to "civil religion" (a concept apparently imported from the history of Antiquity, but whose content must be the new reality of *patriotism*), which proposes the institution that will cement social consensus. "By making their country an object of adoration to the citizens, it teaches them that to serve the State is to serve the tutelary God."[5] By assuming that such a religion is constant, that it can be instituted in place of or next to traditional religions (without "placing man in contradiction with himself"), and finally that it doesn't unleash generalized war between peoples making them "bloody and intolerant"—and these are significant assumptions—one can effectively assume that the general interest, made sacred, prevails over every other.

Pact, general will, general interest, civil religion: such is, in short, the system with which Rousseau resolved his own problem. In the face of naturalist and theocratic traditions, or of monarchical *raison d'état*, it represents a democratic alternative, the *liberal* current. For the first time a proposition to found the law is constructed not on an original community (naturalism), or on divine grace (transcendentalism), or on an arbitrary convention (artificialism), but on the liberty and equality that it itself implies: a kind of *self-foundation of the law*. The aporias, however, arise precisely from this novelty.

In the first place, the very notion of a people proves equivocal. That which Rousseau terms a people or sovereign, the French Revolution calls a "nation": "the source of all sovereignty is located in essence in the nation."[6] Here the term clearly designates a *political body*, a collectivity of citizens united by the rights which they mutually recognize and by the act of liberation which they undertake together. It is for this reason that the scope of the Declaration of the Rights of Man and the Citizen is absolutely universal (and will be understood as such). But in the course of following years, the word "nation" acquired another significance: invaded, the Republic fixes its sights on the conquest of "natural boundaries" and therefore becomes the "Great Nation." This enterprise develops into an enterprise of hegemony which seems to reactivate the dream of a universal monarchy; the conquered and threatened states develop, for their part, a *nationalist* ideology. The term "people," now understood as nation, no longer refers exclusively to a political body, but to a *historical unity* whose identity must be explained and whose claims must be justified. The notion of patriotism undergoes the same evolution.

Second, the notion of equality harbors a formidable alternative. On one hand it can be understood formally: all individuals have the same rights and the same duties, signifying that they are *treated equally by the law* (*droit*). Not only does this equality fail to imply the suppression of social differences, but, in a sense, it presupposes them: the function of the law is precisely constructed so that, beyond these differences, universal rules are observed so that everyone is "represented" by the State. We have thus returned to the themes of liberalism. Or—the interpretation seen emerging in Rousseau, which will be taken on in part by Robespierre and which will attempt to prescribe the Conspiracy of Equals—equality is thought to be a "real" equality of *individual rights* (*droits*) (of that to which individuals have the right (*droit*)) and thus an equality of social conditions: for in every society where conditions are unequal, the relationships of power are inevitably an obstacle to the relationships of right (*droit*), and the rights (*droits*) of man are constantly negated in practice. Thus, the question of class struggles comes to the foreground.

Consequently, the Rousseauian notion of general will, spread by the Revolution as a veritable slogan, continuously oscillates between the two poles of *constitution* and *insurrection*. It can be referred to in order to legitimate a State, but it can also be reclaimed to legitimate the revolution. Political thinkers of every camp realize that it harbors an element contesting *every* established order, since "people" (or "nation," or "society") and "State" are not identical realities:[7] hence the necessity, in the eyes of many of these thinkers, to challenge or at least profoundly transform the concept.

In this precise conjuncture, Rousseau's utterance remains unavoidable; that is, it bars every possibility of returning to a problematic of the State as corporation (*corporation*) or as civil society. However, instead of constituting a satisfactory response to the political problem, it becomes a *question*. Kant, and after him Fichte, Hegel, Saint-Simon, later Comte or Marx, each in his own way continued to reformulate it to supply another response.

Kant's Response: A Citizen Is (Always Still) a Subject

The Kant in which we are interested here is the "critical" Kant, exactly contemporary with the events of the Revolution.[8] It is also the Kant who can be regarded, in matters of morality, as a disciple of Rousseau—not without noting the evolution that took place over the years. The principal difficulty, however, resides in the gap that divides seemingly very similar statements.

The undiscoverable people

When Kant takes up the notion of contract, he appears to rediscover precisely the same conception as Rousseau:

> The act by which a people forms itself into a state is the *original contract*. Properly speaking, the original contract is only the Idea of this act, in terms

of which alone we can think of the legitimacy of a state. In accordance with the original contract, everyone (*omnes et singuli*) within a *people* gives up his external freedom in order to take it up again immediately as a member of a commonwealth, that is, as a people considered as a state (*universi*). And one can say: A man in a state has sacrificed a *part* of his innate outer freedom for the sake of an end, but rather, he has relinquished entirely his wild, lawless freedom in order to find his freedom as such undiminished, in a dependence upon laws, that is, in a rightful condition, since this dependence arises from his own lawgiving will.[9]

Where might the difference lie? Kant just told us that the "universal sovereign" of the State, "considered according to the laws (*lois*) of freedom, can be no other than the united people *itself.*" The constitution of the people and of the State thus reciprocally imply one another: the people *do* not precede the State (in fact, a people have no existence independent from the State), but conversely, the State (at least that which conforms to its rational Idea) is nothing other than the instituted representation of the people.

However, Kant clarifies this himself: it is a question of a people *in a juridical sense* that articulates the institutions of an Idea (later called the "fundamental norm"). Such a people should not be confused with the *empirical people*, or rather must be considered the result of a transformation of an empirical people according to a juridical norm and by means of its being put into practice. The empirical people will therefore appear to us at once as anticipation, the condition of the possibility of a juridical people (that is, of the State), and contradictorily, as the obstacle its constitution must overcome, the element of naturalness that always remains to be reduced. However, this transformation will not be simple to demonstrate, for the idea of empiricism contains, *at once*, a reference to the "natural" ties of sociability that singularize nations in relation to each other, and a reference to the "cultural" relationships that bring social conditions into play. In the representation of the people as a state of nature which must become a state of law, these two aspects are inextricably mixed.

Another text, taken this time from *Anthropology From a Pragmatic Point of View* (1798), is relevant. From the paragraph entitled "The Character of Nations" (itself inserted between the "The Character of the Sexes" and the "Character of Race") we read this:

By the word people (*populus*) we mean the number of inhabitants living together in a certain district, so far as these inhabitants constitute a unit. Those inhabitants, or even a part of them, which recognize themselves as being united into a civil whole through common descent, are called a nation (*gens*); the part which segregates itself from these laws (the unruly group among this people) is called the plebeians (*vulgus*), and when they form a coalition against the laws, this is called a revolt (*agere per turbas*).[10]

Rather than denounce the incoherence of this juxtaposition, or seek an explanation in the complex circumstances of the text's composition and publication, it is worth granting it the value of a symptom. Indeed, we see an element irreducible to the law which is in fact of a political nature (the unruliness of the masses as an aporia of citizenship) inscribed here as an effect of nature. How can we not wonder whether it is precisely this element which will indefinitely confer on the common origin of the people—what can very well be called an "ethnicity"— a necessary regulatory function of the law itself? Without such an element, there is no certainty that the mass would recognize itself in all circumstances as "united in a civil totality," in other words, that it would subject itself to the juridical form which collectively liberates it and makes it a people "constituted by the State."[11]

These formulations therefore turn our attention to two major differences between the Rousseauian people and the Kantian State.

First, there is the fact that in Kant's texts the distinction between "active citizens" and "passive citizens" is constituent.

> The only qualification for being a citizen is being fit to vote. But being fit to vote presupposes the independence of someone who, as one of the people, wants to be not just a part of the commonwealth but also a member of it, that is, a part of the commonwealth acting from his own choice in community with others. This quality of being independent, however, requires a distinction between *active* and *passive* citizens, though the concept of a passive citizen seems to contradict the concept of a citizen as such.[12]

To become an active citizen, it therefore does not *suffice* to be a party to a contract: it is also necessary to have the "properties" which are the equivalent of a nature, or, more likely, which make possible a certain "free" relationship to nature (and it is perhaps, as we will see later on, in the mode of this relationship where the entire "contradiction" lies). Those who work in the service of others—minors, women, *dependants* in general—"lack civil personality and their existence is, as it were, only inheritance."[13]

From this moment on, a distinction must be made between "rights of man" and "rights of the citizen" (or between "natural liberty and equality" on the one hand, and "civil constitution" on the other). *The notion of the people is split.* The idea of representation thus acquires a double signification: on the one hand, citizens who actively form the people *represent themselves* in the State (and in the system of its different "powers"); on the other hand, certain citizens *represent others* who precisely "depend naturally" on them and consequently cannot become autonomous subjects of the law (*droit*). These are doubtless the same ones who have the tendency to revolt because they always risk preferring the imperative of happiness (or the "right (*droit*) of existence") to the categorical imperative or the Idea of reason.[14] We can risk the hypothesis that if the people as such must be represented by the State, only certain "parts," certain "elements," *within* the people must represent others.

A second pronounced difference is the fact that the Kantian political community is explicitly inscribed in a system of States. This is the reason why an individual cannot be characterized univocally as subject of the law (*droit*) (even as subject of *public* law (*droit*)). But the individual must be recognized and must conduct his activity in a *plurality* of juridical orders to which correspond as many "citizenries": not only the national juridical order and the international juridical order, but also Kant's own innovation, the "cosmopolitical" order (*Weltbürgerrecht*).

The meaning of this innovation is exactly the inverse of that preceding it: not restriction, but extension of citizenship. It is concerned with making sure that, *even* beyond the limits of the State, the individual is still, in certain respects, a citizen (and not simply the subject of a power that uses it as its property and its instrument). Here, Kant means to confront the problem of war. One of Rousseau's essential arguments, as we know, consists of assuming that war is not a relationship between individuals, but solely a relationship between States.[15] The fact remains nevertheless that, in these very particular "relationships" (*rapports*), the States *use* the individuals who are their subjects as property, or as instruments, at their disposal, *aiming* to strike individual subjects of other States. The objective of the Kantian cosmopolitical law is to limit this utilization by *juridically* imposing on States certain *moral* forms of respect for the human person which anticipate a regime of "perpetual peace."

However, a contradiction presents itself here as well. For such a limitation to be effective, it must be imposed by an authority: but this would assume the constitution of a "State of States" either in the form of a supranational State, or in the form of a federation. Since this constitution is not possible (for it assumes that the problem of a moralization of humanity, the obstacle to which is precisely wars, is resolved), it can only concern an *Idea*, toward the realization of which different convergent forces will work. Which forces? According to Kant, one must seek them on two sides simultaneously: in the republican constitution of each particular State, and in the civilizing effects of universal commerce.[16] But this hypothetical solution assumes that the intermediary level will be maintained—that of the membership of individuals, as "subjects" (*Untertan*), in a natural, or quasi-natural, community. The two levels of citizenship (*Staatsbürgerrecht, Weltbürger-recht*), whose union alone would make the general condition of man and of the citizen coincide exactly, remain separated by a *Völkerrecht*, in which individuals confront the powers they do not freely constitute. This is perhaps why Kant maintained here the analogy of the people and the family:

> As natives of a country, those who constitute a nation can be looked upon analogously to descendants of the same *ancestors* (*congeniti*) even though they are not. Yet in an intellectual sense and from the perspective of rights, since they are born of the same mother (the republic) they constitute as it were one family (*gens, natio*), whose members (citizens of the state) are of equally high birth.[17]

The people is a nation, that is, a fictional family. Confusion seems now more than ever to prevail between the order of law and the order of nature. But the heart of the question lies in Kant's observation that a perfect coincidence of the concept of the people with itself in a univocal definition is impossible due to historical realities, the explanation of which he reduces to human nature.

What relationship can be established between these two problems: that of the representation, *in the State*, of "passive" citizens by "active" citizens, and that of the establishment of a cosmopolitical right limiting the freedom of national States in relation to their own subjects? There is first a negative relationship: in both cases, the equilibrium between the idea of right and the reality of social antagonisms is obtained by the *republican* form. This form is defined, according to Kant, by a double exclusion, of both despotism and democracy—two extremes that paradoxically join one another in their negation of the division of powers and in their attempt to make men happy to the detriment of their liberty. Next, there is a positive relationship from the viewpoint of humanity's progress: it is enough that the constitution is not contradictory "to the liberty and equality of men *as men*, who together make up a people"[18] and who can "work [their] way up from this passive condition to an active one."[19] It is enough that a republican State (or to begin with, even a *single* republican State) assign itself the objective of making communication (*Verkehr*) between men and their material advantages prevail over war so that the universal reign of law (*droit*) becomes at least thinkable, or realizable "by approximation."

We are finally very far from Rousseau. The ideal notion of the people as the "common self" (*moi commun*) of the citizens is dissolved into a realism of human nature. But at the same time, its essential content, the identity of the subject and of the citizen, which can be considered as the very existence of liberty, has been sublimated under the form of a regulatory "Idea" of historical progress. We can also truly say that it is a certain idea of the subject's liberty, irreducible to Rousseauian citizenship and susceptible to initiating this dissolution– sublimation. We must attempt to reconstruct it.

The divided subject: heroic humiliation

We cannot say unconditionally that Kant formulated a definition of human nature, for the recognition of the anthropological motif in his works is surrounded by curious precautions.[20] The explicit wording of the question "What is man?" must be suspect in marginal texts (the *Course on Logic*, a collection of notes published in 1800 by Jäsche). What is more, the *Course on Logic* is the only text in which philosophy as such is identified with an anthropology and its completely developed program ("philosophy is not in any real sense a science of representations, concepts, and ideas, or a science of sciences . . . but a *science of man*, of his representation, his thought, and his action").[21] Kant borrows this anthropology from a disciple to insert it in his own piece of writing which, at the same time, allowed him to maintain a certain distance.[22] It is fair to say that this overcautiousness betrays not only the difficulty of introducing a neologism of meaning,[23] but also a persistent tension internal to the very notion of man, or of human nature. Indeed, this notion is neither that of the theological tradition and of metaphysical substantialism (of dualism of soul and body), nor that of psychological empiricism, nor that of anthropological positivism.

To think this notion, Kant forges precisely the concept of the subject in its modern usage—or at least he names it—free self-consciousness (*conscience de soi*). But this usage is inseparable from a double interior conflict: sensibility and reason, theoretical reason, and practical reason.

In the order of knowledge—within its limits—the conflict of sensibility and of reason is able to resolve into complementarity, into harmony (even though the foundation of this harmony—the self-affection of the subject—always remains for us unknowable, "mysterious"). In the order of practice, the conflict proves irreconcilable, for sensibility and reason present incompatible impulses (*mobiles*). Those of sensibility are "pragmatic." They express for each individual the desire for personal happiness, the pursuit of personal interest, and the search for corresponding means. Those of reason are reducible to the unique imperative of duty, which imposes itself unconditionally on the consciousness (*conscience*) and resumes the obligation of always treating others as a person (as an "end in and of itself") and never as just a thing (or a "means"). Thus, the subject finds himself caught in what we call in modern terminology a *double bind*: he is *incapable* of not desiring happiness, the "synthesis" of morality and affectivity, but *cannot*, either, shirk the categorical imperative that presents itself to him as the obligation to disregard motives (*mobile*) of sensibility, and thus, in practice, to resist them "heroically." Finally, that which constitutes the subject is its division from itself which can only be lived in the admiration and the displeasure, even the humiliation, "in our own consciousness (*conscience*)."[24] One could say that the specific mode of moral sentiment in Kant's texts is that of *heroic humiliation*. Here is undoubtedly the central question: how can one make sure that the division of sentiment does not exclude identity (self-consciousness (*la conscience de soi*), self-presence (*la présence à soi*)) but actually constitutes it?

It certainly seems that Kant himself evolved toward an increasingly tragic reading of the practical conflict and of the division which he induces in the subject.[25] But it is this very tragic quality that allows him to pose his solution, for he sets aside every substantialist temptation, every representation of the subject as a "thing," in order to identify it with its own "practical" activity. From the beginning, the antithesis of sensibility and of reason appeared purely and simply as the expression of a conflict between nature and freedom, between affective inclination and "good will" in conformity with duty. In the end, in a Pauline and Augustinian manner, the conflict is reinscribed in freedom itself, which is not simply the other of nature (an anti-nature), but is "divided in two." Inclination therefore literally becomes a property of human desire. To express this relationship, Kant plays with the two terms he coins in German, *Freiheit* (moral liberty, autonomy) and *Willkür* (which has been translated rather uneasily as "will" (*arbitre*) or "free will"): freedom is *at once* auto-nomy and hetero-nomy, which means that it carries its other in itself. Indeed, without free will, there is no responsibility and therefore no autonomy: duty only has meaning for a being itself determining its own action according to certain ends. But free will is also the principle of a resistance to morality: it is the "faculty of

desire" inevitably affected by sensibility (which Kant terms "inclination"). Although the sensible impulses (*mobiles*) convey the *passivity*
of the individual in opposition to the free *action* of a subject who
imposes a rule on himself, they do not resist this passivity any less in
the interiority of moral intention. This is why it appears as an obligation
or an imperative which, although it emanates from me, I must "obey,"
and not simply as a personal decision the circumstances of which make
the execution more or less easy for me.[26] Therefore the term "pathological," which Kant uses to designate the sensible impulses (*mobiles*), is
understood as desire. Although the resistance of these impulses is not
the expression of my will (as "good will" whose necessity I cannot
mistake), their resistance is not so much "not me," or other than me.
What I discover in "me" is, in a way, the impossibility of identifying
myself with "my will."[27] In *Religion Within the Limits of Reason Alone*
(1793), Kant will designate this intervention of the pathological in the
very heart of liberty not simply as a "weakness," but as "radical evil," as
the original perversion, the "bad principle" with which "we secretly
communicate" and which human forces have no power to extirpate,
but which can, in a way, condemn them to the infinite task of a
liberation from freedom.

Kant actually means to say that the moral or practical experience or
practice, like the experience of internal division, is precisely our access
to human nature, the available means by which we can connect the
representation (and the self-consciousness) of the individual with a
general idea of humanity. At the same time, this also allows us to
measure the gap that always continues to separate any given individual
from the *human* as such. But what he also attempts to show is that the
division of the subject is tightly linked to the social or commercial
being of man. If the subject can interiorize his own membership in a
community that, for him, will be the realization of a moral idea and
not simply a coalition of interests, or an exterior entity (more or less
constraining, useful, just, etc.), it is not in spite of, but precisely *because
of*, his own division (*clivage*) into which society will be inserted. However, reciprocally, if society (the people, the State) must be constituted
as an organic "community," it is because it can be interiorized by
subjects, spontaneously "willed" (*voulue*) by them as the means of their
own freedom. One senses here that the Kantian "dualism" is nothing
but a negative function. On the one hand, it engages in a perpetual
flight forward. On the other, it becomes the theoretical means *par
excellence* of the construction of politics and history.

We must now consider as the very core (*noyau*) of practical philosophy the system of categories that allows for a conceptualization of the foundation of the community on the liberty of the subject and, correlatively, the insertion of the community into the division of the subject. The categories whose recovery Kant has systematically effectuated are, as we know, those of *duty* and *right* (morality and legality), *interiority* and *exteriority, freedom* and *constraint.*

The presentation of the Other: right (*droit*) and morality

Morality is "interior," or rather it moves from the interior to the exterior. It consists in acting in such-and-such a way according to an immediate necessity experienced by the *conscience/consciousness* (*la conscience*) (in the double sense of *Bewusstsein* and of *Gewissen*). But for this "fact of reason" to lead to determinate acts (and nothing is more foreign to Kant than the indifference to acts) *judgment* is necessary: it is here that "maxims," or principles that translate duty into the language of the universal, intervene. Formally, this means that particular duties (for example: to each his own, to keep one's word) will be perceived as expressions *of* duty when they will have been subsumed under the universal rule deduced from moral conscience/consciousness (*la conscience morale*). Substantially, this means that *my* duties bind me by means of mediation of my own representation of the existence of others, of their unconditionally respected humanity. The *representation of the Other as Man* is the internal criterion of the morality of my intentions.

Does this mean that moral subjectivity is conceived here as *intersubjectivity*, that is, as the original constitution of the "self" (*moi*) from the interior presence of the "non self" (*non moi*) (the I-You of Fichte, Feuerbach, and later Buber)? Or as *transindividuality*, that is, as practical or symbolic "social relationship" (Spinoza, Hegel, Marx)? It is neither one nor the other, for a formal mediation is required without which the "Other" would not be able to assume the universal form that governs the maxims of the categorical imperative. It is doubtless necessary to state that moral conscience/consciousness (*conscience*) unites the individual subject and the human community in the element of interiority. But this mutual belonging is not original. Its realization is necessarily through its contrary: law, or rather its "idea." This universal Other that I must represent to myself to assure in myself the primacy of morality is *presented to me by the law* (*droit*) insofar as it identifies me as a "person," as another real freedom in the realm of the exterior. *All possible subjects of right* (*droit*) (of which I am a part)[28] are Men for morality (and therefore universally respectable Others). The idea of the law (*droit*) ("the sum of the conditions under which the choice of one can be united with the choice of another in accordance with a universal law of freedom")[29] thus appears as the minimum exteriority for duty to be *determined*, for it to have an *object*.

The law (*droit*) is indeed the inscription of law (*loi*) in exteriority, defined by its natural setting (space, time). It is the system of actions in external conformity with the law (*loi*) in the sense that it *anticipates* a certain rule of behavior for a certain type of situation and that it requires individuals to follow it. It is thus a "machine" that, from certain principles and with the idea of organizing the relationships of individuals between themselves and with "things," divides human actions into two classes: those of legal actions and illegal actions (all that is not illegal being legal, and vice versa). However, this division makes sense only because human individuals have the capacity to determine themselves by themselves: for they are free in the sense of *Willkür*. The game of law (*droit*) therefore includes a subjective moment: that of the comprehension of juridical rules and of the decision to apply them. A second opposition must intervene here: *freedom and constraint*.

Morality is free, law (*droit*) is always constraint. It would be even more accurate to say that morality *is liberty*, for there is no liberty without law (*loi*) that imposes itself on desire, nor will liberty exist without the law that *I* can formulate myself *as if* I were the author or "legislator." This is precisely and uniquely what takes place with moral law. Consequently, with morality, I not only attain my own freedom, but I inscribe freedom in general *on* the world, at least as an *end* according to which the events or the course of the world become intelligible. But what is this end? The ends of liberty can be nothing other than the realization of liberty itself, that is, a *transformation of the world*—let us understand, of the human world—so that morality rules it "spontaneously." In other words, morality is that activity or that practice by which men freely attempt to transform themselves into naturally free beings, to institute a "reign of freedom," a "reign of ends."

This is admittedly a strange formulation. To prevent it from concealing both an insoluble contradiction and a pure tautology, one must consider the means that allow for a collective realization of the task thus prescribed to each particular subject: that is, once again, the law (*droit*). Yet we are thus immediately confronted with a brutal contrast. The law (*droit*), Kant tells us, is *constraint*. He does not mean, undoubtedly, that the essence of the law is constraint, for all constraint is neither juridical nor legitimate *a fortiori*. But the essence of the law (*droit*) implies constraint, by means of which the law (*la loi*) must be enforced and without which it cannot be. In other words, the concept of the law (*droit*) is obtained from that of moral obligation while *adding* the necessity of an external constraint (in a way, to make one respect respect). One can therefore ask how the "addition" to the constraint of that which constitutes freedom in oneself makes itself purely and simply free without destroying itself.

This paradox is resolved in the very utterance of the reasons explaining the necessity of constraint. The first is that different individual liberties *do not coexist spontaneously* as liberties of "choice" or of "decision." On the contrary, they collide with one another, they "block" one another. Hence Kant's superb formula: the law (*droit*) is "the hindering of a hindrance to freedom."[30] This means that right is the expression (and the formulation) of a reciprocal constraint that individuals exercise on one another to prevent their liberties from being destroyed. In this way, individuals, by subjecting themselves to it, act *as if* they agree to have their liberties coexist and to render them mutually compatible. It is in this way that we must first read Kant's expression: "right and authorization to use coercion therefore mean one and the same thing."[31] To this reason is nevertheless added a second, which appears the moment we search for the reason why individual liberties contradict one another: juridical constraint is necessary to require each individual to act kindly toward others *even when* he is inclined to forget his duty, that is, to act as "external" substitute of the internal moral strength or of the truth. But these two reason are in reality only one and this is the solution of our paradox. For if individual liberties do not immediately agree, it is precisely because each individual does not always have the interior strength (*force*) to do his duty, to humiliate himself heroically. Reciprocal juridical constraint appears as the means to transform a freedom that destroys itself into a nonconflictual freedom that passes into acts. At the heart of constraint is freedom, and at the heart of freedom is constraint.

In the structure of the juridical relationship we therefore rediscover exactly the same duality which in the subject itself constituted morality—but in an *inverted* form. Juridical constraint has exactly the same finality as morality: to make sure that men become what they essentially are—at once betrayed and sublimated in the consciousness of obligation—free beings who freely recognize each other as such. However, while in the concept of morality the internal duality of the freedom affected by its "pathological" other was, in a way, repressed, the concept of law (*droit*) itself exhibits the subjective conflict in its own exteriority at the same time that it proposes the means by which to sever it. Why has this correlation between morality and law (*droit*) continued to cause difficulty? Apparently it is because it can be read in two complementary but non-symmetrical ways.

On the one hand, it can be read in relation to morality, as Kant himself incites us to do by defining duty as an unconditioned imperative. It is understood that even if the organization of social relationships in accordance with juridical norms moved indefinitely closer to the moral idea of a human community founded on an absolute respect for persons, a gap would always remain. The rule of law (*droit*) will never be the pure consciousness of duty, just as the observance of laws (*lois*), no matter how "voluntary," will never be "good will." From this gap can be inferred an optimistic reading (further effort must always be made for men to be fully human), or a pessimistic reading (whatever they do, men will never be truly human: at least, they will always be conscious of what they lack to become human). In a way, Kant has practiced both readings on his own doctrine.

On the other hand, his doctrine can be read in relation to the law (*droit*). It is rationally conceivable, compatible with the general laws (*lois*) of nature, and, on the other hand, it is empirically achievable given certain conditions.[32] But the condition par excellence *is the morality* of individuals: understood not in the sense that they will always do "their duty from a sense of duty," but that they will always hear the voice of the conscience which will never be silenced in them. In return, juridical constraint morally educates individuals, conferring upon moral obligation the force of a constant disposition: the power to enforce. Finally, the opposition between the law (*droit*) and morality is resolved with the idea of *educating* the individual (and, in fact, juridical constraint as Kant describes it is essentially educational).

All of this can be stated in yet another way: the *subject of the law* (*droit*), by himself, would not be a *subject* if he was not identical to the subject of morality. But the subject of morality who tries his best, more or less successfully, to do his duty, is *already* inscribed in a juridical order that requires this morality and that, when needed, helps him overcome his weaknesses. It has been stated above that a juridical order is needed to *present* to moral consciousness (*conscience morale*) the other man from whom it demands respect. Now this can be clarified: the law presents the Other to the conscience as a person, as an "end in and of itself," confronting the object of desire or of interest (which can also be called the other man "in me"). It is up to morality to "choose" between them. But this choice consists precisely in treating the Other in oneself as a subject of the law (*droit*). Law (*droit*) and morality are therefore, reciprocally, the conditions of their effectiveness: faced with the divided subject (*sujet clivé*), the law (*loi*) divides and gives itself the supplement necessary to its realization. In the division of moral law (*loi*) and of juridical law, the conflict internal to human existence that makes the struggle between the pathological "self" and the universal "subject" a way of life, and that, in a way, places the subject "outside of itself," is immediately resolved by making itself explicit: in the community.

The idea of organization

Let us therefore observe the political consequences. Just as the idea has been too often repeated that Kant's morality is a morality of intention, indifferent to acts or to their consequences, so Kantian politics have often been presented as *moral politics,* or even as politics that can be reduced to morality, having turned away from the real world.[33] But it is clear that the notion of politics, as Kant conceived of it, is not the practical "synthesis" of its two interdependent elements, neither on the side of morality and duty, nor on the side of the law (*droit*) and its effectiveness, that is, precisely the articulation or practical synthesis of two interdependent elements. It consists in governing men in such a way that they behave toward each other according to these two obligations. The duality of morality and of law is constitutive of the citizen just as the citizen is, for the same reasons, constitutive of the subject. Consequently, this duality is necessary in order to think the historico-political notion of the *people* that we had abandoned to the struggle with the aporias of "nature" and "sociability." Formally, the people will come to inscribe itself in the Kantian topic in exactly the same place as the subject: in the conflictual in-between of the law (*droit*) and of morality—itself required by the *internal* conflict between freedom and nature. In a moment we will see that history is also inscribed in the same place. This is why these three terms are continually juxtaposed.

To govern is to organize the people. Better yet: it is to supply the people with the means for its *self-organization by an "art,"* not hidden but public (a "cybernetic"). A note added by Kant to Section 65 of *The Critique of Judgement* (1790) has often been cited in regard to this: "Only a product of such a kind can be called a *natural purpose,* and this because it is an organized and self organizing being ... the organization of nature has in it nothing analogous to any causality we know."[34]

> We can conversely throw light upon a certain combination (*Verbindung*), much more often met with in idea than in actuality (*mehr in der Idee als in der Wirklichkeit*), by means of an analogy to the so-called immediate natural purposes. In a recent complete transformation (*gänzlichen Umbildung*) of a great people into a state the word *organization* for the regulation of magistracies, etcetera, and even of the whole body politic (*des ganzen Staatskörpers*), has often been fitly used. For in such a whole every member should surely be purpose as well as means, and, while all work together toward the possibility of the whole, each should be determined as regards place and function by means of the Idea of the whole (*durch die Idee des Ganzen*).[35]

It is possible to read such a text as one of numerous manifestations of philosophy's propensity to think the political (or social, or historical) totality according to the model of a living organism. A link will therefore be made insuring the transition between the medieval representations of the *corpus mysticum* (of which the physics of the "political body" during the Classical Age only represented in many respects a materialist reversal) and the future socio-biologisms of the twentieth and twenty-first centuries.[36] How would such an interpretation be reconciled with the primacy, constantly reaffirmed by Kant, of the point of view of liberty in the judgment that exerts itself over law (*droit*), politics, and history? Would it do so through the intermediary of the antithesis, which romantic idealism would expand to an extraordinary degree: that of *mechanical* totality and *organic* totality, which oppose one another like interiority and exteriority, heteronomy and autonomy? But Kant is characterized precisely[37] by the fact that such an opposition is not pertinent in his work: the correct opposition is that which appears between mechanism and liberty and which refers back to the two sides of the *antinomy of pure reason*.

One must doubtless wonder, as does G. Canghilhem, at the fact that "when Kant abandons the recourse to every technological model of organic unity, justifying himself as he does so, he hastens to present this organic unity as the possible model of a social organization."[38] Indeed, this analogy transgresses the criteria for the distinction that will be proposed between "exterior finality" (certain things and beings are destined to serve others in view of an end) and "internal finality" (different parts of a whole exist not only for one another, but also by one another: they reciprocally cause one another in view of a common end).

I will suggest a solution by reversing the perspective. Kant has always affirmed that *practical* finality is clearly (and even originally) defined, *natural* finality being the problematic element. This entire discussion rests on two theses. First, certain natural productions will remain unintelligible if we fail to see that their organization is regulated (*régie*) by (internal) final causes: with living bodies, "a hint, as it were, given us by nature"[39] leading to an analogy between life and intentionality, "spontaneity." Second, it is impossible for us to effectively determine through experience (or even to pass from a regulatory hypothesis to a constituted knowledge), and to discover, *a fortiori*, a principle common to mechanical causality and to final causes (which would base the specificity of organisms on reason), for these two types of causes are to our understanding radically contradictory. The status of a science of natural organisms (or of automatons) as such is thus irremediably hypothetical.[40] But what is impossible for natural organisms is at once possible and necessary for political organizations. Indeed, the idea that parts of a whole "cause" one another—or reciprocally cause one another's actions in as much as they *represent* each other's existence as an "end"—is exactly the idea of a community regulated (*régie*) by juridical relationships based on the fundamental norm of the Law (*Droit*).

This is what the Introduction to the *Doctrine of Right* states: "strict right [that is, 'based on everyone's consciousness of obligation in accordance with a law,' but abstracting it from consciousness 'as impulse'] rests instead on the principle of its being possible to use external constraint that can coexist with the freedom of everyone in accordance with universal laws."[41] And this is in terms of the notion of *civil society* (the *bürgerliche Gesellschaft*: society of citizens) that "Idea for a Universal History from a Cosmopolitan Point of View" of 1784 had already developed:

> The greatest problem for the human species, the solution of which nature compels him to seek, is that of attaining a civil society which can administer justice universally. The highest purpose of nature—i.e., the development of all natural capacities—can be fulfilled for mankind only in society, and nature intends that man should accomplish this, and indeed all his appointed ends, by his own efforts. This purpose can be fulfilled only in a society which has not only the greatest freedom, and therefore a continual antagonism among its members, but also the most precise specification and preservation of the limits of this freedom in order that it can co-exist with the freedom of others. The highest task which nature has set for mankind must therefore be that of establishing a society in which *freedom under external laws* would be combined to the greatest possible extent with irresistible force in conformity with the law (*eine vollkommen gerechte bürgerliche Verfassung*), in other words of establishing a perfectly *just civil constitution*. For only through

the solution and fulfillment of this task can nature accomplish its other intentions with our species.[42]

This will be restated more briefly on page 83 of *The Critique of Judgement*.

The construction of the concept of right (*droit*) inasmuch as it represents freedom in the opposing element of constraint and therefore allows its realization by way of reciprocity, is thus the key to the idea of organization, and not its inverse. The complete cycle is as follows: by secretly affecting one another, nature and freedom determine (interior/exterior) the antagonism which, in turn, develops a (exterior/interior) reciprocal constraint. This constraint then induces regulation and inscribes freedom as an (interior) end in (exterior) nature. Let us attempt this formulation: articulating freedom and nature by means of juridical constraint without eliminating their conflict, but revealing the possibility of a solution through a complete development of the antagonisms that such a conflict implies, society *conceptually* defines the type of organization according to which it can itself, in return, appear *analogically* as a "whole." We have most likely come as close as we possibly can to what makes a people a people: the self-organization of a community that tends to transform nature by its own natural means. But the means of this self-organization has never ceased to be freedom's constraining of itself.

The master of masters: State and progress

The proper name of this generic constraint is the *State*. This can be shown from both the legal (*droit*) and the moral point of view. It is necessary to understand, as Kant constantly instructs us to do, that organization is not a *given*, or even less an original fact, but a task in process, a practice that inscribes itself in history. Better yet, it is that which confers on history its progressivity and its specific temporality. The time of history is, in reality, nothing other than the time of the community's self-organization.

The statements concerning society or civil constitution that I have reproduced below are inserted between two more frequently cited statements. On the one hand is the *fourth proposition*: "The means which nature employs to bring about the development of innate capacities is that of antagonism within society, in so far as this antagonism becomes in the long run the cause of a law-governed social order."[43] And, on the other hand, there is the *sixth proposition*: "*This problem is both the most difficult and the last to be solved by the human race.*" The difficulty (which the very idea of this problem clearly presents) is this: "if he lives among others of his own species, man is *an animal* (*Tier*) *who needs a master* (*einen Hern nötig hat*)." The State is the master of masters, the only one that is at once effectively constraining and absolutely legitimate because it is the only one that does not occupy this dominant position because of particular circumstances. By virtue of its very conception, it is the only one which, in the exercise of constraint, does not risk ("in law" ... (*droit*)) identifying itself with a point of view, or with particular interests. Only the State incorporates into its *raison d'être* the very representation of the constraint it exercises: the fact that it is destined to ensure the coexistence of freedoms. We must finally explain this transition, but we must also reveal its limitations.

Kant defines antagonism as "*the unsociability* of men (*ungesellige Gesellligkeit*), that is, their inclination to enter into society, an inclination which is nevertheless linked with (*verbunden*) a general repulsion at such an entrance, constantly threatens to break up the society it just created." Social conflicts are nothing other than the phenomena of this antagonism: it is fundamentally a contradiction (a "relationship of forces") between society *and itself* which presents itself with the problem of its own government, better still, of its own "governability." It is therefore nothing other than the deployment, in the space and time of history, of the conflict internal to liberty presenting itself as a conflict of nature. Without this *bad side* of human nature, humanity's moral progression toward the reign of the law (*droit*) would have neither impulse (*mobile*) nor force (even though in *The Critique of Practical Reason* it is the conflict with inclination that gives force to duty). Humanity finds strength in antagonism at the same time that it experiences the necessity to rectify (*redresser*) (and thus to straighten out (*dresser*)) its "deviant" nature (*nature "courbe"*).

This can of course be understood in several ways. The 1784 text privileges an optimistic perspective in accordance with the ideology of the *Aufklärung*. The development of antagonism is presented in a naturalistic language and, as a result, Kant must even have recourse to a providentialistic idea: it is "nature's design," which never fails to evoke the "invisible hand" of Adam Smith, derived from theology and para-doxically transposed from economic nature to the political constitu-tion.[44] One must understand that men's pathological motives (interest, the search for personal happiness) incessantly hurl them into a war of all against all, but that this very "war" calls for regulation. A *sociability* organized in the form of a State thus emerges through an "extorted pathological accord" (that is, itself interested). And the antagonism between these two sides (unsociability, sociability) would progressively result in a preponderance of the latter over the former. This in turn would be "converted" into a second nature, a "moral whole" in which juridical rules are accepted in and of themselves. The State would not become useless, but it would lose the characteristics of violence and arbitrariness that are the price paid for men to unite in an initial phase of barbarism. This barbarism is perpetuated in the war between States (and from there, it constantly threatens to penetrate them and to drag them backwards). It is for this reason that the end of progress can be nothing other than a "universal, cosmopolitical State," a "great future state body," a "political community" capable "of conserving itself as an automaton."[45]

But this formulation could not be maintained as such, even and especially if the idea of progression toward the State of universal law [*droit*] had not been abandoned. The reasons are exactly parallel to those I evoked above to justify Kant's own interpretation of his idea of pathology in terms of "radical evil": it is a question of inscribing the conflict in freedom itself (in its tendency and its perversion), and not in nature.[46] Every "natural" spontaneous convergence between two modes of the social bond (that which constitutes the means of individuals' reciprocal utility, that which makes everyone an end in themselves for everyone else) is therefore excluded. Contemporary circumstances also perhaps explain this evolution. It is indeed war itself which appears as the essential revelation of the "wickedness (*Bösartigkeit*) of human nature," which "although it is largely concealed by governmental constraints in law-governed civil society (*im bürgerlich-gesetzlichen Zustande*) . . . is displayed without disguise in the unrestricted relations between peoples,"[47] while in the 1784 text, it appears more as the particular case of a sort of generalized occurrence. "War itself, however, does not require any particular kind of motivation, for it seems to be ingrained in human nature."[48]

The nature here in question no longer has the meaning of a physical naturalism and, correlatively, it no longer appeals to an external idea of Providence. What is essential is the dialectic of freedom grappling with its internal otherness. Unsociable sociability does not univocally produce a free juridical community through the linear development of an embryo. Instead, it produces an antithesis which is perhaps fundamental to what we must call "culture." On the one hand, it produces a "society" of selfish men united and immediately divided by interest: in such a society, *men reciprocally pervert one another* with their moral dispositions and make each other wicked.[49] On the other hand, it produces a moral reaction to this pathological society, an immanent reaction guided by the idea of an "ethical community" that is all the stronger the greater the perversion. Likewise, the State is *at once* this violent instrument which neutralizes the passions by using men against one another (and which Kant tells us can organize "even a people of demons"), *and* this process of self-educating the people which proceeds from the pure Idea of the law (*droit*) as from an interior directive (*Richtschnur*).[50] Such States, *themselves on the road of transformation*, must exist so that the universal commerce can effectively be the agent of a moralization of human behavior. The historical perspective (the "end of history") is therefore open. The triumph of the good principle over the bad in the social order, and the possibility of its triumph in each individual, is *progression toward* a "universal State": but rather in the form of the *universalization of each State*, the incarnation of the universal principle, than in the form of a unique organization. The Idea of self-organization has moved from the register of space to the register of time.

The universalized State, or the *State according to its Idea* (which is necessarily the Idea realizable in empiricity), is exactly what Kant calls republican (taking good care, as we have seen, to distinguish this notion from that of a democratic, egalitarian, and therefore insurrectional government). Such a State is the only "master" able to educate men, "stating the law" which signifies to all the individuals the rule of their own collective freedom. Any other master (the father, the priest, the teacher, even the doctor) can only exercise authority by virtue of his title due to lack of higher authority, so that either freedom collapses into the anarchy of free will, or constraint is exercised by an arbitrary authority (which amounts to the same thing). We can however go further, for the Idea of education is a derivative notion. It is the symptom of a more original link between liberty and constraint. What it aims at is in fact the existence of *the synthetic link between morality and the State*. Employing this category in an extensive way (which always refers to the "secret" of the unity of contraries in Kant), I would say that it is a question of an *a priori* synthetic link. For it is now entirely clear that the State is not (only) an "empirical" concept: it also fulfills a "transcendental" function.

There is undoubtedly no question of claiming that individuals create their duty by representing a political authority who prescribes it to them (we have seen that what they represent is the person, the Other). It is *a fortiori* impossible to see in morality the interiorization of the "repressive" social instance. In the same way, it is impossible to claim that the State, in order to fulfill its political function, should intervene in the "private" morality of the citizens (it would cease to be, for the same reason, a State of law (*droit*)). But there is a link synthetically necessary in the sense that, if the realization of a moral world, demanded by conscience itself—the transformation of the world—was possible, then it would be necessary for the State to exist. It is tempting to say that *there must be "a State,"* for there must be law (*droit*) whose existence implies that of the State. It is this more than the existence of God that must be considered a "postulate of practical reason." Reciprocally, if the State exists and endures, if it tendentiously triumphs from unsociable sociability, it is because men are beings for whom the "voice of consciousness/the conscience" (which is that of a *trial*, of a "judge that everyone carries inside") is not prescribable. And it is this synthetic link which guarantees to us that every State, however contrary to freedom its origin and its contemporary regime may be, can be reformed to become a State of right (*droit*) and serve the perfectioning of humanity. This is also why the State as such is *unsurpassable* in history in so much as it is the history of freedom.[51]

Such a conception doubtless harbors latent ambiguities. Some of these are clarified in Kant's own texts. To say that the State is historically unsurpassable while thinking of history as an indefinite progression is to raise the question of a tendentious sublimation of its coercive function, in favor of an *ethical community* whose idea already guides it. Such a community would be the fusion of legality and morality, of "exterior law (*loi*)" and "interior law (*loi*)." It is more or less inevitable that such a fusion could only be imagined by projecting it on to either exteriority or interiority (even Hegelian Absolute Knowledge, not to mention Marxist Communism, will not escape this constraint). It is for this reason that Kant gives *at times* a juridical presentation (it is the Society of Nations: the "pact of universal and durable peace" of the *Doctrine of Right* and of the opuscule *Toward Perpetual Peace*), and *at times* a religious, although not mystical, presentation (it is the "invisible Church" of *Religion within the Limits of Reason Alone*, the "concept of a people as a community subjected to God as to a human moral leader").

Above all, this conception—these are its limits—is based on two presuppositions. One is metaphysical: the thesis that makes *sensibility* an interior perversion of freedom, its menacing pathology. The other is political (or politico-anthropological): the unification, in a single "pragmatical" concept of empirical humanity, of the *private interest* of individuals, the *natural hostility* of nations, and the *social inequality* of conditions, that is, the forms of conflict which together constitute the obstacle that the law (*droit*) must reduce and codify. Without these presuppositions, the subjective synthesis of morality and of the State is not thinkable. It remains that, thanks to these presuppositions, Humanity can be conceived of as the motor and the end of its own history.

Notes

1. Jean-Jacques Rousseau, "The Social Contract" in *Social Contract: Essays by Locke, Hume, Rousseau,* trans. Sir Ernest Barker (New York: Oxford University Press, 1971), p. 179.

2. A "question" is naturally never absolutely without precedents, especially if it is revolutionary. It must, on the contrary, be inscribed in a *signifying chain* whose effectivity (*prégnance*) it reiterates at the same time that its economy is overturned under the fire of a new conjuncture. A question is now necessary to return to the (Roman) "definition" of a people spoken by Cicero through the mouth of Scipio: "Est igitur, inquit Africanus, respublica, res populi; populus autem non omnis hominum coetus quiqui modo congregatus, sed coetus multitudinis juris consensu et utilitatis communione sociatus" (*De republica*, I, 25). Saint Augustine responds in the *City of God* (XIX, 21) by denying that the Roman Republic, according to its very definition, had never been—the fault of true justice—the "thing of the people": "Quapropter nunc est locus, ut ... secundum definitiones, quibus apud Ciceronem utitur Scipio in libris de re publica, numquam rem publicam fuisse romanam. Breviter enim rem publicam definit esse rem populi. Quae definitio si vera est, numquam fuit Romana res publica, quia numquam fuit res populi, quam definitionem voluit esse rei publicae. Populum enim esse definivit coetum multitudinis juris consensu et utilitatis communione societatum." It is on this alternative that, across the centuries, Rousseau will impose a radical displacement. But to do so, he must "problematize" the entire chain, i.e., state in full the latent question for which different "responses" were available.

3. This is, as we know, the second of the formal definitions of citizen given by Aristotle in Book III of the *Politics* (1277b): "we praise the ability to be governed just as we do that to govern, and it seems that the excellence of a good citizen is, in a way, the capacity to command well and to obey well" (*to dunasthai kai archein kai archesthai kalôs*). Here we must again face a signifying chain whose origin returns at least to the "discourse of Otanes" in Herodotus's *Histories*, III, Vol. II, Thalia 83, trans. George Rawlson (London: John Murray, 1858), p. 477: "Now, as I have neither a mind to rule nor to be ruled" (*Oute gar archein oute archesthai ethelo*). With these three formulas, we have therefore the apparently complete series of logical possibilities: neither command nor obey (the principle of "an-archy"), or (alternatively) command or obey, and (simultaneously) command and obey. Cf. the commentary of E. Terray, *La Politique dans la caverne* (Paris: Le Seuil, 1990), p. 210.

4. Cf. Louis Althusser, "Rousseau: The Social Contract" in *Politics and History; Montesquieu, Rousseau, Hegel, Marx,* trans. Ben Brewster (London: NLB, 1972).

5. Rousseau, *Social Contract,* IV, chapter 8.

6. Paul H. Beik, *The French Revolution,* "The Declaration of the Rights of Man and of the Citizen," (1789), p. 95.

7. Y. Vargas, *Rousseau, Économie politique* (Paris: PUF, 1755, 1986), p. 55: "Revolt fuses individuals into a collective body which has a will created by no one and which each individual recognizes as his own. The dynamic of the revolt replaces the metaphor of the organism. It preserves the common self, but instead of defining it as structural and blind, this dynamic defines it as an objective law of reciprocity and thus immediately reconciles the individual and the group. Only a people *who fights* for its freedom, recognizes itself in the unity of its general Will ... the basic theoretical question is the founding insurrection

of the law (*droit*) of the people. It is the *basis* (*fond*) of the problem, the contract is only the *form*. . . ."

8. In his latest book, *Kant révolutionnaire—Droit et politique* (Paris: PUF, 1988), André Tosel characterizes Kant's position—favorable to the institutionalization of the revolution as opposed to the States of the Old Regime—as "thermidorian."

9. Immanuel Kant, "The Doctrine of Right," *Metaphysics of Morals* (1797), ed. Raymond Geuss, trans. Mary Gregor (Cambridge: Cambridge University Press, 1991), § 47, 127.

10. Immanuel Kant, "The Character of Nations," *Anthropology from a Pragmatic Point of View*, trans. Victor L. Dowdell (Carbondale: Illinois University Press, 1978), p. 225 (translation modified—*trans.*).

11. It is enlightening to oppose Kant's formulation (which, in fact, excludes the plebeians from the category of citizenship) to that, nearly contemporaneous, of Saint-Just, which excludes the right of governments: "Whoever is magistrate, is no longer of the people; he cannot enter into the people with any individual right. If the authorities were part of the people, they would be more powerful than the people. . . . When speaking of a civil servant, one must not say *citizen*; this title is above him" (Fragments of *Institutions Républicaines*, III.4): cf. my essay "Who Comes After the Subject?" (New York: Routledge, 1991).

12. Kant, "The Doctrine of Right," § 46, 126.

13. Ibid.

14. "Adversity, pain, and poverty are great temptations leading man to violate his duty" (Immanuel Kant, Introduction to "The Doctrine of Right").

15. Rousseau, *The Social Contract*, p. 4.

16. Cf. Immanuel Kant, "Toward Perpetual Peace," Section 2, in *Kant: Political Writings*, ed. Hans Reiss, trans. H. B. Nisbet (New York: Cambridge University Press, 1991).

17. Kant, "Doctrine of Right," § 53.

18. Ibid., § 46.

19. Ibid.

20. It is Michel Foucault more than Heidegger who sheds light on this question. Cf. G. Lebrun, *Kant et la fin de la métaphysique, Essai sur la "Critique de la faculté de juger"* (Paris: Librairie Armand Colin, 1970), p. 467.

21. *Course on Logic*, collected from notes published in 1800 by Jäsche.

22. Immanuel Kant, "The Contest of Faculties" in *Kant: Political Writings*.

23. I say meaning (*sens*) because the expression "science of man"—coined by Malebranche in its modern sense where man is no longer "subject," in opposition to a "science of God," but "object" of knowledge—appears during the eighteenth century in Diderot and in d'Alembert (the article "Encyclopedia" and *Discours préliminaire de l'Encyclopédie*), in Hume, and was later used by French doctors before reaching the Ideologues. Cf. G. Gusdorf, *La conscience révolutionnaire—Les idéologues* (Paris: Payot 1978), p. 384 .

24. Kant, *Critique of Pure Reason*, trans. Picavet (Paris: PUF, 1960), p. 78.

25. I return to this point, among others, interpreted by Franca Papa, *Tre studi in Kant* (Rome: Lacaita editore, 1984).

26. In the *Critique of Practical Reason*, Kant never ceases to link (*enchaîner*) the series of terms duty (*Pflicht*), responsibility (*Schuldigkeit*), obligation (*Verbindlichkeit, Zwang*). The *Doctrine of Truth* (1797) will speak of "dictatorship."

27. What *The Groundwork of the Metaphysics of Morals* (1785) calls in Latin *antagonisms*.

28. Cf. in particular "The Amphiboly of the Moral Concepts of Reflection," *The Doctrine of Virtue*, I., 1.2., § 16.

29. Kant, Introduction to "The Doctrine of Right," p. 56.

30. Ibid., p. 57.

31. Ibid., p. 58.

32. The importance of the French Revolution for Kant is first that it shows that these conditions have coincided at least once in contemporary history.

33. Kant himself has employed the expression "moral politics," but in a very specific context: by opposing it both to "moralizing politics" and to "political morality" (i.e., a morality flexible according to political imperatives). Cf. Tosel's commentary in *Kant révolutionnaire*, p. 19.

34. Immanuel Kant, *The Critique of Judgement* (1790), §65.

35. Kant, *Critique of Judgement*, trans. J.H. Bernard (New York: Hafner Press, 1951), p. 221.

36. Cf. Judith Schlanger's book, *Les Métaphores de l'organisme* (Paris: 1971).

37. As Domenico Losurdo shows so convincingly in his book where one finds summarized and related to the anti-mechanistic thematic its immediate political stakes: see *Hegel, Questione nazionale, Restauration, Pubblicazioni dell'Università di Urbino* (1983), p. 18.

38. G. Canghilhem, "Le tout et la partie dans la pensée biologique," in *Études d'histoire et de philosophie des sciences* (Paris: Librairie Vrin, 1968), p. 327.

39. Kant, *Critique of Judgement*, § 72.

40. What is even more striking, as again Canguilhem shows, is that here, Kant is the first, between Lavoisier and Claude Bernard, to clearly conceive in philosophical terms the specificity of life as regulation.

41. Introduction to "The Doctrine of Right" (translation modified), § E.

42. Kant, "Idea for a Universal History from a Cosmopolitan Point of View," Fifth Proposition, in *Kant: Political Writings*, p. 45 (translation modified—*trans.*).

43. Ibid., Fourth Proposition, p. 44.

44. See Paulette Taieb, "Tours de mains," in *Revue de Synthèse*, Vol. 2, April–June 1989, pp. 189–203; and Jean-Claude Perrot, "La main invisible et le Dieu caché," in *Différences, valeurs, hiérarchies, Textes offerts à Louis Dumont*, ed. by J. Galley, (Paris, 1984), p. 157.

45. Kant, "Idea for a Universal History with a Cosmopolitan Point of View," *Kant: Political Writings*, Seventh and Eighth Propositions.

46. Jürgen Habermas perceives the question in terms of an exoteric/esoteric doctrine: "In Kant's political philosophy *two* versions can be clearly distinguished. The official one relied on the construction of a cosmopolitan order emerging from natural necessity alone. . . . The other version of the philosophy of history, the unofficial one, proceeded from the notion that politics had first to push for the actualization of a juridical condition. It employed, therefore, the construct of a cosmopolitan order that issued from *both* natural necessity and moral politics." *The Structural Transformation of the Public Sphere*, trans. Thomas Burger (Cambridge, MA: MIT Press, 1989), p. 115.

47. Kant, "Perpetual Peace, A Philosophical Sketch" in *Kant: Political Writings*, Second Definitive Thesis, p. 103.

48. Ibid., First Supplement, p. 111.

49. Kant, *Religion within the Limits of Reason Alone*, Part Three, Introduction.

50. Kant, "Doctrine of Right," § 45.

51. This synthetic unity between morality and the State (comparable to a preestablished harmony) could also be related to that which the entire tradition had established between morality and religion. However, the difference is essential: it is a new economy of "interiority" and of "exteriority," the formula of which we have seen above, thus a new conception of the "subject." If the State is *directly* identified with the authority which, in the element of the law, corresponds to the existence of moral law (*loi*), this means that this authority is totally *exteriorized* in the historical world and thus secularized: from the sky of revelation, it descends onto the land of men. But, at the same time, it is *interiorized*, as an "absent cause": in the consciousness (*conscience*) of duty, man finds no representation of authority, but the pure form of the law (*loi*) which requires him to consider himself a universal "subject." The commanding figure of God or of the Prophet is not replaced by that of the State or of the State leader, it is foreclosed from consciousness in the very moment when the State appears in the *real* ("phenomenal") as the sole legitimate instance of juridical constraint.

7

The Pressure of the Street:
Habermas's Fear of the Masses

Warren Montag

One of Jürgen Habermas's most effective interventions in the field of contemporary philosophy was to draw a line of demarcation separating philosophy from literary criticism. This "genre distinction"[1] was crucial, given the growing preeminence in the 1980s of works (usually in French) that, although written by individuals whose institutional training and function would appear to qualify them as philosophers, could be excluded from study on the grounds that they were actually specimens of literary criticism and could not accurately be classified as philosophical. Such works might take as their object philosophical concepts, just as they might advance analyses of philosophical texts. They did so, however, in the manner of literary criticism as Habermas conceives it: they not only concerned themselves with the history rather than the truth (and it is well known that the former can only "relativize" the latter) of concepts and the rhetoric rather than the logic of even the recognized texts of the philosophical canon, but they themselves, as analyses, exhibited the primacy of rhetoric over rationality and therefore of ornament over argument. Authentic philosophy, in contrast, follows rational procedures in studying the logical structure of arguments rather than the rhetorical tropes in which they might be expressed. Habermas's intervention had a liberating effect, especially on the English-speaking world; after a brief period of uncertainty and perplexity, philosophers were relieved of any obligation to respond to or even read many of the works produced by their French counterparts, which now were reclassified as non-philosophy (fortunately there are those who continue to study these texts even though disciplinary duty does not compel them to do so). As a result, undergraduates seeking to study Derrida's *Introduction to Husserl's Origins of Geometry* or Deleuze's analyses of Leibniz, Hume, or Kant are routinely sent to departments of literature where "literary criticism" is studied.

Readers will forgive me then if, unauthorized and unwelcome, I cross precisely the boundary between literary criticism and philosophy, not to call into question the existence of truth or reality but precisely to open the way to the rigorous knowledge of history, including the historical circumstances that make possible a given philosophical text. From the perspective of a certain Enlightenment tradition, but one to which Habermas rarely, if ever, refers, to respect the reality of a philosophical work means to grasp how it came to be what it is in its actuality, to explain, not explain away, what it presents to us, contradictions and all. This approach to philosophical texts, which might be called materialist, is drawn not from the poststructuralists or postmodernists, but from the work of Spinoza whose treatment of the incoherence and disorder of the Scripture as indices of its historical existence excited the ire of countless defenders of the faith.

In the same way, if *The Structural Transformation of the Public Sphere* exhibits a specific incoherence, it is not because it expresses a primal transcendental disorder (the obverse of the logic whose advocate Habermas appoints himself) that sets the work against itself but because it embodies the conflicts that traverse the conjuncture in which he writes. It is possible that Habermas's works too, despite their "reasoned" air, their high serious refusal of the metaphor and the wordplay that characterize so much writing across the genres, have their own silent spaces, those gaps that do not interrupt the order of arguments but make that order possible and even believable. And no work exhibits such silences more exorbitantly (if to most readers insensibly) than *The Structural Transformation of the Public Sphere*.

I will take as my point of departure a single sentence: "Laws passed under the 'pressure of the street' [*dem Druck der Strasse*] could hardly be understood any longer as embodying the reasonable consensus of publicly debating private persons."[2] The proposition contained in this utterance is repeated throughout *The Structural Transformation of the Public Sphere*: that if any force other than the mere force of reason is brought to bear in the public sphere, rational debate ceases, the universal is lost and the necessarily violent rule of the particular is established, with the certainty that one particularism will soon be replaced by others. It is not sufficient, however, to treat this utterance as if it were nothing more than one expression among others of one of the essential ideas Habermas advances in *The Structural Transformation of the Public Sphere*. To find out what the specific form of the utterance adds to this idea, we must first place it in its context. It appears in Chapter 15, the last chapter of Part Four, "The Bourgeois Public Sphere: Idea and Ideology," in which Habermas treats the successive theorizations of the public sphere (the historical reality in however partial a form necessarily preceded its idea) from its prehistory in England and France, through Kant, Hegel, and Marx, to its definitive treatment by the "liberalists"[3] Mill and Tocqueville. As such, the sentence captures the apparently inescapable contradiction immanent in the public sphere. Indeed, it will be repeated, if in a different idiom, at the end of *The Structural Transformation of the Public Sphere* where Habermas describes the degradation of the public sphere in the period after World War Two, a degradation that is itself the outcome of the conflict of two opposing forces: monopoly capital and the labor movement to which it inevitably gives rise and which it incessantly provokes. The former is characteristic of late capitalism, the time when the unfettered competition of the market, which while not producing the equality of opportunity that it promised (only the proper kind of state could do that) nevertheless expressed a genuine economic rationality that resulted both in ever-increasing general wealth and the optimization of goods and services, had been abolished by the powerful interests that its own success had created. The latter force, the labor movement, in contrast, had always dogged capitalism even if in the inchoate forms of the plebeian mass not yet conscious of its own interests, but already prone to an unthinking rejection of market rationality even in the absence of an alternative.

With the passing away of the absolutist regimes, the threat to the public sphere would come from these two forces, at certain times one more than the other, but most often both simultaneously, locked in a combat that threatened to dissolve the universal into the particular and reason into force. Of course, Habermas does not take these forces to be equivalent: if the irrational particularity of the monopolies could be curbed by a state itself heeding the directives that issued from rational critical debate and discussion, the rationality of the market could be restored and its wealth socially managed in such a way as to guarantee an "affluent society"[4] in which the harmony of interests would permit the emergence of a genuine universality. The possibility of such a state, however, depends in turn on the existence of a genuine rational–critical public sphere which the monopolies have destroyed through mass media; thus, the impasse at which Habermas arrives at the end of his book, recognizing that of all the critics of the public sphere, it was the great "liberalists" of the nineteenth century who accurately diagnosed its fatal malady.

In its prehistory, the public sphere was practiced rather than theorized, primarily in England. Perhaps because in the seventeenth century England, more than any other state in Europe, suffered from the absence of a public sphere in which differences on matters of religion and politics might be freely argued, critics of the monarchy and church were forced to act out rather than express their disagreements with official policies and dogmas. This, according to Habermas, was the cause of the civil wars; with the emergence of a public sphere in England after 1689, revolution became "superfluous."[5] Henceforth, the state had constantly to legitimate itself in the face of opposition critiques by entering public debate with rational argumentation. In this sense the market, whatever the inequalities it introduced into social life, also provided a model of autonomous rationality. Just as the state was advised to withdraw from controlling wages and prices to "let the market decide," so, by the ending of all forms of censorship, reason would become the sole criterion by which arguments would be judged.

This "one blissful moment in the long history of capitalist development" may have "issued from a unique historical constellation in Great Britain"[6] but it found its philosophical expression in the political writings of Kant. In "What is Enlightenment?" in particular, Kant defined the public sphere as a norm; it was to be a realm, free from all coercion or the intrusion of force, in which individuals would express their opinions about all things religious, political, economic, and social solely in words, refraining from any action, content to submit their arguments to the adjudication of reason alone.[7] Only in this way could a public achieve enlightenment, divesting itself of the dogmas and superstitions that are impediments to progress. The world's rulers would thus be well advised to grant the freedom to argue and to withdraw from the public sphere in the same way that they should allow the market to set wages and prices, no matter how temporarily inconvenient such developments might be. And just as the market unhindered always achieves the optimum and restores equilibrium, so the sphere of unimpeded rational–critical debate produces the best arguments possible at a given time. It is here that Habermas, however much he is philosophically and politically indebted to Kant, finds the fatal contradiction of the Kantian public sphere. It is based precisely on a notion of the capitalist market as a natural order not only in the sense that it constitutes a coherent system, but that it produces a social harmony, transmuting, as Mandeville and Smith argued, individual vice into public good, not only independently of the base intentions of individuals but absolutely contrary to them. Motivated by greed and selfishness, the totality of individuals in perpetual interaction could only contribute to the general welfare.

Kant, however, is forced to differentiate between the qualifications necessary for participation in the marketplace and those necessary to participation in the critically debating public sphere. In principle any human being can participate in the marketplace with equal title to any other. This is clearly not the case in the public sphere whose currency is the ability to use one's reason freely. There are those, the majority in fact in any given society, so economically dependent on an other that they cannot reasonably be expected to "think for themselves." Of course, such individuals (Kant calls them "passive" citizens) have the right to all the freedoms guaranteed by law, as well as to all its protections, but they cannot participate in making or even judging laws. Only male property owners are truly *sui juris* and thus capable of being active citizens.[8] The division between active and passive citizens, however, signals the existence of an antagonism in the supposed natural order of the economy, an antagonism all the more likely to explode as a large part of society, and precisely that part with the most grievances, is deprived of the "weapon of criticism" and forced to resort to "the criticism of weapons," that is, force, to voice its concerns.

It was precisely the recognition of the "dialectical" character of civil society and the public sphere that gave rise to the political philosophies of Hegel and the early Marx, united in their difference by a common rejection of Kant's formula for progress and enlightenment. Hegel, especially in the *Philosophy of Right*, acknowledges the contribution of classical political economy, especially Smith, Say, and Ricardo, to the understanding of the universality of what otherwise appeared to be a spectacle of particularities, the way in which individuals precisely in seeking to satisfy their own needs and no one else's constitute a community—to be precise, a civil society—whose interacting members are subject to laws immanent in the totality of their actions. He differs from Kant, however, in that for him civil society as a "system of needs"[9] not only does not produce an order in equilibrium, but by its very nature produces historically unprecedented conflict. Because needs and desires are not essentially natural (and therefore, of necessity, finite in number), but social and therefore illimitable, and because the system of production and accumulation increases continually, so does the mass of individuals necessary to produce the desired goods who find themselves by virtue of market rationality reduced to poverty and want. This is the underside of the progress Kant contemplated, the labor of the negative that would not only undo the movement toward perpetual peace, replacing it with conflict, but would also necessarily bring into existence as a condition of a society's wealth a materially and intellectually deprived mass. Even more perniciously, the means to redress the grievances of the mass within the framework of civil society are conspicuously lacking. Both charity and social welfare would deprive them of a sense of "individual independence and self worth,"[10] but the nature of the system of needs is such that it is impossible to set them to work in the productive sphere; there are already too many unsold products and too few consumers. Civil society may seek in response to expand beyond its borders through conquest or trade and most often a combination of both in search of new markets and cheaper materials, but this merely postpones and generalizes the problem. The world, far from being the cosmopolitan sphere that Kant hoped might be realized one day, would exhibit the poles of surfeit and deprivation that, if abandoned to its own dynamic, would erupt into violence.

Under such conditions, the public sphere could not be expected to address arguments to the state and later to become its legislative branch. For there was nothing rational or universal about the public sphere, which could be no more than the site in which the struggles that traversed civil society would be played out, with opposing forces organizing their own communities or "corporations."[11] On the contrary, the conflicts inevitably produced by the market necessitated the growth of the state, in particular its "police" functions. Only the state could embody the universal.

From the same dialectical perspective, Habermas argues, Marx drew opposing conclusions. The intensity of the conflicts internal to society was so great that no state, not even a police state (in the broadest sense of the term, that is, a state that controls, watches over and cares for its population), could prevent them from exploding into revolutionary crisis. At first, Marx believed that the very notion of the public sphere in which individuals irrespective of their material class position could interact at the level of discourse, a level free from the intrusion of power relations, as equals was purely ideological, the illusion of a disembodied formal equality that helped persuade people to accept their real material conditions of domination and exploitation. At the same time, however, the idea of the public sphere could not be reduced to mere ideology even in Marx; rather, it functioned as the promise (first even as a purely formal reality, later, with the extension of suffrage, in its "authentic" sense) that bourgeois society could not keep, the ideal that under the social conditions that were its foundation could never be realized, a realm of freedom and equality that could only be achieved when the existing social relations were overthrown. Such a revolution would usher in a genuine public sphere in which conflicts would be waged with words alone, force would be unnecessary, and a genuine evolution would begin. Marx thus, according to Habermas, did not so much reject the natural order of bourgeois property as invert it in "a dialectically projected counter-model." This was said to be true not only of the early Marx, but even of the Marx of *The Civil War in France*: the notion that the destruction of the bourgeois state, including parliament, and its replacement by the direct democracy of workers' councils would for the first time permit something like a general public sphere was predicated on the idea of an "ordre naturel" that once achieved would no longer give rise to "extended controversies."[12] In fact, the experience of revolution would show that in place of the withering away of the state, it was civil society itself that would disappear with the rise of postrevolutionary states "incomparably more powerful"[13] than those they replaced.

In this way, Habermas concludes his discussion of the idea of the public sphere by noting its indissociable link to the liberal tradition whose material base, he concludes, remains inescapable and unsurpassable except in the Marxist imaginary which, whenever it has been actualized, has produced something far worse than the unfairness of the market. Marxism, both in its theoretical and its practical forms, is reduced to a variant of liberalism and a particularly weak one at that. Precisely because for the Marxist tradition the limitations and conflicts of the public sphere were merely the effects of causes external to it (the sphere of production) and would vanish into an untroubled universal publicity once the transformation of the infrastructure was achieved, this tradition proved incapable of grasping the contradictions proper to the public sphere, that is, proper to any conceivable public sphere whatever. The task was thus left to the liberal tradition whose strength lay precisely in the fact that, for it, the capitalist market and capitalist social relations were an absolute horizon, beyond which it was not merely undesirable, but impossible, to go. Liberals were thus compelled to look within rather than beyond the public sphere for any explanation of its failures. Accordingly it was such liberals as Mill and Tocqueville who noted the tendency of the public sphere *per se* to degenerate from a sphere of rational–critical debate, the model of which depended upon the ability of individuals to abstract themselves from their material circumstances and allow reason alone to decide their controversies, into an arena in which competing interest groups struggled for power. The general good was lost and the tyranny of the majority, bound not by reason but by interest, over minorities became an ever-present danger. In the period after World War Two, such a development becomes increasingly likely, even inevitable, with the universalization of mass media, the colonization of thought and imagination by advertising, by "publicity" in the degraded sense. Rational–critical debate is reduced to a distant memory as majorities are shaped by the means of communication. Criticism becomes pseudo-criticism, revolt merely the simulacrum of great challenges to established orders past, more likely than not to produce an even more totally administered world. Habermas's claim in 1989 that "*Structural Transformation* moved totally within the circle of a classical Marxian critique of ideology"[14] is inconceivable. It is rather the dilemma that the great "liberalists" identified in response to the mass movements and insurrections of the mid-nineteenth century, far more than anything Hegel or Marx wrote, which remains for Habermas the dilemma of post-war capitalist Europe and North America.

This dilemma, the return of force to what was supposed to be a sphere of objectivity, a force originating not this time from the state but from majorities outside of and opposed to the state, no longer associations of autonomous individuals but unthinking, perhaps manipulated, majorities, unreasoning masses whose violence (threatened or actualized) will provoke even greater state intervention whether against or at the behest of their movements, is precisely the concern of the statement I cited at the beginning of these remarks: "Laws passed under 'the pressure of the street' could hardly be understood any longer as embodying the reasonable consensus of publicly debating private persons."[15] The pressure of the street: Habermas has insisted that rhetoric is as external to reason as literature is to philosophy and that to analyze the rhetoric of a philosophical text is to forsake essence for appearance and content for form and forsake any notion of meaning at all in favor of an infinite self-referentiality independent of history and society. If we would restore to Habermas's text, however, precisely its objective reality and refrain from reducing it to an ideal order in relation to which all that did not pertain to this order would be defined as inessential and insignificant (an operation that is as common to the practice of literary criticism as to philosophical analysis—was it not for this reason that Aristotle declared tragedy the most philosophical form of writing?), we cannot help but examine, at least in this significant case, his recourse to a certain rhetorical figure: metonymy. To do so is not to make the work indeterminate and unknowable but the contrary: to understand the way that historical conflicts inhabit *The Structural Transformation of the Public Sphere* in forms that escape both Habermas's knowledge and his control. In another epoch, this was called a symptomatic reading; I call attention to this name only to point out the very non-literary origins of this practice of reading or, more accurately, analysis which, whatever its success, sought to produce a kind of knowledge in the face of centuries of spiritualism. An innocent reading, the kind Habermas would have us undertake, would take the metonym "the street" simply as a substitution for the sake of variation. But a substitution for what? What exactly is the meaning of "the street" in the utterance? Further, why is the phrase "the pressure of the street" placed in quotation marks? Is it a citation? If so, what is its source and why is there no reference?

To determine the meaning of "the street" we might turn to the preceding sentence in which we are told that the public sphere had become "an arena in which competing interests were fought out in the coarser forms of violent conflict."[16] "Competing interests" here is a bit misleading: it is not all the different interest groups in nineteenth-century Europe fighting among themselves as the phrase seems to suggest, nor does Habermas define these interest groups and their weight in a given society. Instead, if we follow Habermas's argument to the letter, the conflict arises from the group with "needs that could not expect to be satisfied by a self-regulating market," a group which "tended to favor regulation by the state."[17] The same evasiveness appears in a formulation, strikingly similar in meaning to the ideas attributed to the great liberalists, near the end of the *The Structural Transformation of the Public Sphere* in which Habermas, no longer speaking as an interlocutor of the philosophers of the public, argues that unless the social wealth of the "affluent society" can dull "the antagonistic edge of competing needs to the extent that the possibility of mutual satisfaction comes within reach" the advanced industrial societies are doomed to a situation in which "the power relation between pressure and counter pressure, however publicly exercised, creates at best an unstable equilibrium of interests supported by temporary power constellations that in principle is devoid of rationality according to the standard of the universal interest."[18] Here the plural (needs, interests, groups) is a sleight of hand. Although from the juridical view, all interest groups, like the autonomous individuals who make them up, are equal and equivalent, like the two individuals who come together to conclude a contract that alone turns them, after the fact, into employer and employee or ruler and ruled, from the point of view of power, things appear quite differently. And "the street" of course precisely refers to power, physical not legal power; it is the place where the interest group of the majority in any given society, those whose needs are not met even by the rational operation of the market, often "speaks." But to speak from the street is not to engage in authentic discourse (or communicative action) which is necessarily disembodied and disempowered, having surrendered itself, in advance, to the force of reason alone. The realm of discourse not only remains separate from and outside of the material world of forces and interests but, and here again Habermas does little more than cite Kant, it imposes such limits on itself. To speak from the street is to speak from outside the public sphere, not just the bourgeois public sphere, but any public sphere as Habermas defines it. The addition of other, subordinate or subaltern, public spheres does not call Habermas's notion into question; in his later work he refers to a general public sphere that is the totality of particular spheres (the particularity of which may be based on class, race or gender), the site at which they in their discursive existence communicate as equals.[19] The street is then in no way an alternative public sphere; it is precisely not a sphere of rational critique or even discussion at all. The street is the sphere of action for the critique that has violated the limits it ought, if it were in fact rational, to have observed, the border that separates the speech that transcends the world of practice from that world, leaving it untouched and remaining untouched by it in return. The freedom rational critical debate enjoys within its own realm depends upon its scrupulous observance of this territorial imperative. To translate words of criticism into deeds is to remove reason from its adjudicating role and thus contaminate the public sphere and to provoke the imposition of external, artificial laws in response to lawlessness of the critique that attempts to actualize itself.

In fact, the street doesn't speak insofar as it is the materialization of critique, critique become force; in this sense, it communicates nothing intended or even capable of "convincing" or "persuading" those to whom it addresses itself. Rather, it exerts what Habermas's translator has rendered as "pressure," *Druck*, which has the sense of physical force exerted. The street moves or produces effects through the force of its weight, its mass. The words of the group for which "the street" is a metonym are always embodied, immanent in material force. Even its use of language does not constitute communicative action in the rational sense: it does not discuss, it demands, and its demands are chanted or written on banners carried by a mass and backed up by the threat of physical resistance and even violence, if its demands go unheeded.

The street is outside the centers of discussion, exchange and deliberation. In fact, it is the outside of rational exchange in every sense: the exchange of ideas which resembles in so many respects the exchange of commodities (competition, progressive optimalization). But of course, Habermas is an Enlightened man; unlike today's neoliberals, proud descendants of Adam Smith, who have lapsed into a notion of the market as natural order that requires a state that knows not to interfere with its immutable laws, he understands that a market left to its own devices will give rise to precisely those class struggles that Marx predicted without, however, any possibility that these struggles could produce anything better than the market and a great likelihood that they will produce a statist regime far worse. The market, therefore, requires as a condition of its rationality the mediation of a state which will redistribute just enough to dull the edge of need (as well as the edge of the revolt that need is likely to produce) but not enough to interfere with market mechanisms. This mediation alone will save the market from falling victim to the force of its own contradiction. And just as such a state knows enough not to interfere excessively with the market, so it knows not to interfere imprudently with the public sphere which, in our time, is the sum of a plurality of interacting spheres. But if the state is necessary to save the market from itself, so it must help the public sphere observe its limits. In his more recent discussions of the public sphere, Habermas warns that no matter how the current economic system (he doesn't often use the word "capitalism") persistently fails certain groups, even the majority, they must give up their "holistic" goals for a transformation of society. Of course, they may go on arguing for such a transformation, but their arguments must never pass into acts or "take to the street." It is undoubtedly significant in this connection that *The Structural Transformation of the Public Sphere* is largely silent about European history from 1914 to 1945; such an absence is absolutely necessary to Habermas's assumption of a relatively stable capitalist system the greatest fault of which is its failure to guarantee the "affluence" of the population in its entirety. We may see clearly why he prefers Kant and Mill to Hegel and Marx. The latter's insistence that imperialism, war and periodic crisis were necessary attributes of capitalism makes it far more difficult to repress the reasons why so many millions of men and women fought for socialist revolution as the

only alternative to barbarism. Habermas's narrative systematically sup-
presses the events whose dissociation from the history of capitalism and
the processes of capital accumulation in the twentieth century can only
be called a kind of theoretico-political denial: a war of unprecedented
savagery, economic collapse, a revolutionary wave followed by the triumph of fascist reaction, a new war, far more savage than the last,
holocausts and genocides, most but not all carried out by what were
once called "imperialist" states. Of course, it might just as well be pointed
out that even the "one blissful moment" of public life in eighteenth-
century Britain, the moment of polite conversation in drawing rooms
and coffee houses, rested on a foundation of dispossession and slavery
and that the most important commodity for the market whose rationality
was so celebrated was human flesh. In Habermas's narrative, however,
the cause of the convivial life has disappeared into its effects.

But the opposition between the public sphere and the street, as an
opposition between communicative action and corporeal action, reason
and force, rests on an even more fundamental hypothesis. If Habermas
doesn't like the word capitalism, he likes the word "ideology" even less.
Habermas must categorically reject the idea that capitalist property
relations require as a condition of their reproduction anything more
than simple "market forces," what Marx called "the silent compulsion
of capital"[20] which, having separated the producers from the means of
production, leaves them no other choice but to sell their labor merely
to survive. It is of course to this "something more" that most of the
great texts of Marxism have been devoted. To take only one of the
most influential cases, Gramcsi argued that in addition to market
pressure, systems both of coercion and violence, on the one hand, and
of persuasion, on the other, are necessary elements of any capitalist
society. There can be no genuine competition between arguments and
ideas, because between ideas there are relations of force, in that they
are embodied in the broader relationship of forces in a society characterized by a perpetual, if latent, civil war that renders some dominant
and others subordinate, usually in inverse proportion to their validity
or truth and certainly in inverse proportion to the degree of their
"criticality." To go beyond Gramsci, Althusser—writing under the direct
influence of Spinoza—argued that if "whatever diminishes the power
of the body to act simultaneously diminishes the power of the mind to
think,"[21] ideological subjection is less a matter of ideas than of forces,
less a matter of minds than of bodies, a notion of subjection taken up
by Foucault who described domination as the effect of subtle forms of
physical, corporal coercion. From such a perspective, the possibility of

a genuine critical analysis of the existing social order rests on a balance of power favorable to those subject to domination: critical theory depends upon critical practice, upon struggles that diminish the effects of coercion and discipline in workplaces and communities. Indeed Kant, who argued that reason may be advised but cannot be expected to police itself and that a high degree of "civil freedom" (that is, freedom to act) "sets up insuperable barriers" to "intellectual freedom," advanced as a necessary condition of the public's enlightening itself a "well-disciplined and numerous army to guarantee public security"[22] against the "unthinking mass" that is such an object of fear for Kant. Behind reason, force; behind rational–critical debate the unceasing struggle of "pressure and counter-pressure [*Druck und gegen-Druck*]," that is, the authorities and those critics loyal enough never actively to contest them against the mass whose *Druck* makes them an object of fear.

Can we not now assign a certain function, if not exactly a meaning, to Habermas's recourse to the metonymy of "the street"? If we could not immediately determine for what "the street" was a metonymic substitute, if behind the term was not a presence but an absence, is not this absence precisely the absence of a rational foundation of political reason? Does it not signal the fact that the force of reason exerts no pressure or has no effect at all, except insofar as it rests on real, physical force? If Machiavelli, Spinoza and Marx seem nearly alone in their recognition of this fact, we may rest assured that there is not a single figure in the history of political thought whose work does not register this idea, if only in the form of a fear of the masses. Habermas too, fundamentally committed to the existing social and economic order, can only experience "the street" as an abyss above which both civil society and the state so precariously hover. It may be, however, that we have nothing to lose and indeed everything to gain in regarding the triumph of the market as itself the abyss from which "the street" is the only way out.

Notes

1. Jürgen Habermas, "Excursus on Leveling the Genre Distinction Between Philosophy and Literature," *The Philosophical Discourse of Modernity* (Cambridge, MA: MIT Press, 1987), pp. 185–210.

2. Jürgen Habermas, *Strukturwandel der Offentlichkeit* (Neuwied: Hermann Luchterhand Verlag, 1962), p. 147.

3. Jürgen Habermas, *The Structural Transformation of the Public Sphere*, trans. Thomas Burger (Cambridge, MA: MIT Press, 1989), p. 130.

4. Ibid., p. 234.

5. Ibid., p. 62.

6. Ibid., p. 79.

7. Immanuel Kant, *Political Writings* (Cambridge: Cambridge University Press, 1970), pp. 54–60.

8. Kant, "On the Common Saying: 'This May Be True in Theory, But It Does Not Apply in Practice,'" *Political Writings*, p. 77.

9. G.W.F. Hegel, *Philosophy of Right*, trans T.M. Knox (Oxford: Oxford University Press, 1967), paragraphs 189–95.

10. Ibid., paragraph 245.

11. Ibid., paragraphs 250–56.

12. Habermas, *Structural Transformation*, p. 140.

13. Ibid.

14. Jürgen Habermas, "Further Reflections on the Public Sphere," in *Habermas and the Public Sphere*, ed. Craig Calhoun (Cambridge, MA: MIT Press, 1992).

15. Habermas, *Structural Transformation*, p. 132.

16. Ibid.

17. Ibid.

18. Habermas, *Structural Transformation*, p. 234; *Strukturwandel*, p. 254.

19. See Habermas's comments in "Further Reflections," pp. 425–7, and *Between Facts and Norms* (Cambridge, MA: MIT Press, 1996), pp. 329–87.

20. Karl Marx, *Capital*, Vol. 1 (London: Penguin, 1976), p. 899.

21. Benedict Spinoza, *Ethics*, Part III, Proposition 11; Louis Althusser, "Machiavelli–Spinoza: The Only Materialist Tradition," *The New Spinoza* (Minneapolis: University of Minnesota Press, 1997).

22. Kant, "What is Enlightenment," *Political Writings*, p. 59.

8

A Displaced Transition:
Habermas on the Public Sphere

Ted Stolze

In order for a critical theory of society to be adequate, Jacques Bidet has contended, it must include at least three key components: a description of actually existing injustice, a normative ideal of justice, and a strategy for transition from unjust to just social orders.[1] Like most contemporary political philosophers, Jürgen Habermas has primarily focused on the first two components. In what follows, though, I want instead to draw attention to, and express reservations about, his scattered observations regarding how to a bring about a just society.

It is worth noting at the outset that Habermas has always been clear about the kind of political mobilization that he rejects, namely, the classical Marxist project of contesting with the hope of supplanting state and class power by setting up alternative institutions of workers' and popular power—what Antonio Negri has strikingly called new forms of "constituent power."[2] In *The Structural Transformation of the Public Sphere*,[3] for example, early on in his philosophical development Habermas expresses a certain admiration for Marx's politics:

> Marx shared the perspective of the propertyless and uneducated masses who, without fulfilling the conditions for admission to the bourgeois public sphere, nonetheless made their way into it in order to translate economic conflicts into the only form holding any promise of success—that is, into political conflict. In Marx's opinion the masses would employ the platform of the public sphere, institutionalized in the constitutional state, not to destroy it but to make it into what, according to liberal pretense, it had always claimed to be.

Yet he immediately adds the following qualification:

> In reality, however, the occupation of the political public sphere by the
> unpropertied masses led to an interlocking of state and society which
> removed from the public sphere its former basis without supplying a new
> one. For the integration of the public and private realms entailed a corre-
> sponding disorganization of the public sphere that once was the go-between
> linking state and society.[4]

Indeed, one of the key underlying themes of *The Structural Transformation of the Public Sphere* concerns the failure of working-class struggles to
make good the promise of liberalism (represented by the rise, temporary flourishing, and fall of bourgeois literary and political public
spheres). The revolutions of 1848 and the 1871 Paris Commune
illustrate for Habermas not only a proletarian inability to bring actually
existing capitalist social and political institutions into conformity with
such professed bourgeois ideals as freedom, equality, and democracy
but also the grave danger that mass movements—especially when
successful—pose to the separation between civil society and the state.[5]
Since the original publication of *The Structural Transformation of the
Public Sphere* in German in 1961, Habermas has maintained this position
with remarkable consistency. Consider the following recent examples.

After making his famous "linguistic turn" and subsequently formu-
lating a theory of "communicative action,"[6] in an article published in
the early 1980s Habermas discerns an "exhaustion of utopian energies"
associated with a "shift of paradigm from a society based on social labor
to a society based on communication."[7] Especially in light of the failed
hopes of the 1960s and 1970s, he concludes, the left must henceforth
abandon "the methodological illusion that was concerned with projec-
tions of a concrete totality of future life possibilities." Instead:

> the utopian content of a society based on communication is limited to the
> formal aspects of an undamaged intersubjectivity. To the extent to which it
> suggests a concrete form of life, even the expression "the ideal speech
> situation" is misleading. What can be outlined normatively are the necessary
> but general conditions for the communicative practice of everyday life and
> for a procedure of discursive will-formation that would put participants
> *themselves* in a position to realize concrete possibilities for a better and less
> threatened life, on *their own* initiative and in accordance with *their own* needs
> and insights.[8]

Thus, according to Habermas, the traditional socialist project requires
significant modification, for the "social containment of capitalism" has
become more than a matter of drawing up "simple recipes of workers'

self management." Indeed, he argues that there is a pressing need for "something new, namely a highly innovative combination of power and intelligent self-restraint." This is because "not only capitalism but the interventionist state itself" must be "socially contained." Moreover, the task has consequently become "considerably more complicated," because "that combination of power and intelligent self-restraint can no longer be entrusted to the state's planning capacity" but must emerge from the activity of "autonomous, self-organized public spheres."[9]

In an article published in the immediate aftermath of what he designates the "rectifying revolution" of 1989, Habermas likewise insists that the "non-communist Left has no reason to be downhearted."[10] Indeed, it continues to have an important political role. In Habermas's view, the "socialist Left . . . can generate the ferment that produces the continuing process of political communication that prevents the institutional framework of a constitutional democracy from becoming desiccated."[11] However, political aspirations must be constrained, as socialist ideas are transformed "into the radically reformist self-criticism of a capitalist society, which, in the form of a constitutional democracy with universal suffrage and a welfare state, has developed not only weaknesses but also strengths."[12] Habermas then offers, and elaborates on, a telling biblical metaphor:

> With the bankruptcy of state socialism, this is the eye of the needle through which everything must pass. *This* socialism will disappear only when it no longer has an object of criticism—perhaps at a point when the society in question has changed its identity so much that it allows the full significance of everything that cannot be expressed as a price to be perceived and taken seriously. The hope that humanity can emancipate itself from self-imposed tutelage and degrading living conditions has not lost its power, but it is filtered by a falliblist consciousness, and an awareness of the historical lesson that one would already have achieved a considerable amount if the balance of a tolerable existence could be preserved for the fortunate few—and, most of all, if it could be established on the other, ravaged continents.[13]

Habermas tries, then, to preserve what he takes to be an *ethical* socialism. Although a long-term utopian hope remains in order (Kant's regulative idea of humanity one day freed from its "self-imposed tutelage"), the immediate task before the left is modest: to help shore up, indeed to strive to *universalize*, the welfare state.

In the preface to *Between Facts and Norms*[14] Habermas returns to this theme and urges the left—"after the collapse of state socialism and the end of the 'global civil war'"—to cease envisioning socialism as "the design—and violent implementation—of a concrete form of life." "If, however," he adds, "one conceives of 'socialism' as the set of necessary conditions for emancipated forms of life about which the participants *themselves* must first reach an understanding, then one will recognize that the democratic self-organization of a legal community constitutes the normative core of this project as well."[15] It is worth noting that here again Habermas intentionally retains the term "self-organization" and dismisses any notion of workers' "self-management."[16]

Indeed, in a 1993 "Conversation about Questions of Political Theory" Habermas insists that:

> [W]e have to let go of interpretations that have become dear to us, including the idea that radical democracy is a form of self-administering socialism. Only a democracy that is understood in terms of communications theory is feasible under the conditions of complex societies. In this instance, the relationship of center and periphery must be reversed: in my model the forms of communication in a civil society, which grow out of an intact private sphere, along with the communicative stream of a vital public sphere embedded in a liberal political culture, are what chiefly bear the burden of normative expectations.[17]

What is the significance of these references? First of all, although Habermas has regularly called attention to the failures of advanced capitalist societies, he has equally insisted that capitalism itself cannot be superseded. In a word, the capitalist market and capitalist state are the unsurpassable horizons of political theory and practice. No doubt Habermas has on occasion granted that "capitalism is just as insensitive to harming the moral equilibrium of society as technology is to the way it disturbs the ecological balance of nature"; and so "there is a practical need for the economic system to be reined in by the welfare state and ecologically restructured." Yet in customary fashion he quickly cautions that such reforms are "easier said than done, because society is indebted for both its productivity and its permanent crisis to the uncoupling of self-directed systems from the life-world—the autonomizing of the rationalities of partial systems with regard to the imperatives of life-forms integrated by way of values, norms, and achievements of understanding is an ambiguous phenomenon."[18]

Habermas's desire to achieve a realistic social theory has thus led him to stress not only the increasing complexity and functional differentiation of modern capitalist societies but also the inadequacies of previous socialist strategies of transition. In fact, if we can speak of a transition any longer, it is not in the sense of superseding the capitalist mode of production but merely of striving to counteract the worst effects—the "insensitivities"—of market maldistribution and state bureaucratization. Since the late 1980s Habermas has tried to scale back and reconfigure socialism in terms of "radical democracy" and has advanced two "models" of how such radical democratization might occur under conditions of advanced capitalism.

In a 1988 article on "Popular Sovereignty as Procedure" (included as an appendix to *Between Facts and Norms*) Habermas proposes a "siege" model for how citizens can criticize and influence the state without actually trying to supplant state power and thereby—at least according to this line of reasoning—undermine the very autonomous public spheres and communicative freedoms that serve as the conditions of possibility for such criticism and influence.[19] Habermas's overriding concern in this article is to develop a "desubstantialized" idea of a popular sovereignty. In other words, sovereignty should be located not in the people themselves but

> in those subjectless forms of communication that regulate the flow of discursive opinion and will-formation in such a way that their fallible outcomes have the presumption of practical reason on their side. Subjectless and anonymous, an intersubjectively dissolved popular sovereignty withdraws into democratic procedures and the demanding communicative presuppositions of their implementation. It is sublimated into the elusive interactions between culturally mobilized public spheres and a will-formation institutionalized according to the rule of law. Set communicatively aflow, sovereignty makes itself felt in the power of public discourses. Although such power originates in autonomous public spheres, it must take shape in the decisions of democratic institutions of opinion- and will-formation, inasmuch as the responsibility for momentous decisions demands clear institutional accountability. Communicative power is exercised in the manner of a siege. It influences the premises of judgments and decision making in the political system without intending to conquer the system itself. It thus aims to assert its imperatives in the only language the besieged fortress understands: it takes responsibility for the pool of reasons that administrative power can handle instrumentally but cannot ignore, given its juridical structure.[20]

Although the basic point is clear, there follows no detailed account of the means by which these autonomous public spheres are supposed to hold state power in check and redirect its activities to serve the common good. Moreover, the type of siege to be conducted via the public sphere is a largely symbolic affair, a kind of communicative "sublimation" of actually existing forms of social struggle. This is a most peculiar siege too: it is permanent and yet must never succeed. If the siege were in fact ever to succeed by supplanting the market and state through the establishment of alternative forms of workers' or popular power, the siege would in fact already have failed, for the autonomy of the public sphere would supposedly collapse.

In the preface to a new printing of *The Structural Transformation of the Public Sphere* (published in Leipzig just prior to German reunification and doubtless intended for readers in the German Democratic Republic)[21] Habermas equally stresses the siege model, which he now presents as a kind of "democratic dam." He reiterates, too, the "implications for his concept of democracy" arising from the "two-tiered concept of society as lifeworld and as system" advanced in *The Theory of Communicative Action*. As an implied self-criticism, Habermas indicates that he has come to consider

> state apparatus and economy to be systematically integrated action fields that can no longer be transformed democratically from within, that is, switched over to a political mode of integration, without damage to their proper systemic logic and therewith their ability to function. The abysmal collapse of state socialism has only confirmed this. Instead, radical democratization now aims for a shifting of forces within a "separation of powers" that itself is to be maintained in principle. The new equilibrium to be attained is not one between state powers but between different resources for social integration. The goal is no longer to supersede an economic system having a capitalist life of its own but to erect a democratic dam against the colonializing *encroachment* of system imperatives on areas of the lifeworld. Therewith we have bid farewell to the notion of alienation and appropriation of objectified essentialist powers, whose place is in a philosophy of praxis. A radical-democratic change in the process of legitimation aims at a new balance between the forces of societal integration so that the social-integrative power of solidarity—the "communicative force of production"—can prevail over the powers of the other two control resources, i.e., money and administrative power, and therewith successfully assert the practically oriented demands of the lifeworld.[22]

With the publication of *Between Facts and Norms* in 1992, though, Habermas finds this "image of the democratically 'besieged' fortress of the state apparatus" to be "misleading," since it fails to allow for the possibility of a "democratization" of the state that goes "beyond special obligations to provide information" and could "supplement parliamentary and judicial controls on administration from within."[23] Lately, too, he has reflected that his purpose in proposing the image of a "siege" of the bureaucratic power of public administrations by citizens making use of communicative power was to oppose the classic idea of revolution—the conquest and destruction of state power. The unfettered communicative freedoms of citizens are supposed to become effective through—as Rawls says with Kant—the "public use of reason." But the "influence" of the opinions that compete in the public sphere, and communicative power formed by means of democratic procedures on the horizon of the public sphere, can become effective only if they affect administrative power—so as to program and control it—without intending to take it over.

However, the model of citizens forming autonomous public spheres of such size and strength that they can surround, besiege, and limit abuses generated by the administrative power of the state has come to seem inadequate to Habermas. He now regards

the siege model [as] too defeatist, at least if you understand the division of powers in such a way that administrative and judicial authorities *employing* the law are to have limited access to the grounds mobilized in their full scope by legislative authorities in justifying their decisions. Today, the matters that need regulation are often such that the political legislator is in no position sufficiently to regulate them in advance. In such cases, it is up to administrative and judicial authorities to give them concrete form and to continue their legal development, and these require discourses that have to do with grounding rather than with application. However, to be legitimate, this implicit subsidiary legislation . . . also requires different forms of participation—a part of the democratic will-formation must make its way into the administration itself, and the judiciary that creates subsidiary laws must justify itself in the wider forum of a critique of law. In this respect the sluice model counts on a more far-reaching democratization than the siege model does.[24]

It is indeed such a sluice model of democratization that Habermas defends in Chapter 8 of *Between Facts and Norms*, a chapter devoted to the descriptive and normative aspects of civil society and the public sphere. Let us consider the sluice model in some detail. Habermas acknowledges his debt to the work of Bernard Peters and explains that he wants "to give a more precise form to, and seek a tentative answer to, the question of whether and how a constitutionally regulated circulation of power might be established."[25] Habermas proposes that

processes of communication and decision making in constitutional systems display the following features: they lie along a center–periphery axis, they are structured by a system of "sluices," and they involve two modes of problem solving. The core area of the political system is formed by the familiar institutional complexes of administration (including the incumbent Government), judicial system, and democratic opinion- and will-formation (which includes parliamentary bodies, political elections, and party competition). Hence this center, distinguished from the periphery in virtue of formal decision-making powers and actual prerogatives, is internally organized as a "polyarchy." Within the core area, to be sure, the "capacity to act" varies with the "density" of organizational complexity. The parliamentary complex is the most open for perceiving and thematizing social problems, but it pays for this sensitivity with a lesser capacity to deal with problems in comparison to the administrative complex. At the ends of the administration, a kind of *inner* periphery develops out of various institutions equipped with rights of self-governance or with other kinds of oversight and lawmaking functions delegated by the state (universities, charitable organizations, foundations, etc.). The core area as a whole has an *outer* periphery that, roughly speaking, branches into "customers" and "suppliers."[26]

By "customers" Habermas has in mind public agencies and such private organizations as business associations, labor unions, and interest groups that give rise to "complex networks . . . [that] fulfill certain coordination functions in more or less opaque social sectors." "Suppliers," by contrast, consist of those "groups, associations, and organizations that, before parliaments and through the courts, give voice to social problems, make broad demands, articulate public interests or needs, and thus attempt to influence the political process more from normative points of view than from the standpoint of particular interests."[27]

The image evoked by the sluice model is straightforward enough: we are to envision a filtering process from social periphery to administrative center. Public opinion is generated in a wide variety of informal ways and eventually washes through to influence formal decision-making processes. The upshot of this model is that binding decisions within a society can be legitimate only if they are

> steered by communication flows that start at the periphery and pass through the sluices of democratic and constitutional procedures situated at the entrance to the parliamentary complex or the courts (and, if necessary, at the exit of the implementing administration as well). That is the only way to exclude the possibility that the power of the administrative complex, on the one hand, or the social power of intermediate structures affecting the core area, on the other hand, become independent vis-a-vis a communicative power that develops in the parliamentary complex.[28]

Habermas is, of course, well aware that the institutions of actually existing capitalist democracies hardly operate in such a smooth, friction-free manner. The sluice model is equally intended to draw attention to the extent to which social crises can and do arise:

> In cases in which perceptions of problems and problem situations have taken a conflictual turn, the attention span of the citizenry enlarges, indeed in such a way that controversies in the broader public sphere primarily ignite around the normative aspects of the problems most at issue. The pressure of public opinion then necessitates an extraordinary mode of problem solving, which favors the constitutional channels for the circulation of power and thus actuates sensibilities for the constitutional allocation of *political responsibilities.*[29]

It would appear, then, that for Habermas a theoretical advantage of the sluice over the siege model is precisely that the former model better captures the alternation between normal and extraordinary socio-political circumstances. In turn, the sluice model lends an important nuance to the concept of the public sphere. Henceforth, the public sphere should not be regarded as simply a

> sounding board for problems that must be processed by the political system because they cannot be solved elsewhere. . . . From the perspective of democratic theory, the public sphere must, in addition, amplify the pressure of problems, that is, not only detect and identify problems but also convincingly and *influentially* thematize them, furnish them with possible solutions, and dramatize them in such a way that they are taken up and dealt with by parliamentary procedures.[30]

However, despite any advance that the sluice model of democratization might mark over the siege model, neither model is adequate. In my view, both models of democratization unduly restrict the scope of collective action. A striking illustration of this restriction can be found in the important distinction made in *Between Facts and Norms* between the specific forums organized around administrative bodies of the state and the more general forums constituted by the citizenry at large. Using language strikingly reminiscent of Karl Popper's writings on the philosophy of science, Habermas explains that the former are "structured predominantly as a *context of justification*" and "rely not only on the administration's preparatory work and further processing but also on the *context of discovery* provided by a procedurally unregulated public sphere that is borne by the general public of citizens."[31]

Appropriating a distinction first made by Nancy Fraser,[32] Habermas calls this general public sphere "weak" inasmuch as it only forms opinions but, unlike a "strong" public sphere, makes no decisions. It consists of an "open and inclusive network of overlapping, subcultural

publics having fluid temporal, social, and substantive boundaries."[33]
Habermas adds that

> on account of its anarchic structure, the general public sphere is, on the
> one hand, more vulnerable to the repressive and exclusionary effects of
> unequally distributed social power, structural violence, and systematically
> distorted communication than are institutionalized public spheres of parlia-
> mentary bodies. On the other hand, it has the advantage of a medium of
> *unrestricted* communication. Here new problem situations can be perceived
> more sensitively, discourses aimed at achieving self-understanding can be
> conducted more widely and expressively, collective identities and need
> interpretations can be articulated with fewer compulsions than is the case in
> procedurally regulated public spheres. Democratically constituted opinion-
> and will-formation depends on the supply of informal public opinions that,
> ideally, develop in structures of an unsubverted public sphere. The informal
> public sphere must, for its part, enjoy the support of a societal basis in which
> equal rights of citizenship have become socially effective.[34]

Again we see that the chief function of the general public sphere is
to mediate between social and administrative power. Yet Habermas's
refinement of the concept of the public sphere through the introduction of a strong/weak nuance fails to resolve a fundamental problem
in his account of democratic transition. Although Habermas explicitly
permits citizens within "weak" public spheres to *discuss* anything they
like—presumably even the large-scale structural overthrow of capitalist
social relations—nonetheless his allowance for such freewheeling discussion has a political price to be paid. These opinions, no matter how
urgently or persuasively expressed, remain mere opinions; and ultimately citizens must be content either symbolically to storm an administrative fortress (the siege model) or else generate certain messages
from the periphery that at best will eventually filter across to be
interpreted, and legitimated, by the administrative center (the sluice
model). Either way, their ability to carry out genuinely collective *action*
has been seriously undercut. Despite his professed search for "post-
metaphysical" means to legitimize modern societies "in which normative orders must be maintained without metasocial guarantees,"[35]
Habermas nonetheless retains what amounts to a transcendent moral
barrier to prevent citizens—to say nothing of workers—from exercising
their immanent power to change the basic structure of their society.
Here is a contradiction that cannot be resolved; it can only be
displaced.[36]

Notes

1. In this regard Bidet has especially identified the shortcomings of both John Rawls's theory of justice and Jürgen Habermas's discourse ethics. See *John Rawls et la théorie de la justice* (Paris: Presses Universitaires de France, 1995), pp. 93–105 and *Théorie générale* (Paris: Presses Universitaires de France, 1999), pp. 399–426.

2. For Negri's brilliant rereading of Marx in terms of the concept of "constituent power," see *Le Pouvoir constituant* (Paris: Presses Universitaires de France, 1997), pp. 44–50, 295–306, 331–52.

3. Jürgen Habermas, *The Structural Transformation of the Public Sphere*, trans. Thomas Burger with the assistance of Frederick Lawrence (Cambridge, MA: MIT Press, 1989).

4. Ibid., p. 177.

5. Habermas makes his case largely on the basis of a reading of Marx's early philosophical writings, especially *On the Jewish Question*; arguably, he undervalues the richness and subtlety of such later historical works as *The Civil War in France*. See *Structural Transformation*, pp. 122–9, 139–40. Also, see the contemporaneous article "Natural Law and Revolution," in Jürgen Habermas, *Theory and Practice*, trans. John Viertel, (Boston: Beacon Press, 1973), especially pp. 109–13.

6. See Jürgen Habermas, *The Theory of Communicative Action, Volume One: Reason and the Rationalization of Society*, trans. Thomas McCarthy (Boston: Beacon Press, 1984) and Jürgen Habermas, *The Theory of Communicative Action, Volume Two: Lifeworld and System: A Critique of Functionalist Reason*, trans. Thomas McCarthy (Boston: Beacon Press, 1987).

7. Jürgen Habermas, "The New Obscurity: The Crisis of the Welfare State and the Exhaustion of Utopian Energies," in *The New Conservatism: Cultural Criticism and the Historians' Debate*, ed. and trans. Shierry Weber Nichelsen (Cambridge, MA: MIT Press, 1989), p. 68.

8. Ibid.

9. Ibid., pp. 63–4.

10. "What Does Socialism Mean Today? The Rectifying Revolution and the Need for New Thinking on the Left," trans. Ben Morgan, *New Left Review*, no. 183, September/October 1990: pp. 3–21.

11. Ibid., p. 21.

12. Ibid.

13. Ibid.

14. Jürgen Habermas, *Between Facts and Norms*, trans. William Rehg (Cambridge, MA: MIT Press, 1996).

15. Ibid., p. xli.

16. In this regard, also note an interview that Habermas gave in February 1997 to *L'Humanité*, the newspaper of the French Communist Party. He insists that autonomy and democracy are tied to the idea of 'self-organization.' I can give the example of the university, with the forms of research that currently exist to popularize knowledge. That has nothing to do with the self-management of companies in a market in which everything is decided in advance.

17. Jürgen Habermas, "Conversation about Questions of Political Theory," in his *A Berlin Republic: Writings on Germany*, trans. Steven Rendall (Lincoln: University of Nebraska Press, 1997), p. 133.

18. "The Germans' 'Sense of Being Special' Is Regenerating Hour by Hour: An Interview with the *Frankfurter Rundschau*," *A Berlin Republic*, p. 71.

19. Kenneth Baynes has been one of the few commentators to draw attention to Habermas's use of the siege model, but he does not distinguish this model from the later sluice model. See Kenneth Baynes, *The Normative Grounds of Social Criticism: Kant, Rawls, and Habermas* (Albany: State University of New York Press, 1992), p. 179, and "Democracy and the *Rechtsstaat*: Habermas's *Faktizität und Geltung*, in *The Cambridge Companion to Habermas*, ed. Stephen K. White (New York: Cambridge University Press, 1995), p. 217.

20. Habermas, *Between Facts and Norms*, pp. 486–7.

21. Available in English as "Further Reflections on the Public Sphere," trans. Thomas Burger, in *Habermas and the Public Sphere*, ed. Craig Calhoun (Cambridge, MA: MIT Press, 1992), pp. 421–61.

22. Ibid., p. 444.

23. Habermas, *Between Facts and Norms*, p. 440.

24. Habermas, *A Berlin Republic*, pp. 135–6.

25. Habermas, *Between Facts and Norms*, p. 354.

26. Ibid., pp. 354–5.

27. Ibid., p. 355.

28. Ibid., p. 356.

29. Ibid., p. 357.

30. Ibid., p. 359.

31. Ibid., p. 307.

32. On the distinction between "strong" and "weak" publics, see Nancy Fraser's article "Rethinking the Public Sphere: A Contribution to the Critique of Actually Existing Democracy," in *Habermas and the Public Sphere*, pp. 132–6.

33. Habermas, *Between Facts and Norms*, p. 307.

34. Ibid., pp. 307–8.

35. Ibid., p. 26.

36. Thanks to Warren Montag for his much-needed encouragement and critical remarks on an early draft of this article.

9

The Withering of Civil Society

Michael Hardt

The concept of civil society has enjoyed a new life in recent years, not only in Western Europe and North America, where indeed it has had a long and varied career in support of various political positions, but in countries throughout the world, particularly in those today making the transition from socialism to capitalism in Asia and eastern Europe and in the postdictatorial and postauthoritarian regimes in Latin America. Civil society is proposed as the essential feature of any democracy: the institutional infrastructure for political mediation and public exchange. It is important, however, while recognizing the democratic functions that the concept and reality of civil society have made possible, also to be aware of the functions of discipline and exploitation that are inherent in and inseparable from these same structures. Furthermore, we must question whether the social foundations necessary for the construction and sustenance of civil society are themselves present in contemporary social formations. I want to argue, in fact, that in recent years the conditions of possibility of civil society have progressively been undermined in North America, Europe, and elsewhere (if indeed they ever really existed outside the European world).[1] Even if we were to consider civil society politically desirable, any invocation of the concept under present conditions can only remain empty and ineffectual.

Focusing specifically on the concept of civil society will also afford us a new perspective on a more general contemporary problematic. In other words, recognizing the withering of civil society gives us terms for grasping more adequately the phenomena that are all too often vaguely indicated by references to the end of modernity or the end of modern society. The terms "modern" and "postmodern" lack the specificity to be useful beyond a certain point. The society we are living in today is more properly understood as a postcivil society.

Society of the Organization of Abstract Labor

In political philosophy civil society is fundamentally linked to the modern notion of labor, and the thinker to make this connection clearest is Georg Hegel. The concept of civil society is perhaps Hegel's greatest contribution to political philosophy, but he was certainly not the first social theorist to employ the concept. Throughout the early modern period, from Hobbes to Rousseau at least, the distinction between natural society and civil society, or rather between the state of nature and the civil state, played a fundamental role, as the dualism that founded and justified the political order. In these early modern theories, the primary concern was that the rational order of civil society be contrasted with the irrational disorder of natural society. The movement from the natural to the civil was thus the historical and/or theoretical movement of human civilization.

By the time that Hegel developed his political theory, however, the axis of this fundamental social distinction had shifted, so that Hegel focused primarily on the contrast not between natural society and civil society, but between civil society and political society, that is, between civil society and the State. When we look at Hegel's usage of "civil society" against the backdrop of the early modern theories, then, we have to be struck by two closely related innovations. The first, which should be credited as much to the tenor of Hegel's times as to Hegel himself, is that civil society has gained a more complex economic definition, due at least in part to the progressive spread and maturation of capitalism. Many commentators have pointed out that Hegel developed his conception of civil society on the basis of the writings of English economists of the time, and that the standard German translation of the English "civil society," which Hegel used, was "bürgerliche Gesellschaft" or "bourgeois society." This fact alone should lead us to focus on the relationship between Hegel's conception of civil society and the conceptions, which were widespread at the time, of the civilizing process contained in market exchange and capitalist relations of production. According to Hegel, through needs, work, exchange, and the pursuit of particular self-interests, the "unorganized atoms of civil society"[2] are to be ordered toward the universal—not exactly through the mysterious actions of Adam Smith's invisible hand, but rather though the competitive institutions of capitalist production and circulation. In this respect, then, the economic medium of civil society can be said to fill the role of nature, to which Hegel can contrast the rational order of the political realm.

The second innovation in Hegel's usage of the concept of civil society, which is closely tied to the first but specific to Hegel in its formulation, is the emphasis on the educative aspect of civil society. Here it should be clear that Hegel does not merely replace the earlier dualism (natural society–civil society) with another dualism (civil society–political society), but rather sets up a three-part conception (natural–civil–political). The state of nature, as a realm of needs and unrelated self-interest, has no direct relation to the political State in Hegel, but must instead pass through or be mediated by civil society before becoming political. Civil society shares with natural society the fact of being a realm of needs and self-interest, Hegel emphasizes, but civil society is also a "sphere of relatedness—a sphere of education."[3] In other words, civil society takes the natural human systems of needs and particular self-interests, puts them in relation with each other through the capitalist social institutions of production and exchange, and thus, on the basis of the mediation and subsumption of the particular, poses a terrain on which the State can realize the universal interest of society in "the actuality of the ethical Idea."[4] Hegelian education in civil society is a process of formal subsumption, that is, a process whereby particular differences, foreign to the universal, are negated and preserved in unity.

Hegel combines and highlights these economic and educative aspects in his conception that civil society is primarily a society of *labor*. This can be our first approximation of a definition of the concept. Labor produces and labor educates. In his early writings on the State, in the Jena period, Hegel conceived the process of the abstraction of labor from its concrete instantiations as the motor driving the civilizing social institutions. Concrete labor is the elemental, substantial conversation, the basic foundation of everything, but it is also "blind and savage," that is, uneducated in the universal interest.[5] Concrete labor, which in this early period Hegel imagines as the labor of peasants, is the human activity closest to nature. Just like nature, concrete labor, since it is the foundation of all society, cannot be simply negated, but neither can it be simply integrated since it is savage and uncivilized; "like a savage beast," Hegel writes, "[it] must be constantly subjugated and tamed (*Beherrschung und Bezähmung*)."[6] Labor must be *aufgehoben*, negated and integrated, subsumed. The process of abstraction, then, from concrete labor to abstract labor, is the educative process whereby the singular is transformed into the universal by negation, by abandoning itself.[7] As a second approximation, then, we should say that civil society is not simply the society of labor, but specifically the society of *abstract* labor.

This same educative process of abstraction is also at the center of Hegel's mature conception of civil society, which he poses in his later writings in less philosophical, more practical terms: through labor the pursuit of the satisfaction of one's particular needs is related to the pursuits of others and thus "subjective self-seeking turns into a contribution to the satisfaction of the needs of everyone else."[8] Hegel finds this educative role of labor, the transformation to the universal, organized and made explicit in the institutional trade unions, the corporations, which structurally orient the particular interests of workers toward the universal interest of society.[9] Civil society consists of not just the unions but all the institutions of capitalist society that organize abstract labor. In its mature formulation, then, and for us as a third approximation, we should say that civil society is the society of the *organization* of abstract labor.

Education, Hegemony, and Discipline

The Hegelian conception of civil society persists in various forms throughout modern and contemporary social and political theory. When we survey the work of the wide variety of twentieth-century authors who in some form or another take up this notion of civil society we quickly recognize that the social dialectic of civil society is presented in two guises, one more democratic and the other more authoritarian. Antonio Gramsci is perhaps the thinker who has gone furthest in theorizing the democratic and socialist potential of civil society. He insists repeatedly in his prison notebooks on the importance of the Hegelian distinction between civil society and political society for any liberal or progressive political theory, but in effect he inverts the relationship between these two concepts, standing the relationship, he might say, on its feet.[10] As we have seen, Hegel conceives the end of social movement and conflict, in both logical and historical terms, as gathered together, subsumed, and thus realized in the ends of State, "the actuality of the ethical Idea." Gramsci casts the historical movement or flow in the opposite direction, proposing instead "that the State's goal is its own end, its own disappearance, in other words, the re-absorption of political society within civil society."[11] The term "re-absorption" indicates a reversal of the social flow: what according to the Hegelian process of subsumption flowed from society toward the State now is reversed from the State to civil society, as a sort of inverted subsumption. Gramsci is able to understand the process of the withering or disappearance of the State as a process of re-absorption because he conceives the State as existing only secondarily, as if it were a placeholder that fills the structural void left by a civil society that is not fully developed. When civil society does manage fully to fill its role, the State as such will no longer exist; or rather, State elements will continue to exist only as subordinated agents of civil society's hegemony. In effect, Gramsci has taken what he finds to be democratic in Hegel's conception of civil society and given those aspects the prominent position, turning the system upside down. Expanding and reinforcing the scope and powers of the various segments and institutions of civil society is thus central to a Gramscian strategy of social progress, which will eventually reverse the flow of the Hegelian process and fill the dictatorial and coercive spaces now occupied by the State with democratic forces organized in terms of social hegemony and consent. This hegemony is grounded finally on a Hegelian form of education, which gives the revolutionary class or party its ability to "absorb" or "assimilate all of society" in the name of general interests. When the State has been effectively subsumed, Gramsci claims, the reign of civil society, that is, self-government, will begin.[12]

The writings of authors who like Gramsci highlight the democratic aspects of civil society focus in general on the pluralism of the institutions of civil society and the avenues or channels they provide for input into the rule of political society, or the State. Seen in this light, the institutional labor union, to take up Hegel's prime example, provides a channel for the representation of the workers' interests in the forum of political society. Juridical reformism might point toward another example, exploiting the channel of the legal institutions and the framework of rights in order to represent diverse interests within the State. Numerous other strategies of political practice and scholarly analysis—focusing for example on interest group politics, the interplay of political parties, segments of the media, church movements, and popular reform movements—all emphasize the possibilities of democratic representation available through the passages opened by the ideological, cultural, and economic institutions of civil society. From this perspective, the social dialectic activated in civil society and the possibilities of mediation make the State open to the plurality of social flows channeled through the institutions. The activation of the forces of civil society makes the State porous, destabilizing its dictatorial powers or rather "re-absorbing" them within the expanding hegemony of civil society.

In the work of other authors, however, the mediatory institutions that define the relationship between civil society and the State are shown to function toward not democratic but authoritarian ends. From this second perspective, then, the representation of interests through the channels of the institutions does not reveal the pluralistic effects of social forces on the State, but rather highlights the State's capacities to organize, recuperate, even produce social forces. Michel Foucault's work has made clear that the institutions and *enfermements* or enclosures of civil society—the church, the school, the prison, the family, the union, the party, etc.—constitute the paradigmatic terrain for the disciplinary deployments of power in modern society, producing normalized subjects, and thus exerting hegemony through consent in a way that is perhaps more subtle but no less authoritarian than the exertion of dictatorship through coercion. The disciplinary perspective, then, might recognize the same channels passing through civil society, but sees the flows moving again in the opposite direction. The institutional labor union, for example, is viewed not so much as a passage for the expression of worker interests to be represented in the plurality of rule, but rather as a means to mediate and recuperate the antagonisms born of capitalist production and capitalist social relations—thus creating a worker subjectivity that is recuperable within and will actually support the order of the capitalist State. This is not only the sense in which Foucault analyzes the institutions of civil society, but also the very same way in which Hegel celebrates them. As we saw earlier, the labor union and the other institutions of civil society are intended to "educate" the citizens, creating within them the universal desires that are in line with the State. "Actually, therefore," Hegel writes, "the State as such is not so much the result as the beginning."[13] The social dialectic thus functions in order that antagonistic social forces be subsumed within the prior and unitary synthesis of the State.

In order to situate Foucault's work on the terrain of Hegel's civil society, however, we need to take a step back and elaborate some of the nuances of Foucault's theoretical perspective. Hegel's understanding of the historical rise of civil society and the generalization of its educative social role does correspond in several respects to the process that Michel Foucault calls the governmentalization of the State. The State of sovereignty, which according to Foucault served as the dominant form of rule in Europe approximately from the Middle Ages to the sixteenth century, positioned itself as a transcendent singularity with respect to its subjects. The transcendence of the sovereign State afforded it a certain detachment from the pressures of conflictive particular interests in society. In the passage to the modern State, however, the transcendence and singularity of the State were overturned through the rise of what Foucault calls "governmentality." The rule of the governmental State is characterized instead by its immanence to the population through a multiplicity of forms. "The art of government . . .," Foucault said, "must respond essentially to this question: how can it introduce the economy, in other words, the manner of adequately managing individuals, goods, and wealth, as can be done within a family, like a good father who knows how to direct his wife, his children, and his servants."[14] The management of people and things implied by this governance involves an active engagement, exchange, or dialectic among social forces and between social forces and the State. The same educative social processes that Hegel casts in terms of abstraction and organization, Foucault recognizes in terms of training, discipline, and management. The channels or striae in which these processes function, recognized as social institutions by Hegel, are characterized by Foucault in terms of deployments (*dispositifs*) and enclosures (*enfermements*). Civil society, from this perspective, is the productive site of modern economy (economy understood now in the large sense); in other words, it is the site of the production of goods, desires, individual and collective identities, etc. It is the site, finally, of the institutional dialectic of social forces, of the social dialectic that gives rise to and underwrites the State.

In his extensive work on the nature of power, however, Foucault not only refuses Gramsci's inversion of the priority between civil society and political society (that is, civil society and the State), he goes one step further and argues that we can make no analytical distinction at all between them. When Foucault argues that power cannot be isolated but is everywhere, that it comes from everywhere, that there is no outside to power, he is also denying the analytical separation of political society from civil society. In what is now a famous passage Foucault writes, "relations of power are not in a position of exteriority with respect to other types of relationship (economic processes, knowledge relationships, sexual relations), but are immanent to the latter . . . they have a directly productive role, wherever they come into play."[15] In the disciplinary and governmental society the lines of power extend throughout social space in the channels created by the institutions of civil society. The exertion of power is organized through deployments, which are at once ideological, institutional, and corporeal. This is not to say that there is no State, but rather that it cannot effectively be isolated and contested at a level separate from society. In Foucault's framework, the modern State is not properly understood as the transcendent source of power relations in society. On the contrary, the State as such is better understood as a result, the consolidation or molarization of forces of "statization" (*étatisation*) immanent to social power relations.[16] The causes and intentions that inform and order power relations are not isolated in some headquarters of rationality, but immanent to the field of forces. Foucault thus prefers to use instead of "State" the term "government," which indicates the multiplicity and immanence of the forces of statization to the social field. While this denies all the moral and teleological elements of Hegel's social theory, Foucault's understanding of the disciplinary and governmental society does in certain respects take the Hegelian notion of civil society to its logical conclusion. In particular, Foucault emphasizes the "educational" aspect of civil society whereby particular social interests are enlightened to the general interest and brought in line with the universal. Education means discipline. More accurately, Foucault reformulates the educational process of civil society in terms of production: power acts not only by training or ordering the elements of the social terrain, but by actually producing them—producing desires, needs, individuals, identities, etc. I see this not so much as a contradiction as an extension of Hegelian theory. The State, Hegel says, is not the result but the cause; Foucault adds, not a transcendent but an immanent cause, statization, immanent to the various channels, institutions, or enclosures of social production.

Let me take a moment to summarize before moving on. Disciplinary society can be characterized as civil society seen from a different perspective, approached from underneath, from the microphysics of its power relations. While Gramsci highlighted the democratic potentials of the institutions of civil society, Foucault made clear that civil society is a society founded on discipline and that the education it offers is a diffuse network of normalization. From this perspective, Gramsci and Foucault highlight the two contrasting faces of Hegel's civil society. And in all of this what is primary is the way our labor or our social practice is organized and recuperated in social institutions and educated in the general interest of political society. In presenting the arguments this way I do not intend to charge that either Foucault or Gramsci is finally too Hegelian. Foucault's work on disciplinary societies, while of course in certain regards decisively non-Hegelian, does remain on the same terrain as Hegel's social analysis, as does Gramsci's, primarily because they are all oriented toward understanding the same social formation, the historical phase of European civil society. As Marx said, however, neither Hegel nor anyone else should be blamed for theorizing the existing relationship between the State and society; they *should* be blamed only when they cast that formation as necessary and eternal, outside of history.

The Infinite Undulations of the Snake

When we look the contemporary societies of Western Europe and North America, however, it seems that these various, rich, promising, and frightening theoretical visions of civil society, both in the Hegelian version and in the Gramscian and Foucauldian reformulations, no longer hold—they no longer grasp the dominant mechanisms or schema of social production and social ordering. The decline of the paradigm of civil society correlates to a passage in contemporary society toward a new configuration of social relations and new conditions of rule. This is not to say that the forms and structures of social exchange, participation, and domination that were identified by the concept of civil society have ceased entirely to exist, but rather that they have been displaced from the dominant position by a new configuration of apparatuses, deployments, and structures.

This is the context in which I understand Gilles Deleuze's claim in a brief and enigmatic essay that we have recently experienced a passage from a disciplinary society to a society of control. Deleuze's notion can serve us here as a first attempt to understand the decline of the rule of civil society and the rise of a new form of control. Disciplinary societies, as I said earlier, are characterized by the enclosures or institutions that serve as the skeleton or backbone of civil society; these enclosures define the striae of social space. The coordinated striation formed by the institutions of civil society branch out through social space in structured networks, as Deleuze says, like the tunnels of a mole.[17] Gramsci in fact takes this same image and casts it with a military metaphor: "The superstructures of civil society are like the trench systems of modern warfare."[18] Lines of power or lines of resistance, the striae of civil society are the skeleton that defines and supports the figure of the social body.

Deleuze insists, however, that these social enclosures or institutions are today everywhere in crisis. One might interpret the crisis of the factory, the family, the church, and the other social enclosures as the progressive crumbling of various social walls that subsequently leave a social void, as if the striated social space of civil society had been smoothed into a vacant free space. One of the most important lessons that Foucault tried to teach us, however, is that power never leaves a vacuum, but always in some form fills social space. Deleuze suggests that it is more adequate, then, to understand the collapse of the walls defined by the enclosures not as some sort of social evacuation but rather as the generalization of the logics that previously functioned within these limited domains across the entire society, spreading like a virus. The logic of capitalist production perfected in the factory now invests all forms of social production. The same might be said also for the school, the family, the hospital, and the other disciplinary institutions. "The prison," Foucault notes, "begins well before its doors. It begins as soon as you leave your house"[19]—and even before. Social space is smooth, not in the sense that it has been cleared of the disciplinary striation, but rather in the sense that those striae have been generalized across society. Social space has not been emptied of the disciplinary institutions, but completely filled with the modulations of control. The relationship between society and the State no longer primarily involves the mediation and organization of the institutions for discipline and rule but rather sets the State in motion directly through the perpetual circuitry of social production.

We should be careful to point out, however, that the passage from disciplinary society to the society of control is not merely a shift in the institutional structures of rule. Foucault insisted, as we saw earlier, that the institutions do not occupy a primary position, as the sources of power relations; instead, institutions represent the consolidation or assemblage of the strategies of power. What underlies the various institutions is the diagram: the anonymous or abstract strategic machine, the unformed or non-stratified schema of power relations. The diagram transcends, or better subtends, the various institutional assemblages. Foucault's most successful attempt to grasp the diagram of disciplinary society is his analysis of the panopticon. "Is it surprising that prisons resemble factories, schools, barracks, hospitals, which all resemble prisons?"[20] The disciplinary diagram runs throughout the various institutions defining the conditions of possibility, the conditions of what can be seen, said, and known, the conditions of the exertion of power. The passage to a society of control, then, will certainly manifest symptoms at the institutional level, but it should be grasped also and above all at the diagrammatic level. If we are to follow Foucault's method, then, first we should ask, what are the diagrams that define the conditions of possibility in the societies of control? And then, in what kinds of social assemblages will these diagrammatic forces be consolidated, and how?[21]

The metaphors available to us can at least give us an indication of the nature of this passage. We can no longer, for example, use the metaphor of structure and superstructure that was central to the conception of the mediating institutions of civil society. The image of the intersecting burrows of the mole that characterized the structures of disciplinary societies no longer holds in this new domain. Not the structured passages of the mole, Deleuze insists, but the infinite undulations of the snake are what characterize the smooth space of the societies of control.[22] Similarly, the Gramscian metaphor of a system of trenches that supported the war of position in civil society has been definitively surpassed by the contemporary techniques of warfare. Fixed positions have become a liability, not a strength, in combat; instead, monitoring, mobility, and speed have become the dominant characteristics. The Iraqi army certainly learned this lesson in the Gulf War. Iraqi soldiers were literally buried alive when their trenches were smoothed over by the U.S. war machine. The metaphorical space of the societies of control is perhaps best characterized by the shifting desert sands, where positions are continually swept away; or, better, the smooth surfaces of cyberspace, with its infinitely programmable flows of codes and information.

These metaphors suggest an important shift marked by the diagram of the society of control. The panopticon, and disciplinary diagrammatics in general, functioned primarily in terms of positions, fixed points, and identities. Foucault saw the production of identities (even "oppositional" or "deviant" identities, such as the factory worker and the homosexual) as fundamental to the functions of rule in disciplinary societies. The diagram of control, however, is not oriented toward position and identity, but rather mobility and anonymity. It functions on the basis of "the whatever,"[23] the flexible and mobile performance of contingent identities, and thus its assemblages or institutions are elaborated primarily through repetition and the production of simulacra. Fordist and Taylorist production schema elaborated long ago a model of interchangeability, but that interchangeability was based on common roles, fixed positions, and defined parts. The fixed identity of each part is precisely what made interchangeability possible. The post-Fordist productive model of "the whatever" and contingent performativity proposes a broader mobility and flexibility that fixes no identities, giving repetition free rein. In this sense the societies of control preserve the anonymous character common to all diagrams and refuse the particularization that previously accompanied the translation of the diagram into molar assemblages or institutions. Elaborate controls over information flows, extensive use of polling and monitoring techniques, and innovative social use of the media thus gain prominent positions in the exertion of power. Control functions on the plane of the simulacra of society. The anonymity and whateverness of the societies of control are precisely what give them their smooth surfaces.

We should not get carried away, however, with applying these metaphors absolutely. Claiming the decline of civil society, of course, does not mean that all the mechanisms of rule and organization that characterized civil society no longer exist or function. Similarly, recognizing a passage from disciplinary societies to societies of control does not mean that disciplinary deployments and the attendant potentialities of resistance have completely disappeared. Disciplinary deployments remain, as do elements of sovereignty in the regimes of control. Even more important, the smoothing of social space does not bring an end to social striation; on the contrary, as Deleuze and Guattari are careful to point out, within this process of smoothing, elements of social striation reappear "in the most perfect and severe forms."[24] In other words, the crisis or decline of the enclosures or institutions gives rise in certain respects to a hypersegmentation of society. For example, while in recent years factory production has declined and the social striae that it defined have been smoothed, it has been at least partially replaced by forms of flexible production that have segmented the labor force in extreme forms, creating mobile, anonymous networks of home labor, part-time work, and various forms of undeclared or illegal labor. While wage labor seems to disappear, its relations are really proliferated and generalized throughout society. The shift from factory production to flexible production paradoxically combines the smoothing and the hypersegmentation of social space. Although extreme, the new segmentation is nonetheless mobile or flexible—these are flexible rigidities. What is primarily at issue, though, is not simply the existence of certain apparatuses, mechanisms, or deployments, but rather their predominance within a specific paradigm of rule. Our task is to discern the salient characteristics of the social formation that succeeds civil society; the smooth spaces of the societies of control constitute our first attempt.

We can formulate a second, complementary approach to this problematic by casting the passage not in Foucauldian but rather in Marxian terminology, which will highlight the contemporary change in the social organization of labor. Straining their periodizations a bit, we could say that Foucault's societies of sovereignty correspond to feudal relations of production; disciplinary regimes rely on what Marx calls the formal subsumption of labor under capital; and the societies of control point to the real subsumption of labor under capital. This periodization is central to both Marx's and Foucault's understandings of the historically specific relationships among the State, society, and capital. The State today has moved beyond Hegel and his dialectic, not limiting but perfecting the State's rule.

Marx recognized the passage from the formal to the real subsumption in nineteenth-century society as a tendency, but it seems to me that this passage has only come to be generalized in the most completely capitalist countries in our times.[25] Let me take a moment to explain Marx's understanding of this passage within capitalism. According to Marx, in the first of these two phases, the formal subsumption, social labor processes are subsumed under capital, that is, they are enveloped within the capitalist relations of production in such a manner that capital intervenes as the director or manager. In this arrangement capital subsumes labor the way it finds it; capital takes over existing labor processes that were developed in previous modes of production or at any rate outside of capitalist production. This subsumption is *formal* insofar as the labor process exists within capital, subordinated to its command *as an imported foreign force*, born outside of capital's domain. Actually, as Hegel clearly recognized in his early writings (in the Jena period), capital cannot directly integrate concrete labor but must first abstract it from its concrete forms. The various processes of abstraction, the resistances these give rise to and the potential lines of social conflict between concrete labor and abstract labor are thus principal characteristics of the phase of the formal subsumption.

Capital tends, however, through the socialization of production and through scientific and technological innovation, to create new labor processes and destroy old ones, transforming the situations of the various agents of production. Capital thus sets in motion a specifically capitalist mode of production. Marx calls the subsumption of labor *real*, then, when the labor processes themselves are born within capital and therefore when labor is incorporated not as an external, but as an internal force, proper to capital itself.

As we move to the phase of the real subsumption, Marx explains, labor processes evolve so that, first of all, production is no longer a direct and individual activity but instead an immediately social activity. "*Direct labor* as such," Marx writes, "ceases to be the basis of production, since, in one respect, it is transformed more into a supervisory and regulatory activity; but then also because the product ceases to be the product of isolated direct labor, and the *combination* of social activity appears, rather, as the producer."[26] Furthermore, this socialized labor-power itself seems to disappear as it is displaced from its position as the source of capitalist production. "This entire development of the productive forces of *socialized labor*, and together with it the *use of science*, takes the form of the *productive power of capital*. It no longer appears as the productive power of labor."[27] In very brief summary, then, Marx identifies a three-stage shift in the apparent source of capitalist production, from individual labor to social labor and finally to social capital. In the *specifically* capitalist mode of production, that is, in the phase of the real subsumption, productive labor—or even production in general—no longer appears as the pillar that defines and sustains capitalist social organization. Production is given an objective quality, as if the capitalist system were a machine that marched forward of its own accord, without labor, a capitalist automaton.

In this light the real subsumption appears as the completion of capital's project and the fulfillment of its long-standing dream—to present itself as separate from labor, and pose a capitalist society that does not look to labor as its dynamic foundation. "The political history of capital," Mario Tronti writes, is "a sequence of attempts by capital to withdraw from the class relationship," or more properly "attempts of the capitalist class to emancipate itself from the working class through the medium of various forms of capital's political domination over the working class."[28] This is how we should understand the passage from the formal to the real subsumption. The society of the formal subsumption was characterized by the dialectic between capital and labor: as a foreign force subsumed within capital, labor had to be abstracted, recuperated, disciplined, and tamed within the productive processes; but labor nonetheless was continually recognized as the source of all social wealth. (Consider, for example, the opening sentence of the Italian Constitution of 1948: "Italy is a republic founded on labor.") In the society of the real subsumption this dialectic no longer holds the central role, and capital no longer needs to engage labor or represent labor at the heart of production.[29] What is subsumed, what is accepted into the process, is no longer a potentially conflictive force but a product of the system itself; the real subsumption does not extend vertically throughout the various strata of society but rather constructs a separate plane, a simulacrum of society that excludes or marginalizes social forces foreign to the system. Social capital thus appears to reproduce itself autonomously, as if it were emancipated from the working class, and labor becomes invisible in the system. The contemporary decline of labor unions in both juridical and political terms, as the right to organize and the right to strike become increasingly irrelevant in the constitution, is only one symptom of this more general passage.

The State of the formal subsumption was indeed, as Hegel saw, defined by the organization of abstract labor. The State of the real subsumption is interested no longer in mediation or "education" but instead in separation, interested no longer in discipline but instead in control. The State of the real subsumption operates on a separate plane, a simulacrum of the social field, abstract from labor itself. (We can recognize here, parenthetically, the utility of an investigation of Guy Debord's society of the integrated spectacle and the separateness it implies as a third approximation of this passage.) Once again, my general point here is simply that in this passage the democratic and/or disciplinary institutions of civil society, the channels of social mediation, as a particular form of the organization of social labor, have declined and been displaced from the center of the scene. Not the State but civil society has withered away! In other words, even if one were to consider civil society politically desirable—and I hope to have shown that this position is at least contestable—the social conditions necessary for civil society no longer exist.[30]

The Postcivil Condition

As I stated at the outset, I consider each of these attempts to register adequately the fundamental changes in contemporary society coherent with the various social theories of postmodernism, at least to the extent that they are all focused on the same social terrain. The difficulty with many of these discourses, however, arises from the fact that they have not defined their field accurately enough. The end of modernity is a notion too vague and abstract to be very useful. Reformulating the problematic as the analysis of not postmodern but postcivil society is already a great step forward. Civil society, as we have seen, is central to a form of rule, or government as Foucault says, that focuses on one hand on the identity of the citizen and the processes of civilization, and on the other hand on the organization of abstract labor. These processes are variously conceived as education, training, or discipline, but what remains common is the active engagement with social forces (through either mediation or production) to order social identities within the context of institutions. What has come to an end, or more accurately declined in importance in postcivil society, then, is precisely these functions of mediation or education and the institutions that gave them form.

The formulation "postcivil," however, like "postmodern," is finally limited by its backward gaze; it is too reactive to do justice to the new paradigm of social relations. More important than the social elements and techniques that have faded from prominence are those that have newly taken the dominant positions. The deployments of control and the social constitution of the real subsumption give us a framework to begin to grasp the novelties of our situation. Instead of disciplining the citizen as a fixed social identity, the new social regime seeks to control the citizen as a whatever identity, or rather as an infinitely flexible placeholder for identity. It tends to establish an autonomous plane of rule, a simulacrum of the social—separate from the terrain of conflictive social forces. Mobility, speed, and flexibility are the qualities that characterize this separate plane of rule. The infinitely programmable machine, the ideal of cybernetics, gives us at least an approximation of the diagram of the new paradigm of rule.

Analyzing the new techniques of social control is only worthwhile to the extent that it allows us to grasp also the new potentialities for contestation and freedom emerging within this new paradigm. Foucault suggested in an interview in 1978 that we have to begin thinking politics in a society without discipline.

> In the last few years society has changed and individuals have changed too; they are more and more diverse, different, and independent. There are ever more categories of people who are not compelled by discipline [*qui ne sont pas astreints à la discipline*], so that we are obliged to imagine the development of society without discipline. The ruling class is still impregnated with the old technique. But it is clear that in the future we must separate ourselves from the society of discipline of today.[31]

I would suggest that in order to begin thinking these new potentialities we should return again to investigate the form and nature of labor, or creative social practices, in contemporary society. This is one way that we can begin to separate ourselves from the society of discipline and begin to think the lines of power and potentiality in the new society. Labor practices have certainly changed and so too should our notion of what constitutes labor—not just in the sphere of wage labor (which indeed has undergone radical transformation in some sectors) but also in the sphere of desiring production, intellectual creativity, caring labor, kin work, and so forth.[32] The phase of the real subsumption is characterized by the increasingly pervasive eclipse of labor in the production and reproduction of society, but that does not negate in any way the fact that labor is still the source of wealth and sociality. Even in the society of control, labor is still the "savage beast" that Hegel feared, refusing to be subjugated and tamed—and perhaps its potential is even greater today when it is no longer engaged, mediated, and disciplined through the institutions of civil society as it was in the previous paradigm. The networks of sociality and forms of cooperation embedded in contemporary social practices constitute the germs for a new movement, with new forms of contestation and new conceptions of liberation. This alternative community of social practices (call it, perhaps, the self-organization of concrete labor) will be the most potent challenge to the control of postcivil society, and it will point, perhaps, to the community of our future.

Notes

The principal ideas of this chapter were first developed with Antonio Negri as part of a study of the contemporary juridical formation of the capitalist State. See Michael Hardt and Antonio Negri, *Labor of Dionysus: A Critique of the State-form* (Minneapolis: University of Minnesota Press, 1994), in particular pp. 257–61. I would like to thank Marianne Constable and Rebecca Karl for their comments on earlier versions of this chapter.

    1. I will focus in this chapter on the genealogy of civil society in the Euro-American context, but I hope that this genealogy will be relevant also for evaluating the question of civil society in other parts of the world. In nearly all countries outside of North America and Western Europe, proposals for the contemporary establishment of a civil society seem to serve only as part of an imagined re-creation of one of the stages of civilization that Europe has already passed through, specifically the historical processes of the development and consolidation of capitalism in eighteenth- and nineteenth-century Europe. As Partha Chatterjee says in "A Response to Taylor's 'Modes of Civil Society,'" *Public Culture*, 1990, vol. 3, no. 1: 119, 131: "the central assumption of this proposal is that it is only the concepts of European social philosophy" such as civil society "that contain within them the possibility of universalization." Hence, he continues, "the provincialism of the European experience [is] taken as the universal history of progress."
    2. G.W.F. Hegel, *Philosophy of Right*, trans. T.M. Knox (Oxford: Oxford University Press, 1952), p. 255.
    3. Ibid., p. 209.
    4. Ibid., p. 257.
    5. G.W.F. Hegel, *Jenenser Realphilosophie*. (Leipzig: Meiner, 1932), vol. 2, p. 268.
    6. Hegel, *Jenenser Realphilosophie*, vol. 1, p. 240.
    7. Alexandre Kojève notes in his famous reading of the *Phenomenology of Spirit* in *Introduction à la lecture de Hegel* (Paris: Gallimard, 1947), p. 30, that "labor is what 'forms or educates' man, distinguishing him from the animals." The educative laboring process that Kojève recognizes, however, is one oriented toward the recognition and self-consciousness of the laborer, while the conception that interests us here is oriented instead toward the alignment of the particular interest of the laborer with the universal interest of the State.
    8. Hegel, *Philosophy of Right*, p. 199.
    9. Ibid., p. 251.

10. In his now classic analysis, "Gramsci and the Conception of Civil Society" in *Which Socialism?* (Minneapolis: University of Minnesota Press, 1987), p. 149, Norberto Bobbio makes clear the Hegelian roots of Gramsci's notion of civil society. "In fact, contrary to what is commonly believed, Gramsci does not derive his concept of civil society from Marx but is openly indebted to Hegel for it."

11. Antonio Gramsci, *Selections from Prison Notebooks*, trans. Quintin Hoare and Geoffrey Nowell Smith (New York: International Publishers, 1971), p. 253; Gramsci, *Quaderni del carcere* (Einaudi: Turin, 1975), p. 622.

12. See Gramsci, *Quaderni del carcere*, p. 1020.

13. Hegel, *Philosophy of Right*, p. 256.

14. Michel Foucault, "La gouvernementalité," *Dits et écrits* (originally 1978; Paris: Gallimard, 1994), vol. III, pp. 641–2. In the course from which this text was taken, "Sécurité, territoire et population" (given at the Collège de France, 1977–78), Foucault makes a distinction between the techniques of discipline and those of governmentality, not in the sense that they pertain to different historical periods but rather in the sense that they pertain in a parallel fashion to different domains of society. "Can one speak of something like governmentality that would be to the State what the technologies of segregation were to psychiatry, what the technologies of discipline were to the penal system?" (February 8, 1978). This quote should also indicate to us that Foucault does not deny the existence of the State (any more than he would deny the existence of the penal or psychiatric systems), but rather that he finds it more useful to formulate his problematic in terms of the technologies of governmentality that in some sense constitute the power of the State.

15. Foucault, *The History of Sexuality. Volume I: An Introduction*, trans. Robert Hurley (New York: Vintage Books, 1978), p. 94.

16. See Gilles Deleuze, *Foucault* (Paris: Minuit, 1986), p. 84.

17. Deleuze, "Postscript on the Societies of Control," *October*, 1993, No. 59: 5.

18. Gramsci, *Selections from Prison Notebooks*, p. 235; Gramsci, *Quaderni del carcere*, p. 1615.

19. Michel Foucault, "Le prison partout," *Dits et écrits* (originally 1971; Paris: Gallimard, 1994), vol. II, p. 194.

20. Foucault, *Discipline and Punish*, trans. Alan Sheridan (New York: Vintage Books, 1977), p. 228.

21. See Deleuze, "Postscript on the Societies of Control," p. 7.

22. Ibid.

23. I use the term "whatever" to translate what Giorgio Agamben refers to in Italian as "il qualunque" and what Deleuze and Foucault indicate in French with "le quelconque." See Giorgio Agamben, *The Coming Community* (Minneapolis: University of Minnesota Press, 1993).

24. Gilles Deleuze and Félix Guattari, *A Thousand Plateaus*, trans. Brian Massumi (Minneapolis: University of Minnesota Press, 1987), p. 492.

25. See Antonio Negri, *Marx Beyond Marx*, trans. Harry Cleaver, Michael Ryan, and Maurizio Viano (South Hadley: Bergin and Garvey, 1984), pp. 113–23.

26. Karl Marx, *Grundrisse*, trans. Martin Nicolaus (New York: Vintage Books, 1973), p. 709.

27. Marx, *Capital*, trans. Ben Fowkes (New York: Vintage Books, 1977), vol. 1, p. 1024.

28. Mario Tronti, "The Strategy of Refusal," *Italy: Autonomia*, Semiotext(e), 1980, vol. 3, no 3: 32.

29. This eclipse of labor in the society of the real subsumption is very close to Fredric Jameson's claim of the heightened role of commodity fetishism in postmodernity, or rather, in the era of late capitalism. See his essay, "Actually Existing Marxism," *Polygraph*, 1993, no. 6/7: 170–95. Commodity fetishism, after all, refers to the fact that in capitalist society commodities seem to present themselves and relate to each other autonomously, without revealing the various forms of labor and the social circuits of laboring cooperation that went into their production.

30. Once again, I am arguing here that the social conditions for civil society no

longer exist in Western Europe and North America. In order to consider the question of civil society outside the Euro-American context, one would first have to look to its primary condition of possibility, that is, the organization of abstract labor in the institutions of a specific phase of capitalist society.

31. Foucault, "La société disciplinaire en crise," *Dits et écrits* (originally 1978; Paris: Gallimard, 1994), vol. III, p. 533.

32. Antonio Negri and I have proposed in *Labor of Dionysus*, pp. 7–11, 275–83, that the concept "labor" be considered a site of social contestation that depends in large part on the way that value is produced in a given social context. In the course of our investigation of the contemporary nature, forms, and organization of labor we individuate a series of "prerequisites of communism" already existing in our postcivil society.

Part III

Public Knowledge

10

Print-Capitalism?

David McInerney

To the memory of Wallis Arthur Suchting (1931–97), my friend and mentor

In the introduction to his *Imagined Communities*, Benedict Anderson presents that work as an attempt to inaugurate a "Copernican Revolution" in nationalism studies.

> [N]ationalism has proved an uncomfortable *anomaly* for Marxist theory and, precisely for that reason, has been largely elided, rather than confronted. . . . The aim of this book is to offer some tentative suggestions for a more satisfactory interpretation of the "anomaly" of nationalism. My sense is that on this topic both Marxist and liberal theory have become etiolated in a late Ptolemaic attempt to "save the phenomena"; and that a reorientation of perspective in, as it were, a Copernican spirit, is urgently required.[1]

In reducing "Marxist and liberal theory" to a "perspective" Anderson elides, rather than confronts, the radical disjunction between Marxism and liberalism that constitutes them as theoretical problematics; *this chapter argues that the elision of this disjunction, in effect, allows the operation of a theoretical discrepancy that constitutes the basis of Anderson's theory of nationalism.*[2] The elision of this disjunction enables the substitution of non-Marxist concepts of "capitalism" for the Marxist concept, and "capital" to stand in for the capitalist mode of production. This chapter analyzes some of the effects of this substitution on Anderson's account of the origin of nationalism.

Anderson's book constitutes an attempt to construct a general theory of the origin and spread of nationalism. This chapter does not attempt to produce an alternative theory, nor does it discuss Anderson's account of the spread of nationalism. Rather, this chapter is a philosophical work, in the sense of Locke's dictum that philosophers should act as "under-laborers" to the sciences: materialist philosophers clear away theoretical obstacles to the development of the sciences, rather than provide idealist guarantees of "Science."[3] The work of developing Marxism, as a *science* for political strategy (as opposed to a "philosophy of history" or a political ideology), remains a labor without End.

"Imagined Communities"

> Essentially, I [that is, Anderson] have been arguing that the very possibility of imagining the nation arose historically only when, and where, three fundamental cultural conceptions, all of great antiquity, lost their axiomatic grip on men's minds. . . . Combined, these ideas rooted human lives firmly in the very nature of things, giving certain meaning to the everyday fatalities of existence (above all death, loss, and servitude) and offering, in various ways, redemption from them.
>
> The slow, uneven decline of these interlinked certainties, first in Western Europe, later elsewhere, under the impact of economic change, "discoveries" (social and scientific), and the development of increasingly rapid communications, drove a harsh wedge between cosmology and history. No surprise then that the search was on, so to speak, for a new way of linking fraternity, power and time meaningfully together. *Nothing perhaps more precipitated this search, nor made it more fruitful, than print-capitalism,* which made it possible for rapidly growing numbers of people to think about themselves, and to relate themselves to others, in profoundly new ways. (*IC*: 40)

This quotation gives a first impression of the central role of the concept of "print-capitalism" in Anderson's account of the origin of nationalism. In this section I shall attempt, by way of a first approximation, to give a summary of Anderson's theory of the relation between "print-capitalism" and the origin of nationalism.

Anderson's theoretical schema, at least for our purposes, is as follows:

1.   Society becomes possible with the imagining of a communal bond between individuals. There are two basic types of imagined community: the religious (premodern) community and the secular (modern) community. The conditions for the modern secular community are incompatible with those of the premodern religious community, in that they imply opposing conceptions of the social function of language, of the character of political power, and of time and space. Nations are secular and modern.

2.   The undermining of the religious community, and formation of

the secular community, coincides with the expansion of mercantile activity in Europe, the discovery of sea routes to non-European societies in the Americas and Asia, and a period of technological and scientific innovation. This is the onset of the modern (and *capitalist*) age.

3.   One of the most important innovations was that of printing, and the combination of this innovation with the expansionary character of capitalist production resulted in the undermining of many of the ideological foundations of the religious communities, and constituted the conditions for the production of the new secular communities.

4.   The expansionary and homogenizing character of capitalism, and certain unchangeable facts of human nature, combined to produce a plurality of *national* communities.

These points formalize aspects of the quotations above and of passages cited below. The important points for the discussion here are those relating to the periodization of capitalism and to the historical agency attributed to "print-capitalism" in the origin of nationalism. I shall give a fuller account of Anderson's theory of "print-capitalism," in terms of its agency in the decline of the religious communities and the formation of the national communities, before specifying the problems relating to Anderson's (explicit and implicit) definitions of capitalism and his periodization of capitalism's emergence and dominance.

Print-Capitalism and the Death of Latin

The merchants and political functionaries of Europe faced the practical task of learning non-European languages with the expansion of European trade routes after 1400. Anderson claims that the solutions to these practical problems raised questions of the cosmological status of Latin, ancient Greek, and Hebrew. The existence of languages possessing a sacred or ritual "truth" function, such as Sanskrit, belonging to religious communities that were not "Judeo-Christian" in character, undermined previous assumptions regarding language and languages. There was also an earlier problem of the formation of new languages-of-state. The struggles between the emerging absolutist states, and between them and the Holy Roman Empire, produced vernacular languages-of-state, and resulted in the production of written materials in those languages. Similarly, the Reformation meant the production of religious texts in the vernacular languages and the use of those languages in religious rituals. At the same time Latin underwent a literary resurgence with the emergence of a secular intelligentsia in

Renaissance Europe, with new editions of ancient Latin texts (and new philosophical and scientific works) appearing in Latin and thus altering the social function of that language.

According to Anderson, all of these changes combined to "demote" church Latin from its status as a "truth-language," thus enabling the formation of secular communities:

> At bottom, it is likely that the esotericization of Latin, the Reformation, and the haphazard development of administrative vernaculars are significant, in the present context, primarily in a negative sense—in their contributions to the dethronement of Latin and the erosion of the sacred community of Christendom. It is quite possible to conceive of the emergence of the new imagined communities without any one, perhaps all, of them being present. What, in a positive sense, made the new communities imaginable was a half-fortuitous, but explosive, interaction between a system of production and productive relations (capitalism), a technology of communications (print), and the fatality of human linguistic diversity. (*IC*: 46)

The "negative" and "extraneous" character of the former changes lies in the facts that print made these negative conditions possible (through vernacular religious, literary, and governmental printed materials), and that these factors *in themselves* only "dissolved" the basis for the old "imagined communities," and did not *in themselves* constitute the basis for the new "imagined communities." These "extraneous factors" only add "further impetus" to "the revolutionary vernaculariz-ing thrust of capitalism." (*IC*: 42)

It is only the assumption that printing was always-already "capitalist" that precludes the conclusion that these "extraneous factors" produced the expansion of printing necessary to the formation of a capitalist printing industry, rather than being the product of "the revolutionary vernacularizing thrust of [print-] capitalism." This assumption of a super-human ability of capitalism to generate its markets is necessary to the "logic" of Anderson's "print-capitalism" thesis.

From this vantage point we can see the function of the "fatality of human linguistic diversity" in Anderson's argument. If "capitalism" is to possess this "superhuman" agency and still necessarily produce a world divided into "monoglot reading publics," there needs to be an unsurpassable limit (imposed by human nature) upon its homogeniz-ing power.

> The element of fatality is essential. For whatever superhuman feats capitalism was capable of, it found in death and languages two tenacious adversaries. Particular languages can die or be wiped out, but there is no possibility of man's general linguistic unification. Yet this mutual incomprehensibility was

historically of only slight importance until capitalism and print created monoglot reading publics. (*IC:* 46)

It is the *strictly derivative* character given to political and ideological factors relative to the economic—*which enables "print-capitalism" to function as a general explanation*—that requires this theoretical fiction of a limit imposed by "human nature."

This necessity also imposes a historicism in Anderson's account of the rise of vernacular printing, in that "print-capitalism" is assumed suddenly to shift from Latin publishing to vernacular publishing once "the Latin market" becomes "saturated," rather than this being understood in terms of different markets for print-commodities, constituted in the ideological and political struggles that he understands as being derivative of, rather than necessary conditions of, the development of new markets for Europe's printing presses.

Anderson explains the move of "print-capitalism" from publishing Latin texts for the bilingual intelligentsia to the production of vernacular texts through reference to the expansionary "logic" of "[print-] capitalism's search for new markets":

> One of the earlier forms of capitalist enterprise, book-publishing, felt all of capitalism's restless search for markets. . . . The initial market was literate Europe, a wide but thin stratum of Latin-readers. Saturation of this market took about 150 years. The determinative fact about Latin—aside from its sacrality—was that it was a language of bilinguals. Relatively few were born to speak it and even fewer, one imagines, dreamed in it. . . . Then and now the vast bulk of mankind is monoglot. The logic of capitalism thus meant that once the elite Latin market was saturated, the potentially huge markets represented by the monoglot masses would beckon. (*IC:* 41–2)

For Anderson, the expansionary "logic" of a capitalism already engaged in the "inherently limited" Latin market requires the "assembly" of regional spoken dialects into national print-languages, as far as is possible, to provide the conditions for further expansion:

> In pre-print Europe, and, of course, elsewhere in the world, the diversity of spoken languages . . . was immense; so immense, indeed, that had print-capitalism sought to exploit each potential oral vernacular market, it would have remained a capitalism of petty proportions. But these varied idiolects were capable of being assembled, within definite limits, into print-languages far fewer in number. The very arbitrariness of any system of signs for sounds facilitated the assembling process. . . . Nothing served to "assemble" related vernaculars more than capitalism, which, within limits imposed by grammars

and syntaxes, created mechanically-reproduced print-languages, capable of dissemination through the market. (*IC*: 46–7)

Thus it appears that capitalism, for Anderson, provides the conditions for its emergence and expansion. Similarly, we can see that this always-already capitalist character of printing is what explains its "superhuman" capacity to "assemble" new markets in the event of the "saturation" of its old markets.

This discussion of Anderson's concept of "print-capitalism," and its historical role in the dissolution of the religious communities, gives us a first approximation of Anderson's account of the character of capitalism and of his periodization of its emergence and dominance. His account presumes that "capitalism" explains the changes of the modern era—which, on this account, constitutes the very first point at which the feudal political order began to crumble—and thus the emergence of capitalism must coincide with the expansion of mercantile activity and the formation of absolutist empires. This also presumes that the emergence of absolutism, and the corresponding global expansion of European mercantile activity, signifies the dominance of capitalism over precapitalist modes of production, through the subjection of the "closed" feudal societies to the effects of a world commodity market.

Nationalism and the Consumption of the Print-Commodity

The theoretical function of this concept of "print-capitalism" in Anderson's account of the origin of nationalism becomes clearer when we move from his account of the "assembly" of "print-languages" to his account of how print-capitalism enabled new forms of subjectivization.

This part of Anderson's account focuses upon differences in the concept of "simultaneity" between the modern secular communities and the premodern religious communities. The different concepts of "simultaneity" presume different concepts of "time." Anderson defines the premodern concept as the opposite of the modern concept: premodern time is one of "prefiguring and fulfillment" (where earlier events prefigure and fulfill later events, thus suggesting the presence of the latter in the former as its telos), whereas the modern concept of time is one of a mechanistic chain of "cause-and-effect" (*IC*: 28–30). The premodern concept corresponds to a concept of "simultaneity-*along*-time" whilst the modern concept corresponds to a concept of "simultaneity-*across*-time" (*IC*: 30).[4] The modern concept of time presupposes that "simultaneity is, as it were, transverse, cross-time, marked not by pre-figuring and fulfillment, but by temporal coincidence, and measured by clock and calendar" (*IC*: 30).

This section (and subsequent sections) will show that *Anderson's account depends upon a teleological sense of earlier events prefiguring later ones, in explaining the development of printing and its relation to the development of nationalism. Contemporary forms of print production and consumption reveal the essential characteristics of "print-capitalism" that, on the assumption of the origins of "print-capitalism" in the fifteenth century, then form the basis for the explanation of the origin of nationalism.*

Anderson's explanation proceeds through the following argument: the imagining of modern forms of "simultaneity" and "community" presumes a mechanism for their imaginary representation, and "print-commodities" (novels and newspapers) provided this mechanism.

I need not provide a detailed exposition of Anderson's account of the novel here. The significance of the novel consists largely in the homology that Anderson asserts between the realist novel and the newspaper in terms of their shared capacity to represent the modern concept of simultaneity, which he sees as a condition of the modern concept of community (*IC*: 31). If "print-capitalism" is to provide a *general explanation* of the origin of nationalism, the structure of the realist novel *must precede* changes in conceptions of time and simultaneity. Otherwise it could simply be a product of those changes, rather than constituting their explanation. However, unless Anderson also presumes that this structure allows representations in terms of the older concepts of time and simultaneity—and therefore it does not necessarily correspond to "modern" social relations—then there is no way in which the novel can constitute an explanation for those changes. However, this produces the paradox that then neither can we pose the difference between premodern and modern communities in such starkly historicist terms, unless we attribute this to a change of ideas.

The novel only acquires its significance in Anderson's argument because its structure, in his view, prefigures that of the newspaper. It is the newspaper that explains the process of subjectivization in which subjects become members of secular, national communities existing in "homogeneous, empty time." However, as we shall see, even the newspaper (of the period of the origin of nationalism) can only perform this function insofar as it somehow prefigures the contemporary newspaper that forms Anderson's example.

Anderson claims that the newspaper provides a *device* through which an *imaginary linkage* (of temporal coincidence) between events becomes possible:

[I]f we now turn to the newspaper as a cultural product, we will be struck by its profound fictiveness. What is the essential literary convention of the newspaper? If we were to look at a sample front page of, say, *The New York Times*, we might find there stories about Soviet dissidents, famine in Mali, a gruesome murder, a coup in Iraq, the discovery of a rare fossil in Zimbabwe, and a speech by Mitterrand. Why are these events so juxtaposed? What connects them to each other? Not sheer caprice. Yet obviously most of them happen independently, without the actors being aware of each other or of what the others are up to. The arbitrariness of their inclusion and juxtaposition (a later edition will substitute a baseball triumph for Mitterrand) shows that the linkage between them is imagined. (*IC*: 37)

The "simultaneity" of these events exists only on the pages of the newspaper. In itself, the thesis of the possibility of producing an imaginary linkage between disparate events through the device of the newspaper is not objectionable, nor an especially startling revelation. However, the exact character of this imaginary linkage plays a pivotal role in Anderson's arguments on print-capitalism and nationalism.

Anderson claims that this "imagined linkage" between the events represented on the front page of his copy of the *New York Times* "derives from two obliquely related sources":

The first is simply calendrical coincidence. The date at the top of the newspaper, the single most important emblem on it, provides the essential connection—the steady onward clocking of homogeneous, empty time. Within that time, "the world" ambles slowly ahead. The sign for this: if Mali disappears from the pages of *The New York Times* after two months of famine reportage, for months on end, readers do not imagine for a moment that Mali has disappeared or that famine has wiped out all its citizens. The novelistic format of the newspaper assures them that somewhere out there the "character" Mali moves along quietly, awaiting its next appearance in the plot.

The second source of imagined linkage lies in the relationship between the newspaper, as a form of book, and the market. . . . In a rather special sense the book was the first modern-style mass-produced industrial commodity. The sense I have in mind can be shewn if we compare the book to other early industrial products, such as textiles, or bricks, or sugar. For these commodities are measured in mathematical amounts (pounds or loads or pieces). A pound of sugar is simply a quantity, a convenient load, not an object in itself. The book, however—and here it prefigures the durables of our time—is a distinct, self-contained object, exactly produced on a large scale. One pound of sugar flows into the next; each book has its own eremitic self-sufficiency. (*IC*: 37–8)

The important point here for Anderson's argument is that the date at the top of the newspaper—the temporality of its production—determines the temporality of its consumption. We can also see here the teleology between the novel and the newspaper, so that the conception of simultaneity which is only *possible* in consuming the novel becomes *intrinsic* to the consumption of the newspaper. Indeed, in Anderson's view, "the newspaper is merely an 'extreme form' of the book, a book sold on a colossal scale, but of ephemeral popularity" (*IC:* 39).

The importance of the "colossal" and "ephemeral" character of newspaper production and consumption suggests that a more important teleology is at work. The *New York Times* is very different, in terms of the temporality and quantity of its production and consumption, from the early gazettes of the period of the origin of nationalism. A quarterly, monthly, or even weekly local newspaper seems very different from a national newspaper produced in massive quantities in morning and afternoon editions. *In Anderson's world the printing of 1450 prefigures the printing of 1850, the newspaper of 1783 prefigures the newspaper of 1983, and the materiality of the latter always fulfills the essence of the former.*

This cosmological time of Anderson's historical explanation allows the newspaper to function as the mechanism that, in the last instance, explains the imagining of the nation. Anderson's account of the role of these "one day best-sellers" is worth quoting in full.

> The obsolescence of the newspaper on the morrow of its printing—curious that one of the earlier mass-produced commodities should so prefigure the inbuilt obsolescence of modern durables—nonetheless, for just this reason, creates this extraordinary mass ceremony: the almost precisely simultaneous consumption (imagining?) of the newspaper-as-fiction. We know that particular morning and evening editions will overwhelmingly be consumed between this hour and that, only on this day, and not that. (Contrast sugar, the use of which proceeds in an unclocked, continuous flow; it may go bad, but it does not go out of date.) The significance of this mass ceremony— Hegel observed that newspapers serve modern man as a substitute for morning prayers—is paradoxical. It is performed in silent privacy, in the lair of the skull. Yet each communicant is well aware that the ceremony is being replicated simultaneously by thousands (or millions) of others of whose existence he is confident, yet of whose identity he has not the slightest notion. Furthermore, this ceremony is incessantly replicated at daily or half-daily intervals throughout the calendar. What more vivid figure for the secular, historically clocked, imagined community can be imagined? At the same time, the newspaper reader, observing exact replicas of his own paper being consumed by his subway, barber shop, or residential neighbors, is continually reassured that the imagined world is visibly rooted in everyday

life. . . . [F]iction seeps quietly and continuously into reality, creating that remarkable confidence of community in anonymity that is the hallmark of modern nations. (*IC*: 39–40)

Here we are at the point where Anderson's argument flips from a materialist emphasis on a real device for the constitution of an imaginary relation to an idealist argument that "ideas" have an existence that preexists their material effects. If we are to assume that printing *explains* the origin of nationalism, rather than being just *one of its conditions of existence*, we would seem to remain bereft of an argument as to how it does so, unless we believe in this "extraordinary mass ceremony" that brings itself into existence.

What Is Capitalism?

The preceding sections of this chapter indicated the central function of "print-capitalism" within Anderson's argument. As the discussion and citations above show, Anderson presumes that the origin of capitalism coincides with, or even precedes, the innovation of printing and the mercantile expansion of Europe that resulted in the European discovery of the "New World." Needless to say, this allows print-capitalism to preexist the origin of nationalism by a considerable margin, and thus to be able to act as its historical explanation. This section of the chapter aims to show how Anderson's understanding of "capitalism" is inconsistent with the Marxist understanding of capitalism; the following section investigates Anderson's historical evidence for his arguments on "print-capitalism."

The question of a theoretical consistency between the concept of capitalism at work in Anderson's argument and the Marxist concept of capitalism is relevant because it reveals a theoretical inconsistency within Anderson's argument itself. Anderson *explicitly* defines "capitalism" as "a system of production and production relations" (*IC*: 46) and claims that "the bourgeoisie [is] . . . a world class insofar as it is defined in terms of the relations of production" (*IC*: 13). This explicit *definition* of capitalism in terms of "production relations," and definition of the bourgeoisie (as a class) in terms of social relations, suggest that Anderson intends his account to be read in terms of the Marxist conceptual apparatus.

However, Anderson's *periodization* of capitalism, and the concept of "print-capitalism" that it produces suggest otherwise. Anderson's periodization of capitalism, and his assertion of the *essentially* capitalist nature of printing, provide the *raison d'être* of non-Marxist definitions of "capitalism." These definitions of "capitalism" refer either to the level of development of the productive forces and the technical division of labor, or to an imperative for profit maximization and the expansion of commodity exchange. Combined, these latter definitions allow Anderson to define the period stretching from the late fifteenth century to the present as "capitalist" in its essence, and thus to date the emergence and dominance of capitalism from the beginning of printing in Europe.[5]

Capitalism, in the Marxist sense, is a *mode of production*. A mode of production is an articulated ensemble of certain means of production, labor-power, and relations of production, under the dominance of (*and defined by*) determinate *social relations of production*, together with the economic, ideological, and political conditions of existence of these relations and forces of production. The importance of its definition in terms of social relations of production for our purposes here is the following: some means of production might be compatible with more than one set of social relations of production, and may even entail *similar* technical relations of production (the specific form of the *combination* of the productive forces, as the sum of the means of production and labor-power).[6] This is especially relevant to the periodization of the historical existence of a mode of production, as in a transitional conjuncture the productive forces characteristic of an existing mode of production come under the dominance of new social relations of production.[7] Also, the existence of these social relations in some formal sense does not imply that those relations will develop further unless the conditions for that further development arise. This depends upon the articulation of the relations of production in a structure where capitalism is the dominant mode of production, as it requires the conditions for the appropriation of surplus-labor in the form of surplus-value, that is, the generalization of commodity relations and the separation of the mass of producers from the means of production, or, in other words, the existence of labor-power as a commodity.

Precapitalist modes of production that were dominant at the level of the economic system include the modes of production that we might call primitive communist, ancient, and feudal. Another mode of production, the slave mode of production, existed together with those modes that required a monetarized commodity economy and private property (the ancient and capitalist modes) but was never a dominant mode.[8] Following Ernesto Laclau, we can distinguish between a *capitalist mode of production* and a *capitalist economic-system,* and we can also say that the dynamics of the dominant mode of production (and the conditions of that dominance) overdetermine the dynamics of the *economic-system* (and of the modes of production articulated within that system).[9] Each of these precapitalist modes of production can exist as a subordinate mode of production within a capitalist economic-system, though subject to the effects of the reproduction of the economic, ideological, and political conditions of existence of the dominant mode of production.

We can outline the importance of these observations to the issue of the relations between capitalism, printing, and the origin of nationalism as follows. Because Anderson makes no distinction between the existence of "free laborers" and the establishment of a capitalist economic-system, he grounds his argument upon characteristics of capitalism that pertain to a conjuncture in which capitalism is the dominant mode of production. This fact means that Anderson's understanding of the dynamics of print production before that time, and its pertinence to the relation between printing and nationalism, must be inadequate and misleading. *Even if capitalist relations and forces of production were a feature of European printing houses from the beginning*—and this is by no means clearly the case, as the subsequent discussion of Anderson's argument and sources will show—*there is no reason to presume that the dynamics of its development or its mechanism of appropriation were those of capitalist printing in the period of the dominance of capitalist social relations. Neither, then, can we assume that the dynamics of the capitalist mode of production determined those of all print production.* The mechanism of appropriation characteristic of capitalist social relations within a feudal economic-system—the appropriation of *absolute* surplus-labor—differs qualitatively from the dominant variant of capitalism in its mature period, which characteristically appropriates *relative* surplus-labor. If these conditions hold, there is no reason to assume that there was any impetus, at the level of the dynamics of the economic-system, for a "vernacularizing" and "homogenizing" expansion of print production such as Anderson's account presumes.

Christopher Plantin: Print-Capitalist?

We can get a sense of the bases for Anderson's claims regarding the development of "print-capitalism" if we look at his main source, the study by Lucien Febvre and Henri-Jean Martin of the origins and development of printing and publishing in the period 1450–1800, *The*

Coming of the Book.[10] Using their account as his guide, Anderson argues that the printed book was "the first modern-style mass-produced industrial commodity" (*IC*: 38). On the basis of the discussion above of the Marxist concept of a capitalist mode of production we can determine whether printing was capitalist and if the economic system in which it existed was capitalist, and thus if the dynamics of print-production were those of the mature capitalist mode of production (as Anderson presumes).

It seems clear from Anderson's argument that he considers the shift from hand-written manuscripts to printed books—analyzed at the beginning of the Febvre and Martin study—to mark the onset of the age of "print-capitalism," that is, of the capitalist production of "print-commodities." This change coincides with the expansion of commodity exchange and the involvement of mercantile and financial capital in production of these print-commodities, and together these suggest the possibility of capitalist print-production.

It might be the case that the social relations of production that correspond to these other changes are capitalist; however, given all that was said above, this would be a matter for rigorous empirical investigation, rather than a process of deduction from the development of the means of production and the presence of mercantile and financial capital.

To sustain the thesis that printing had always been capitalist, Anderson would have to provide evidence of a *necessary relation* between the existence of the printing press and capitalist social relations of production; it would then be a simple matter of saying "printing *ergo* capitalism." This would require demonstration that printing is incompatible with the precapitalist forms of production as found in manuscript production, and thus necessitates the presence of labor-power as a commodity. There is no such attempt in Anderson's book, nor does such an attempt seem likely to provide the answer that Anderson's argument seems to require. A more limited claim, that capitalist printing enterprises emerged to dominate qualitatively a market in which precapitalist printing enterprises were predominant quantitatively, might seem more plausible.

Anderson uses some impressive-sounding numbers that suggest a considerable volume of print-production, as well as the quantitative predominance of small printers and editions:

> It has been estimated that in the 40-odd years between the publication of
> the Gutenberg Bible and the close of the fifteenth century, more than

20,000,000 printed volumes were produced in Europe. Between 1500 and 1600, the number manufactured had reached between 150,000,000 and 200,000,000. (*IC*: 38)

These figures definitely suggest a considerable increase in the rate of book publication in the sixteenth century, even though the printers and editions were small, as indicated by Anderson's note that the 20,000,000 books in the second half of the fourteenth century consisted of "less than 35,000 editions produced in 236 towns" (*IC*: 38). Editions remained small until the nineteenth century:

> Until the nineteenth century, editions were still relatively small. Even Luther's Bible, an extraordinary best-seller, had only a 4,000-copy first edition. The unusually large first edition of Diderot's *Encyclopédie* numbered no more than 4,250. The average eighteenth-century run was less than 2,000. (*IC*: 38)

These facts together suggest that small printers and editions predominated until the nineteenth century, when the world dominance of the capitalist mode of production enabled the transition to the technical relations of production and means of production that are characteristic of what Marx called "machinofacture."

Anderson does provide some information that we can read as evidence of the existence of capitalist print-production in the sixteenth century. He notes the establishment of a large publishing house in Antwerp, then the major commercial center in western Europe: "The great Antwerp publishing house of Plantin controlled, early in the sixteenth century, 24 presses with more than 100 workers in each shop" (*IC*: 38).

The latter figures are especially significant, as they suggest that in those shops books were produced in capitalist manufacture. However, direct consultation of Anderson's source suggests that this information may be a misrepresentation. The wording used by Febvre and Martin— that "[m]ore than one hundred workers were employed in [Plantin's] shops"—is ambiguous, and closer attention to their text suggests that the more plausible reading would be that "Plantin had [a *total* of] more than 100 workers working on 24 presses"; so, each press had four or five workers, probably with as many as four or five presses to a shop (it is not clear from the account of Febvre and Martin how many shops Plantin had), which suggests a very different scale of production. Nevertheless, it is plausible that these shops could constitute small capitalist enterprises. To determine this we would need to determine the exact social relations of production in Plantin's shops.

From the account of Febvre and Martin we do not get a close and careful description of Plantin's shops, although we do get a sense of the organization of printing shops and of the typical technical and social relations of production in a large printing shop of that time.

The first thing to note is that the early printing shops consisted of three social categories: the master, who owned the means of production; apprentices, who served a period of indenture to the master of between two and five years; and, occasionally, journeymen (itinerant former apprentices who, qualified as printers but without shops of their own, traveled from place to place, working for master printers on a monthly or daily basis) (*CB*: 129–42). Although the journeymen and apprentices were direct producers of a product appropriated and distributed by the master, the master usually worked as the compositor and, in times of labor shortages, even operated the printing presses himself, together with members of his family.

The productive labor being the master, his family, and his indentured apprentices, with the occasional supplement of journeymen, suggests that this is a precapitalist mode of production. Here the employment of free laborers is a supplement to household labor and depends upon the existence of former apprentices who are member of the printers' guild, but without a shop of their own. The apprentice became part of the household for the period of his indenture and—despite the obligation of the master to give his apprentice "pocket money"—his board, lodging and clothing constituted his remuneration (*CB*: 129). The journeymen received wages on a daily or monthly (rather than hourly) basis and the master often supplied their food and drink as part of the remuneration for their labor. The master assigned journeymen and apprentices their work for the day, and the appropriation of surplus-value varied with changes in the length of the period of work, rather than with changes in the organic composition of labor. In cases of labor shortages (and/or large contracts) masters often employed journeymen on a monthly basis. The employment of journeymen changed with the supply of workers and the demand for print-commodities, and was dependent upon financial advances from publishing houses that would enable the supplementation of the household labor (that of the master, his family, and the apprentices) with the journeymen's labor. There was no sense that the employment of these journeymen enabled an ongoing accumulation of surplus-value that would suggest the development of capitalist relations; instead, the availability of journeymen provided the possibility of attracting larger contracts (*CB*: 129–36).

The dependence upon household labor, augmented by apprentices indentured from poor peasant households, and the occasional use of journeymen, suggests a constraint upon the development of capitalist print-production arising from two factors: the limitations of the market for its commodities, and the availability of labor-power as a commodity. Various ideological and political developments provided the conditions for the expansion of the market for print-commodities; however, production would remain limited so long as feudal social relations dominated production in the countryside. We should expect, therefore, the location of larger printing houses near sources of labor and finance capital and the dominance of the publishing houses (merchant and finance capital) relative to the producers of print-commodities—the printing-houses—given the limits on production. This also meant that the productive forces and technical relations of production were for the most part similar between large and small printers, with differences being mainly of scale:

> In the largest [printing houses], like those of Koberger, Froben, Plantin, Blaeu or the Imprimerie Royale at Paris, where there might be as many as 50 men on ten presses, each worker had his task strictly determined. The same was true in the houses which were particularly active and painstaking, like the Estiennes', or Vitré's, each of whom employed four presses. But printing was a craft skill and not always on such massive lines. In Geneva in 1570, out of twenty shops, three had four presses, five had two and the remaining twelve had only one each. In seventeenth-century France the majority had only one or two presses, and the same was true of London. Masters had no means of maintaining a large work force, especially when regular work was lacking; in fact it was usual for the master to work alongside his one or two workmen, helped when work was pressing by his wife and children. In such conditions the compositors must often have had to pull the press themselves. (*CB*: 131)

We should note here that this does not suggest that Plantin had "24 presses with more than 100 workers in each shop"—rather it suggests that Plantin had 100 workers on 24 presses, and that it is unclear as to the number of "shops" this involved. However, we might still character-ize production in Plantin's shops as capitalist, although this would imply only a formal subsumption, and not a real subsumption, of labor under capital—there is no evidence in *The Coming of the Book* to suggest that changes in the scale of production produced anything but a more defined and predictable version of the household production of the small printer. This would remain the case until the nineteenth century, when industrial capitalism established its domination of the world economic-system.

The establishment of a more defined and predictable technical relationship of production, suitable for (relatively) large-scale production of print-commodities, as the reason for the (formal) subsumption of labor under capital becomes more apparent if we examine the case of Plantin—Anderson's example—more closely. Febvre and Martin do speak of Plantin as one of "the biggest capitalist publishers" (*CB*: 136). However, they do not distinguish capitalism (as a mode of production) from financial or merchant capital, so they also refer to some publishers only involved in printing in a financial and mercantile manner as "capitalist":

> [P]ublishers and booksellers . . . [should be studied] together, for the great majority of them carried out both jobs at the same time. Of course many book-shops, especially the small ones which published titles only occasionally, did not own a printing press. But most printers kept a shop as well and invested the profits they made out of publishing books for other people into publishing, either on their account or in collaboration with others. Joost Bade worked this way. And if some of the biggest capitalist publishers who dominated the book trade like Cramoisy or some of the Guintas owned no printing shops, others like Koberger and Plantin kept shops, as we have seen, in which they printed some at least of the books they financed as publishers. (*CB*: 136)

Obviously Febvre and Martin do not demarcate "capital" from "capitalism." But, more important, we can see that the rationale for the intervention of financial and mercantile capital into production was to establish predictability of supply. It may also have originated as a way of recouping debts from defaulting printers. In any case, this reading fits better with the facts as given by Febvre and Martin than Anderson's theory of "print-capitalism" can.

It seems that Plantin was a financier and merchant, who through "connections" established through religion was able to put himself in a monopoly position where he could manipulate prices and advance loans. Such were the means that the mercantile bourgeoisie used to make a profit: buying cheap and selling dear, through manipulating the conditions of the market. In the feudal economic system the most lucrative strategy was to buy noble titles and monopolies from the absolutist monarch, through financing military power (the means of economic expansion in the feudal mode of production). The account provided by Febvre and Martin of Plantin's rise, after humble beginnings, and his return from an exile imposed under accusations of heresy, bears this out:

> The members of the sect, called "The Family of Charity," to which [Plantin] belonged began to show interest in [him], and after his return to Antwerp in 1563 he formed a syndicate of publishers with some of the rich bourgeoisie of the city, including Cornelius and Charles Van Bomberghe, Jacob Scotti, a banker, and Goropius Bunho, a doctor. During the five years of the syndicate's existence, 260 works were published; editions of classical authors, Hebrew Bibles and liturgical books. Once "launched," Plantin could call on powerful patrons like Cardinal Granvelle and Gabriel de Cayas, Secretary to Philip II. Through this connection, he obtained financial and legal support from the Spanish king who bore the costs of his Polyglot Bible, the work which made Plantin famous, and gave him a monopoly of sales in Spain and her colonies. The king also ordered the publishing of the reformed liturgical books authorized by the Council of Trent. By early 1572 tens of thousands of breviaries, missals, psalters and antiphonies were sent from Antwerp to Philip II who ordered the monks of the Escorial to see to the distribution and sale of books in his territories. Plantin at that time had up to 24 presses in active production and had assembled for the purpose a unique collection of punches and moulds. More than one hundred workers were employed in his shops and he had depots and other trade outlets in every European city. . . . A share in Antwerp's available capital and the support of the Spanish State were the mainsprings of Plantin's business and the reason why he could create the most powerful book manufactory to exist before the 19th century. (*CB*: 126)[11]

Plantin was a wealthy merchant and financier, whose ability to monopolize the religious and state market of Latin publishing made capitalist manufacture in printing possible and necessary. Smaller printers would approach Plantin and other members of the financial bourgeoisie for capital to invest in materials and equipment for the riskier vernacular markets, or for contract work and capital to supply Plantin or other publishers.

Considering the evidence presented for the presence of "print-capitalism" prior to the nineteenth century, we can say that printing was not necessarily capitalist, although beyond the smallest scale of household production it was dependent upon supplies of financial capital, upon secured contracts from the mercantile bourgeoisie, and upon the numbers of journeymen laborers of the printing guilds available. The dynamics of its production were those of an economic system dominated by feudal relations of production, in which print-commodities had the status of luxury items. The scarcity of supply suited the mercantile appropriation of capital, which depended not upon the appropriation of relative surplus-value in production, but rather upon value accumulated through exploiting restrictions within, and price differentials between, markets, as much as, or more than, any appropriation of (absolute) surplus-value in production. The limitations of a mechanism of appropriation of *absolute* surplus-value in production are suggested by the predominance of small printers dependent upon household and indentured labor, by the supplemental role of wage-labor, and by the subsequent restrictions upon the development of the productive forces (the means of production and the technical relations of production) as is evident in the fact that production expanded by quantitative expansion the number of presses and workers, rather than the accumulation of fixed capital relative to variable capital, which would imply the accumulation of surplus-labor as relative surplus-value.

The implications of these facts for Anderson's argument are as follows:

1. There is no reason to suggest that printing was necessarily capitalist in character from the beginning, and Anderson's sources and evidence suggest rather the predominance of household and indentured labor (and the importance of journeymen's labor and the organization into guilds) in this early period.

2. Capital intervened in printing largely in a financial and mercantile capacity, and only intervened in production directly to secure the conditions for those activities.

3. The dynamics of the feudal economic system determined the development of capitalist print-production before the nineteenth century, and thus allowed a development of the productive forces corresponding to the limits of the labor supply. This implies the restriction of print-production by the technical relations of production characteristic of the precapitalist forms of printing.

4. This implies the restriction of capitalist print-production to larger markets secured through monopolies, and thus relied upon the expansion of *those* printing markets, such as the Latin market in the Catholic countries. Small printers produced small editions under precapitalist social relations of production, and these printers dominated the riskier markets, such as vernacular printing of religious books, political pamphlets and technical manuals. These small printers would not have been able to exercise much of a "homogenizing effect" upon vernacular print-languages. The formation of national print-languages would have depended upon the transformation of the state market

itself away from Latin toward vernacular languages, thus depriving "print-capitalism" of its explanatory primacy in that transformation.

Marxism and Nationalism: Some Concluding Remarks

In concluding I would like to return to the rather elliptical remarks of my introduction regarding Anderson's attempt to break with the "perspective" shared by Marxism and liberalism with regard to nationalism, and the way in which this indicates an elision of the disjunction between Marxism and what constitutes its ideological prehistory. This produces effects in Anderson's explanation of the origin and development of nationalism in terms of the development of "print-capitalism"; by allowing for the confusion of non-Marxist definitions of "capitalism" with the Marxist concept of capitalism as a mode of production, most notably by the confusion of "capital" with "capitalism," Anderson takes the presence of financial and mercantile capital as evidence of capitalism. This chapter attempts to demonstrate the necessity of this confusion in the attempt to produce a general theory of the relation between capitalism and nationalism through the concept of "print-capitalism." This concept depends upon non-Marxist definitions of capitalism, and this despite the fact that Anderson *explicitly* defines capitalism in Marxist terms.

The elision of the difference between problematics depends upon the existence of the same word—in this case, "capitalism"—to signify very different *concepts,* and thus *objects. When Marxism and liberalism speak of "capitalism" they do not speak of the same thing.* Contemporary liberals typically speak of "capitalism" (if at all) as the accumulation of capital as profit or rent. As we have seen, Marxists define capitalism as a mode of production, which may imply the appropriation of surplus-labor as profit, or the distribution of it as rent, or as other forms of *surplus-value.* Marxists also distinguish between the formal subsumption and the real subsumption of labor under capital, and between the appropriation of absolute surplus-value and relative surplus-value. They would also allow for the mercantile accumulation of surplus-labor as value, but this does not imply a capitalist mode of production. It seems clear that Anderson's arguments imply the dynamics of a dominant and mature capitalism characterized by the appropriation of surplus-labor as relative surplus-value, whilst using the intervention of capital and mechanization in production to demarcate the onset of this form of capitalism. This chapter suggests that this substitution of concepts under one word produces inadequate results.

Furthermore, we can see this substitution as one of a *series* of similar substitutions in Anderson's argument. These substitutions are symptoms of a theoretical *discrepancy* that constitutes the basis of Anderson's explanation. The substitution of mature capitalism for emergent capitalism, of modern newspapers and novels for early print-commodities, of capitalist printing for precapitalist printing, and of capitalism for capital, are all symptoms of the fundamental inadequacy of Anderson's theoretical *Übermensch* for the theoretical role required: that of explaining all of the fundamental ideological changes that Anderson lumps together as distinguishing modern imagined communities. *To play this role, contemporary capitalist printing must become the essence of printing per se, and the development of printing must be the unfolding of that essence. Thus the earlier term of each substitution prefigures the later term, which fulfills its promise.*

The specter of Walter Benjamin's Messianic Time—the "simultaneity of past and future in an instantaneous present"—haunts Benedict Anderson's *Imagined Communities*. The purpose of this chapter has been to demarcate the theoretical basis for this spiritualism, and thus to indicate some of the work that remains to be done, not for the development of a "Marxist theory of nationalism," but rather for the development of the Marxist conceptual apparatus, as the condition for the development of concrete analyses of the uneven development of nationalist discourses and their relations to the emergence of the capitalist world-system in the late eighteenth and early nineteenth centuries.

Notes

This chapter is the product of several papers written during the period 1994–97. It benefited from the comments given at the oral presentations of those papers, and from the comments of supervisors of the undergraduate and graduate research of which these papers together formed a part. I would especially like to acknowledge the efforts of Gerry Pye and Barry Hindess in this latter regard. I would also like to thank friends who gave generously of their time in conversation and correspondence, especially Sasho Lambevski and the late Wal Suchting, with both of whom much ink and coffee was spilt. I would also like to thank Warren Montag for encouraging me to develop this work into something publishable, and his patience with my sporadic attempts at doing so. I would especially like to acknowledge Carole Biewener's comments, encouragement, and support during the process of producing this version for publication. Usual disclaimers apply.

  1. Benedict Anderson, *Imagined Communities* (London: Verso, 1983), p. 13. Subsequent references to this work appear in the text as "*IC,*" followed by the page reference.
  2. On this concept of "problematic" see Dominique Lecourt, *Marxism and Epistemology*, trans. B. Brewster (London: New Left Books, 1975), especially the introduction for English readers, where Lecourt draws a crucial line of demarcation between Althusser's

concept of "problematic" and Kuhn's concept of "paradigm." On this concept of "discrepancy" (*décalage*), see Louis Althusser, *Politics and History*, trans. B. Brewster (London: New Left Books, 1972), pp. 111–60.

3. I say here "should" as Locke did not, as Wal Suchting notes in his essay on "Marx and 'The Problem of Knowledge'," practice what he preached. Wallis A. Suchting, *Marx and Philosophy* (London: Macmillan, 1986), p. 52. To act as such an "under-laborer" is to practice philosophy in a materialist way, and by no means characterizes most philosophy. On materialism and idealism as tendencies in philosophy, see Suchting, *Marx and Philosophy*, and Lecourt, *Marxism and Epistemology*.

4. Anderson borrows the phrase "homogeneous, empty time" from Walter Benjamin to characterize the modern sense of simultaneity, whilst describing premodern time in terms of Benjamin's concept of "Messianic time."

5. Marxist debates on the periodization of the emergence and subsequent dominance of capitalism have turned precisely upon such definitional issues, as the different definitions of "capitalism" imply different definitions of the central concept of the Marxist problematic, that of "mode of production." I have found the arguments of Robert Brenner (in "The Origins of Capitalist Development: A Critique of Neo-Smithian Marxism," *New Left Review*, no. 104, July–August 1977: 25–92) most convincing in this regard.

6. Variants of different modes of production might entail similar *technical* relations of production, but they differ in terms of social relations of production (and mechanisms of appropriation) peculiar to their mode of production (in its different variants). These definitions of the concepts of "productive forces," "technical relations of production," "social relations of production," "mechanism of appropriation," and "variant" come from Barry Hindess and Paul Q. Hirst, *Pre-Capitalist Modes of Production* (London: Routledge & Kegan Paul, 1975), and Wallis A. Suchting, *Marx: An Introduction* (Brighton: Wheatsheaf Books, 1983).

7. On this concept of "transitional conjuncture" see the introduction by Barry Hindess to C. Bettelheim, *Economic Calculation and Forms of Property* (London: Routledge & Kegan Paul), pp. 1–27.

8. This usage is that of Hindess and Hirst in their *Pre-Capitalist Modes of Production*. Following Hindess and Hirst, I have rejected the concept of an "Asiatic" mode of production, and would argue that Asian societies can be analyzed as variants of the same modes of production that are used to analyze non-Asian societies, the applicability of each of these concepts being a matter for rigorous empirical investigation.

9. On the distinction between a "mode of production" and an "economic-system" see Ernesto Laclau, *Politics and Ideology in Marxist Theory* (London: New Left Books, 1977), pp. 15–50. An economic-system is understood here to be defined by the dominant mode of production within it, which determines the dynamics of accumulation of the system as a whole, whilst a mode of production is, as has been stated earlier, defined by the social relations of production.

10. Anderson refers to this book: *The Coming of the Book*, trans. D. Gerard (originally published in French in 1958, trans. Lucien Febvre and Henri-Jean Martin; London: New Left Books, 1976); subsequent references to this work appear in the text as "*CB*," followed by the page reference) many times throughout his arguments on "print-capitalism." Although the *Annales* school (of which Febvre was a founder) has been associated with the understanding of capitalism as a mercantile world-system established in "the 'long' sixteenth century," Febvre and Martin do not use the phrase "print-capitalism," which appears to be of Anderson's coinage.

11. It is not clear from this passage how many *shops* Plantin had; however, from the passage cited above which suggested that five men per press on ten presses was a considerable amount, we might presume that saying that "more than one hundred workers were employed in his shops" implies that more than one hundred men worked in Plantin's shops on twenty-four presses, not that there were twenty-four presses each worked by one hundred men. The latter statement would presume that the presses in those shops were vastly different in kind from the presses used in the shops where the master himself occasionally operated the press, and there is nothing in the account of

Febvre and Martin to suggest this. Rather, the large enterprises seem to consist of an aggregation of presses of the sort used in smaller shops; though they were perhaps newer and better equipped than the presses used in the poorest print-shops, there is nothing to suggest that their use implied distinctively capitalist social and technical relations of production, as would be the case in machinofacture. One should be wary of the presence of the *words* "bourgeoisie," "workers," and "capital" in this passage: none of them are rigorously defined in terms of the capitalist mode of production. The "bourgeoisie" here is a mercantile and financial class, accumulating capital through windfalls that come from buying cheap and selling dear; the "workers" are journeymen and apprentices (and probably even former masters who could no longer compete with the larger printers); and, finally, the "capital" is sums of gold and/or silver advanced by financier merchants to the masters as advance payments on relatively scarce commodities with limited markets.

11

Of Multitudes and Moral Sympathy: E. P. Thompson, Althusser, and Adam Smith

Mike Hill

Now 100,000 people may be collected together and no riot ensue, and why? . . . The people have an object, the pursuit of which gives them importance in their own eyes, elevates them in their own opinion, and thus it is that the very individuals who would have been the leaders of the riot are the keepers of the peace.
—Francis Place

Hard History

A promotional blurb from a recent catalogue provides the following assurance: "this book is a breath of fresh air in the increasingly dusty room of texts without human agents behind them. It is an important book," the pitch continues, "[in] its restatement of 'hard' history against cultural studies. . . . Historians have gone too far down the road with cultural theory and are in danger of negating their own vocation." The atoning book referred to here is Charles Tilly's *Popular Contention in Great Britain, 1758–1834.*[1] Alongside E. P. Thompson, whose rehabilitation of the crowd from its long-standing Burkean dismissal occasions this chapter, Tilly is one of our most eminent and prolific writers on eighteenth-century popular dissent.[2] That aside, the allure of seeing "theory" as advertised is almost irresistible here. After years of disruption, "theory" is alas firmly bracketed by the return of a prodigal discipline, "hard history," which promises to endow "human agency" with an erstwhile pre-theoretical vigor. This alone makes *Popular Conten-tion* an attractive bargain today.

In the wake of "cultural studies," which it ought be said ranges from the "dustiest" of textual preoccupation to the "freshest" examples of transgressive ingenuity, a book that promises to amend current schol-arly practice, while at the same time to secure "the popular" in history, is a doubly urgent read.[3] But on a closer look, this double urgency bespeaks a curious slippage of terms. "The popular" as "human agency" is quietly succeeded by a wary, but effectively recuperative, sideward glance at the apparent overpopularity of "theory." What makes this pitch successful is how it conjoins the "vocation" of writing in a preferred adamantine, "hard histor[ical]" form—certified by the recital of an object's pure evidentiary status—with "popular contention," now freed from the immoderate influence of wayward "theoretical" prose. Again, it is an irresistible sale. But insofar as "the popular" and writing are mutually implicated historical problems, as indeed they are, relent-lessly, my argument by contrast is that writing history is even "harder" than the market allows. Theorists know that this is true, especially when it comes to the market for books.

My general concern here might rightly be described as partial to the continued achievement of theory, despite the sort of post-theoretical retreat that seems increasingly to constitute the current moment.[4] In what follows, I want to approach but finally move through an episode of what Paul de Man would have called the "resistance to theory," an episode which is of some significance to the apparent factual apostasy of "cultural studies."[5] What I have in mind is more precisely located in the related tradition of Western Marxism in the period since, I will argue, its "cultural" turn *from* "theory" sometime in the 1960s.[6] Be it more commonly debated as determinism over agency, economy over experience, base over superstructure, or—in the Cold War register E.P. Thompson used to explore these well-worked combinations—the Soviet march into Budapest and the rise of the British New Left, my interest in "the resistance to theory" is narrow and specific, if still not altogether new.[7]

Of concern here in particular is Thompson's long indictment, in *The Poverty of Theory*, of Louis Althusser. Part measured critique, part heated philippic, *The Poverty of Theory* has since its publication in 1978 acquired due response from divergent Marxist quarters, most capably from Perry Anderson.[8] My concern with Thompson's rare descent into theory follows him into what will be a necessarily digressive middle section of this piece. But it is a digression curtailed, I hope, by the more urgent problem addressed on either side, that is: the relation between the masses and the production of knowledge—specifically, eighteenth-century writing.

The first section of this chapter thus proceeds with a critical assessment of Thompson's work on the eighteenth-century English crowd, meaning those essays written as companion documents to the formidable undertaking of *The Making of the English Working Class*.[9] My aim at the onset is to resolve how this self-proclaimed and widely influential scholar of "culture," whose work is steadfastly optimistic about the prospects of "human agency," identifies the masses in history. Essential to this task is to examine the formative notion of the crowd's "moral economy" as allegedly resistant to the indomitable assent of capitalist market relations. These market relations are famously codified by Adam Smith in *The Wealth of Nations*.

Curiously, though, in the tentative evocations of Smith in Thompson's "moral economy" essays and in the slightly more substantive but still agnostic way Smith appears in later defenses of the argument, Thompson limits his discussion of Smith to the corn trade: book four, chapter five, of *The Wealth of Nations*. That Thompson forgoes sustained critical discussion of Smith's lifelong preoccupation with morality and the "sympathetic spectator" is an infelicitous elision, especially given his interest in the "cultural" or subjective dimensions of the masses.[10] A relative silence on Adam Smith's philosophical writings is perhaps not surprising, since Thompson's particular brand of "cultural studies" was no less prone to sacrifice agency on the altar of structure (or text) than to cross comfortably into overly speculative, lest it be other-than-factual, terrain.[11] Yet it is Thompson's reluctance to extend materialist inquiry to certain tenets of Enlightenment epistemological habit that, under the pressure of 1960s Continental Marxism, would burst forth as polemic in *The Poverty of Theory*.

Thompson's occasional longing to bulwark experience and agency from the exigencies both of the market and—necessarily within markets—knowledge production betrays an occulted mutuality with the very history he attempts to describe: for Smith, moral experience and "the advance of knowledge" were commensurate in their specific relation to the accumulation of wealth. The moral experience *of* classical political economy as found in his *Theory of Moral Sentiments* and, some years later, *The Wealth of Nations* was prefigured in the late 1740s (twenty years before *The Wealth of Nations*) in his *Lectures on Rhetoric and Belles Lettres* and, his first published piece, *The Principles Which Lead and Direct Philosophical Inquiries*.[12] For Smith, the voluntarism implicit in the current use of the term "human agency," the production and reproduction of "impartial" (his term) knowledge, and *laissez-faire* economics were mutually conditional Enlightenment feats.

Thus from an examination of Thompson's "moral economy" thesis, section one of this chapter moves on to show how an unexamined Smithian legacy haunts Thompson's notion of the crowd, and eventually compels the haphazard, but somehow also befitting, collision with Althusser that is addressed in section two.

The third and final section of this essay returns to the topic of the eighteenth-century crowd, here with regard to *The Making of the English Working Class*. The connection between Thompson's early-eighteenth-century food rioters and what, by a domesticated name, Thompson described as the more enlightened crowd of the 1790s, is of particular interest. This domesticated name belongs to men like Francis Place, one-time chairman of the London Corresponding Society and Thompson's self-proclaimed political forebear: in the eighteenth century the crowd becomes a "people."[13] The vexed effect of Methodist earnestness, and the less complicated influence of reading societies and voluntary informational associations that inspire Jürgen Habermas's notion of the public sphere[14] are of particular relevance to the crowd's "transitional" moment as described in *The Making of the English Working Class*. The sacking of Joseph Priestly's Birmingham library in 1791 by Church-and-King mobs is taken as an example, in Thompson's terms, of the 1790s transformation of the "mob," and its violence, into the "people's" faith in moral consensus. That the proliferation of writing mediated this heroic transformation is key.

Thus I turn in the conclusion of this chapter to Priestly's subsequent journal descriptions of the Church-and-King riots that destroyed his library. These descriptions are rich for detailing the presence of the masses as the reluctant object of eighteenth-century writing. For Priestly, the "mob" is writing's immanent cause: the hostile inversion of his own self-recovery through the careful preservation of words; and the occasion by which writing itself recovers from the flames of "riot" in order to produce a more sociable order of thought. The predilection to seek redress by riot is transformed in the eighteenth century by the formation of a "people," now "keepers of the peace." To echo Priestly or Place (or Smith) is no less to hear Thompson: once prone to riot, the "people have an object." My account of eighteenth-century writing as object-finding thus prescribed is evidence less of the Enlightened evolution of the masses in history than of the masses' continued historical burden.

Masses, Morality and Markets

> If by some extraordinary misfortune you are fallen into poverty
> . . . you may generally depend upon the sincerest sympathy of
> your friends.
>
> —Adam Smith

> The market was a place where the people, because they were
> numerous, felt for a moment they were strong.
>
> —E. P. Thompson

It would of course be ungenerous to conclude from the second of the
above two epigrams that, in his "moral economy" thesis, Thompson
evinces an easy celebration of the market. To the contrary. In its
capacity to resist the encroaching advance of the new political economy, Thompson suggests that the eighteenth-century bread riot harks
back to an earlier Tudor notion of traditional rights and consensus
over the price of grain. In opposition to middlemen, samplers, and
forestallers, "grievances operated within popular consensus as to what
were legitimate and illegitimate practices in marketing, milling, and
baking. . . . This constitutes the moral economy of the poor."[15] Thompson's numerous examples of price setting by direct crowd action
throughout the first decades of the eighteenth century would seem
unimpeachable on this count. In the 1740s, and in riots ensuing from
the grain dearths of 1756 and 1766, the crowd is seen to select
deliberate targets, bypassing bakers and pursuing millers and merchants as more appropriate objects of redress.

Moreover, the "moral economy" of the crowd "derived its sense of
legitimation from the paternalist model" ("ME," 208), and the "com-
passionate traditionalism" of the seated country gentleman ("ME,"
211). This suggests a contradiction between Smith's "sincerest sympathy" in the first epigram, and the subjective dimensions of popular
struggle as presented by Thompson's "people" in the second. My
suggestion is that in the "moral economy" essay, the crowd tends
toward a kind of macro-subject. Riot is situated by an underinterrogated
client/gentry "reciprocity" that works at artificial distance from market
imperatives so that experience, "compassion," "mutuality," and "sympathy" (Thompson's terms) underwrite "moral" transgressions of the
market.[16] In question here is by no means the historically inherent
presence of riot within capitalism. Rather, it seems entirely appropriate,
especially given the troubled desire for "human agency" that hovers

over claims for and against "cultural studies," to better specify the "moral economy's" essential terms.

For Thompson, "in the eighteenth century the market remained a social as well as an economic nexus" ("ME," 256). And similarly, from a later essay, "Patricians and Plebes": "they [the pre-industrial workers] favored paternal social control because they appeared simultaneously as economic and social relations, as relations between persons, not as payments for services."[17] At stake in this momentary historical alignment, that is, before "relations between persons" were displaced by "economic rationalization" ("PP," 39), is the inclination in the "moral economy" argument to grant subjectivity allowances that appear to slip too easily beyond its relationship to market forces. The assessment of paternalist good conscience and the client/gentry bond as a fleeting alliance against classical political economy begins to weaken here.

What are the tenets of "morality" as Thompson presents them? We know that there is more at stake in this term than the raw data of the riots themselves. Rather, "moral economy impinged very generally upon eighteenth-century government and thought, and did not only intrude at times of disturbance" ("ME," 189). Indeed, riot itself is eventually sublimated in the "moral economy" argument to "thought," that is, to the consensual dimensions of the plebe/patrician social contract.[18] The "moral economy" gained its benefits in the early part of the eighteenth century "less in riot [than] by threat," "the anxiety of the authorities," "the anticipation of riot" ("ME," 242). "There is a sense in which rulers and the crowd needed each other, watched each other, performed theater and counter theater to each other's auditorium. . . . This is a more active and reciprocal relationship than the one normally brought to mind under the formula 'paternalism and deference'" ("PP," 57).

The efficacy of riot appears here as an intersubjective (precapitalist) experiential imperative, a "consenting alliance" between gentry and client whose "moral" capacity precedes the forces of the market so as to transgress them: the plebe/paternalist relationship, Thompson suggests, "appeals to a moral norm—what ought to be men's reciprocal duties" ("PP," 203). But "morality" as such, as Thompson later begrudgingly conceded, is a good deal closer to the mandates of classical political economy than his contextualization of food riots as a matter of social conscience and mutual "watching" would allow. To say so is not to begin an "academic language game" ("MER," 349), a charge Thompson would make against his critics (though this oversight will return precisely as a question of knowledge). Rather, a closer look at morality in its proximate historical relation to early modern capitalism reveals an unacknowledged debt to the liberal moral philosophy of the eighteenth-century Scottish Enlightenment.[19] This legacy (as we shall see more clearly in the next two sections) will inform Thompson's historical methodology, as it did his formative admiration for the middling sorts who comprised the 1790s tradition of Jacobin intellectual dissent.

For Thompson, Adam Smith's "victory" in the corn trade debates between 1767 and 1772, the year which saw the capitalist repeal of anti-forestalling legislation, is presented in "the moral economy" argument as "a direct negative to the disintegrating Tudor policies" ("ME," 203). Reminded by his Cambridge antagonists[20] of the market's explicit moral imperatives insofar as Smith—a "civic moralist"[21]—would have them, Thompson offered that "the 'morality' of Adam Smith was never the matter at issue" ("MER," 270). He describes his own comments on Smith as in fact "deferential, mild, and agnostic" ("MER," 277). This is an unsatisfactory response given the "general rules of morality" and "sympathetic" observation which Smith saw as central to civil society in its commercial form.

The nature of reciprocity within Smith's capitalist socius, it must be said, begins to blur the "moral" versus "market" antinomy that is foundational to Thompson's early-eighteenth-century crowd. Taking from Hutcheson and Hume and foreshadowing Bentham, Smith's ideal of moral "sympathy" as described in *The Theory of Moral Sentiments*, and nearly twenty years later in *The Wealth of Nations*, is important here. For Smith too, a dynamic of mutual watching produces an intersubjective zone of reciprocity. The inequities experienced by the sufferer strike an experiential, or what Smith calls an "imagined," chord of mutuality in the sufferer's sympathetic witness. "For every rich man, there must be at least five hundred poor, and the affluence of the few supposes the indigence of the many," Smith would write in *The Wealth of Nations*.[22] But the inherent inequities of wealth were for Smith already resolved socially, in the arena of civil society where—according to Smith's Lockean rule[23]—one also finds "the security of property . . . [and] the defense of the rich against the poor" (*WN*, 181). The boundaries of morality for Smith are thus contained within capitalist governability. As is evident in book two, chapter three of *The Wealth of Nations*, which echoes his blueprint of "moral sentiment" in the earlier treatise of 1759, "partial" behavior on either side of class division is reduced to the supra-materialist realm of character, conduct, and mutual respect.[24]

Thus conflict writ as "moral" restraint is a historically necessary condition for the advance of markets, not inimical to them. For Smith, economic contradictions, rather than potentially confronted by a pre- or anti-capitalist moral exchange "between persons" as in Thompson's paternalism, are resolved in precisely that (subjective) arena in the guise of "moral sympathy."[25] In a society necessarily unequal, the capitalist spectator finds experiential "correspondence" within civil society as "fellow feeling" (*TMS*, 10). And this is insufficiently distinguishable from Thompson's allegedly precapitalist gentleman/client relation. Far from standing outside and thereby in opposition to capitalism, sympathetic experience and (unequal) moral reciprocity are seen as effects surreptitiously congenial to the early modern market.

We have not in my account of sympathetic moral experience traveled far from our introductory concern of "human agency" in its alleged transformative, prediscursive, or anti-theoretical capacity. Indeed, underneath current debates over the textual proclivities of "cultural studies" and the hard questions theory asks of history is the tacit endorsement of subjectivity attending Thompson's crowd. Moreover, as shall be seen in further discussion of Smith, the shadowy presence of moral experience is claimed at its microcosmic level through an "advance of knowledge" that runs from the eighteenth century, through Thompson, precisely to the issues of "cultural studies" with which we are struggling today.

Adam Smith's theory of moral sympathy is more complex than it appears on first encounter. "We suppose ourselves the spectators of our own behavior," he writes, "and endeavor to imagine what effect it would, in this light, produce upon us. This is the only looking-glass by which we can, in some measure, with the eyes of other people, scrutinize the propriety of our own conduct" (*TMS*, 16). The primary feature of the moral "looking-glass" is that it is circular: "the creation of an imaginative self-projection into an outsider whose standards and responses we reconstruct by sympathy."[26] In Smith's formula, the expression of outward sympathetic feeling is only the initial step in an infinite spectatorial chain. The sympathizing subject not only corresponds his own experience of pleasure or of suffering with the object of his gaze, but internalizes this correspondence such that the first subject/object relation is reproduced as the secondary "propriety" of voluntary self-restraint.[27] "A prison is certainly more useful to society than a palace" (*TMS*, 30), Smith would remark in anticipation of Bentham's panopticon.

But the disciplinary procedures spelled out by Foucault are in

Smith's much earlier example rather more efficient, softer in appearance but no less material in effect than the bricks and mortar of early modern punishment.[28] For Smith, the "propriety" implicit in his circular moral gaze is at work by epistemological necessity, and indeed, at the level of language itself. Unlike the spectator of Hutcheson and Hume, both of whom gave prominence in their ethical theories to spectatorial experience, Smith's morality is found in the voluntary (read "social" or "cultural") domain of "impartial" communicative exchange. "Society and conversation . . . are the most powerful remedies for restoring the mind to . . . that equal and happy temper, which is so necessary to self-satisfaction" (*TMS*, 23).

A communicative ethic such as the one Smith prescribes, presumed concurrent to the market at its normative core, operates somewhat differently from Habermas's otherwise similar formulation of the Enlightenment "public sphere."[29] Like Habermas's public sphere, Smith's spectator may be traced to the polite conversation of imaginatively presumed equals characteristic of the early-eighteenth-century coffee house. Indeed, Smith's moral "spectator" can be traced directly to Joseph Addison's journal of that very name.[30] But in the place of Habermas's disinterested rational–critical debate, Smith offers room for the more affective and potentially conflict-ridden dimensions of feeling summed up in the term "rational admiration."[31] This term allows for the redoubled correspondence, as we have seen in moral sympathy, first between the spectator and his object, and then in the objectification of the looking-subject as, in turn, appropriate in the eyes of an "impartial" (if also absent) third-party witness. But the term "rational admiration" also, perhaps in a more perfidious fashion, embraces—indeed, would seem to require—the occasional violence of "unnatural objects" so as to extend its seamless observational advance.

In his 1746 essay *The Principles which Lead and Direct Philosophical Inquiries*, Smith sums up "the advance of knowledge" as follows: "Wonder, Surprise, and Admiration, are words which, though often confounded, denote in our language, sentiments that are indeed allied. . . . What is new and singular, excites that sentiment which in strict propriety, is called Wonder; what is unexpected, Surprise; and what is great or beautiful, Admiration."[32] The singular object "stands alone in [the spectator's] imagination as if it were detached from all the other species of that genus to which it belongs" (*EPS*, 40). To "get rid of that Wonder," Smith continues, requires the "connecting principles" of philosophy as an "art which addresses itself to the imagination" (*EPS*, 46).

Smith's definition of philosophy, which is coterminous with the "imitative arts" associated with *belles-lettres* (and later "literature"), is essentially a narratological—or one is tempted in the 1740s to say, novelistic[33]—foray into the self-evident sequencing of phenomena within their proper "species and genera" (*EPS*, 40). In moving from "surprise" to "admiration," the goal of knowledge is to seek in "the class[ification] of things" (*EPS*, 39) the same continuity of objects that is fundamental to moral sympathy. From the "momentary loss of reason" experienced when an object is "dissimilar," "unexpected," "strange," "disjointed," or for that matter, "new," agitation is anesthetized within a "natural order of succession." "Philosophy," as Smith defines it, "by representing the invisible chains which bind together all these disjointed objects, endeavors to introduce order" (*EPS*, 37). This order takes place by "the endeavor to arrange and methodize all [the mind's] ideas" (*EPS*, 37). By thus putting "extraordinary and uncommon objects" into "proper classes and assortments" philosophy redresses the imagination such that it "may fill up the gap, [and] like a bridge, may . . . unite those seemingly distant objects, [so] as to render the passage of thought betwixt them smooth" (*EPS*, 42). For Smith, the "mind takes pleasure," and is therefore "relaxed," "in observing the resemblances that are discoverable between different objects" (*EPS*, 36).

In another early essay, *The First Formations of Language*, Smith refers to the mind's innate generic sensibility as a process of assorting "the great multitudes of objects," a process central to language itself (*LRBL*, 205). For Smith it is the presence of "multitudes" within the association of words that hurries the mind toward object correspondence at the experiential level.[34] The "fellow feeling" between sufferers (below) and witnesses (above), an antagonistic class divide, is thus previously played out in a pre-political, horizontal continuity between objects and language in thought. Multiplicity ("surprise" and "wonder") is immanent to meaningful discourse under capitalism, and always threatens to upset its otherwise natural experiential harmonies ("rational admiration"). But again, interruption within Smith's commercial socius is effectively recuperated—before it ever fully speaks—in the production of knowledge itself, and at the semiological level in the correspondence of words to things. Indeed, the more potentially violent the "uncommon object," the more satisfying its eventual adequation in "metaphysical" exchange (*EPS*, 35).

Thus for Smith, morality is method, subjectivity a careful social grammar. The definition of sympathetic moral spectatorship as "emotions . . . just and proper, and suitable to their objects" (*TMS*, 16) finds its premise according to Smith in the very habits of thought. The social arrangement of the market, one might say, is granted through a philosophico-hermeneutic technique which is itself a matter of associational mandate: "smoothing out" otherwise "unexpected," "violent" or "convulsive" objects by the "habit of the imagination" to arrange each disruption according to its moral "propriety" (*EPS*, 41). It is falsely assumed by the terms "natural," "impartial," "experiential," or "moral," that Enlightenment "habits of imagination" can be cordoned off from, so as to "smooth out," the more pressing (if as yet half-spoken) contradictions that comprise the Enlightenment project as a whole. In my account of Thompson and Smith, to seek from those contradictions a moral foundation for knowledge would be a task, wittingly or not, that is circumscribed within the field each attempts to describe. The "moral economy" of the English crowd is made manifest, not opposed to the accumulation of wealth as Thompson would have it, but by reading back upon mass action a rationale that reproduces a philosophical legacy formed at the moment of mass domestication.

Our introductory conflict stated as the "text" and "agency" debate within "cultural studies" thus rears its troubled head again; but, in discussion of Thompson and Smith, less as a matter of recent "theoretical" excess against Enlightenment objectivity than as an anti-theoretical confusion about the Enlightenment's ongoing effect. The securing of objects of knowledge in experience, like the freedom "hard history" promises to give "agency" at some post-theoretical (or appropriately post-"popular") date, is by now familiar terrain. But perhaps this terrain is even more familiar than that. Perhaps the relationship between "theory" and its current discontents is best understood as the latest example of thought in a centuries-old series of "smooth" repetitions.

Resistance to Theory, Again

> The best method of explaining and illustrating the various powers of the human mind, the most useful part of metaphysics, arises from an examination of the several ways of communicating our thoughts by speech, and from an attention to the principles of those literary compositions which contribute to the persuasion of entertainment.
>
> —Adam Smith

> ... to identify the lacunae in the fullness of [political economy's] discourse, the blanks of the crowded text, we need something quite different from an acute or attentive gaze.
>
> —Louis Althusser

The preceding section of this essay began with an attempt to connect Thompson's "moral economy" with Smith's notion of "moral sympathy." Here an unsustainable opposition in Thompson's work on the eighteenth-century crowd is revealed. This opposition was alleged to exist between a precapitalist, moral "reciprocity"—as Thompson put it: "between persons"—and the allegedly antagonistic advent of market relations. On Smith's account, however, an intersubjective moral "looking-glass" close to Thompson's paternalism occurs within the very moment of—not prior to—capitalism. The growth of commercial society as documented by Smith required "moral experience" and "human agency" at every turn.

What Althusser rejects above as an "attentive gaze" retains for Smith and Thompson a "morality" embedded in the protocols of social interaction. Moreover, for Smith, "moral" experience is fundamental to the very activity of thought. The "violence" of "uncommon objects" is heard at its appropriate "metaphysical" level only to be calmed in the anodyne reaches of sympathetic self-reflection. In thus coupling a liberal philosophical ethic with the accumulation of wealth, Smith sought two far-reaching objectives: first, that commensurate human experience be placed over capitalist inequality in the social realm ("moral sympathy"); and, second, that this should happen as a matter of epistemological reflex ("rational admiration"). The "habit" of inquiry, according to Smith, seeks continuity between otherwise "violent" or "uncommon objects" in order to "fill in the gaps." This occurs above all by the proper classification of "uncommon objects" within the experiential harmonies of "a people." In Smith's philosophy, a seamless combination between identity, collectivity, and understanding has built within it a silent guarantee, a frail, potent mechanism—and one I want to follow Althusser in associating with the materiality of writing—which is designed to ensure that the moral gaze is certain and eternal.

In the second part of this chapter I want to make a "theoretical" interruption to examine the legacy of moral spectatorship in a more recent philosophical ruse. My charge in examining Thompson's antitheoretical, at times emotive defense of "experience," "reason," and their essential continuity, is that in such a defense Smith's legacy itself struggles to continue.

Motivating Althusser's call thirty-odd years ago for the delimiting features of "theory" is the notion, put simply, that objective facts emerge and circulate as social and historical forces. In relation to these forces, consciousness and experience play a secondary role. This is by now a boilerplate Marxist proposition.[35] But here Althusser takes up the more difficult issue posed by Sartre of "a plurality of epicenters of action."[36] History through a Sartrean template contains no unidirectional force conversing with human consciousness—especially consciousness writ as "moral experience"—which somehow remains anterior to the historical forces that consciousness may one day seek to describe. For Althusser, in contradistinction to Smith and, as we shall see, Thompson, a convenient shorthand would be to say that the objects of materialist history retain the status of a "multitude." They are, to repeat a well-known term, "overdetermined" by a mass of incommensurable—but nonetheless real—influences and meanings. The totality of this complex arrangement is never wholly available to description because there is no place for writing history that is wholly anterior to the historical forces that knowledge seeks to measure. Thus Althusser's enigmatic phrase: while the economy is determinate in the last instance, that instance never comes.[37] The status of this generative absence, to which I will return at the end of this section, remains one of the most difficult, and perhaps richest, contributions of the Althusserian legacy.

But as Thompson presents it, the only conceivable consequence of a formulation of history as both "overdetermined" and (at least, in part) internal to capitalist forces of production is to rephrase the slogan with which this chapter began: "theory" presents "a structuralism of stasis."[38] It is an escape from this stasis—recalling our introduction—that the more reliably objective way of thinking called "hard history" presumes to guarantee. Purportedly, Althusser's critique of empiricism, "that slender and rotten epistemological pillar" (*POT*, 2), as Thompson puts it with characteristic hyperbole, "destroys every space for the initiative or creativity of the mass of the people—a domination from which only the Enlightened minority of intellectuals can struggle free" (*POT*, 185). Thus it is that Althusser "confuses empirical dialogue with empiricism" (*POT*, 5); and thus it is that this confusion over "empirical dialogue" betrays a "contempt of the people [and of] an old and arduous rational tradition" (*POT*, 25).

The term "empirical dialogue" is essential in Thompson's corrective account of history as the untroubled persistence of the "people's" "rational tradition." Indeed, the way "dialogue" is used throughout *The Poverty of Theory* (pages 9, 37, 39, 40, 43, 50, etc.) allows Thompson to set up a familiar eighteenth-century arrangement—*pace* the same charge against Althusser—between "the people," "intellectuals," and a "freedom" that right reason somehow always guarantees. Thompson suggests that the historian proceed according to "disciplined moral critique" (*POT*, 176). As such, history finds its eighteenth-century correlate in "human experience," which is handled by "the people" in the pre-political realm of "consciousness and . . . culture" (*POT*, 164). "Change takes place," Thompson writes, "within social being, which gives rise to changed *experience*: and this experience is *determining* in the sense that it exerts pressures upon social consciousness" (emphasis in the original) (*POT*, 9). The world changes experience, which in turn changes the world. Althusser's "freak[ish]" (*POT*, 3) offense in attempting to break this circle, it is therefore said, is to rule out "the dialogue between social being and social consciousness" (*POT*, 9). This works to "blackguard out of the club of thought . . . [the] handling of experience within . . . culture" (*POT*, 164). The "cultural studies" debate over agency thus ought to be located here, in a second-order circularity: not in a recent excess of "cultural theory" which "empirical dialogue" eventually contains, but in a "cultural" turn *from* "theory" played out more than thirty years ago in the rise of the British New Left, and, indeed, played out two centuries more before that in the late eighteenth century.[39]

In an account of knowledge production as a "moral" imperative where experience is determinate, collective agency is reduced to the unfettered collation of objects in the inquirer's mind. Between the Marxist terms "social being" and "social consciousness," Thompson inserts an "experiential" or "cultural" zone to which the archivist retains an unmediated pass. But a closer look at this arrangement—again *pace* the charge against Althusser—reveals how the troubled term "culture" prohibits an account of the relation between "experience" and an "openness [to] . . . knowledge" as itself an historically specific relation. What the term "culture" ensures in this guise is an act not of dialogue however one may configure it, but again of a quiet circularity. "Empirical dialogue" in the "cultural" zone functions the same for effective historical agents as it does for the right-thinking historian: the "rational evidence . . . adduced by men and women" in history (*POT*, 175) mimics the historian's "dialogue . . . between thought and its objective materials" (*POT*, 39). Indeed, Thompson presents a historical method that betrays a kind of mirroring of mirroring. The historian's mandate to maintain "the openness with which one must approach all knowledge" (*POT*, 168)—an initial mirroring—is mirrored in a second sense by the way "the people" are themselves supposed to have risen to self-consciousness in their own historical circumstance. The apparent slippage with which we began, between historical method and historical object, remains one of the most troubling features of *The Poverty of*

Theory. Bearing in mind Smith's "moral looking glass," the spontaneous and circular nature of Thompson's historical object ("the people") is a reduplication not only of his own historical method but also, in the end, of the limits of eighteenth-century philosophy in its ability to reduplicate the mirroring process itself.

But the desire to seek an untroubled alliance between experience and object is itself no more actively "mirrored" than in Thompson's evocation of history as the "imperial . . . unitary discipline" (*POT*, 70). Recall that Smith's account of philosophical inquiry is above all a socially monitored classificatory procedure. When anomalous, "violent," or "uncommon" objects create in the mind an agitated state ("surprise"), philosophy reclassifies "the multitude" into their "proper [read: already known] classes and assortments" (*EPS*, 42). By doing so philosophy "fills in the gaps," and the mind may rest secured in the consensus of "rational admiration." Smith's philosophical sequence of excess, recovery, and succession is identical in *The Poverty of Theory* with Thompson's stop-gap evocation of the "unitary discipline of history" (*POT*, 70).[40] Insofar as "theory," in Thompson's agitated response, sets loose "the determinate properties of the object, then no discipline remains" (*POT*, 41). In order to avoid the setting loose of the object, Thompson insists that "the unitary discipline [of history must] always keep watch over the isolating premises of other disciplines" (*POT*, 70). "History," he immodestly continues, ". . . must be put back on her throne as the Queen of the Humanities" (*POT*, 70).

It is the imperial disposition of historical method to keep objects within their classificatory restrictions, evoking Smith, in order to "fill in the gaps." The anti-theoretical ire so renowned in *The Poverty of Theory* might be seen in this light as a foiled philosophical succession. An "arduous [and decidedly British] rational tradition," to again evoke Thompson against Althusser, is derailed in the 1960s by a (continental) "surprise." That this "surprise" was in turn left unrecovered as "rational admiration" would appear to break the Enlightenment rule that knowledge reduplicates itself.[41] The "discipline of moral critique" in this sense would seem to function to preserve the mandates of "*the* discipline," a classificatory procedure that is itself the "mirrored" extension of an earlier philosophical task. Thus the "stasis" Thompson pins on Althusser is rather more evident in his own continuation of eighteenth-century protocols of thought. The bait-and-switch attendant to our current debates over "cultural studies" thus emerges once again: popular dissent is subsumed by the veiled reproduction of a particular order of writing.

What else is Althusser's first essay in *Reading Capital* but the provisional invitation precisely to challenge this bait-and-switch? In "From 'Capital' to Marx's Philosophy," Marx's own reading of Smith (as Althusser's rereading of Marx) is presented as an interrogation of "the mirror myth of immediate vision and reading."[42] In defiance of Smith's various subjective correspondences, Althusser recalls Spinoza to posit "a theory of the opacity of the immediate" (*RC*, 16). This evocation of "theory" seeks a "protocol of reading [for] what classical economy does not see," namely the generative absence in Smith's *The Wealth of Nations* which Marx called "labor power" (*RC*, 23). On the basis of this absence, then, the first of Smith's philosophical goals is diminished: capitalist contradiction is no longer resolved in the "social" or "cultural" field of "imagined" reciprocity, but is brought to bear within knowledge in its materialist potential for subjective and social interruption. Althusser defines a "fact" as: "a mutation in the existing structural relations" (*RC*, 102). That he refuses to seat historical knowledge too far outside these "existing structural relations," as we have seen with Thompson's evocation of the term "culture," marks the challenge to Smith's second philosophical accomplishment: to move knowledge from the realm of experience to a concern with "the conditions of its production" (*RC* 25). The relentless identification by "theory" of precisely the objects that experience forbids hinders the empirical reflex by which Smith sought his silent, social guarantees.

So I return here, by way of transition to the final segment of the essay, to the epigram on silence with which this section began: "to identify . . . the blanks" in political economy's "crowded text" is to emphasize once again the (necessarily) unasked questions of a materialist history of eighteenth-century thought. In such an account, the masses would be immanent to the history of writing, not the transparent exterior to which our reading so blithely refers.

Writing Down a Riot

A sort of Socratic spirit will necessarily grow up, whenever large bodies of men assemble. . . . Though it may generate some vices, [it] is favorable to the diffusion of knowledge, and ultimately promotive of human liberty.

—John Thelwall

Knowledge remains suspended and undecided to action, to the extent that a responsible decision as such will never be measured by any form of knowledge.

—Jacques Derrida

In the limited space remaining, I want to glimpse the nettlesome presence of the eighteenth-century crowd as historically inherent to Thelwall's call for efforts to secure a general "diffusion of knowledge." The "liberty" of the eighteenth-century masses and the presumptions of eighteenth-century writing are mutually conditional historical problems. A full examination of this mutuality, which one might be allowed to say is apparent within current historical scholarship precisely by its absence, is something I should like to pursue at greater length another time. For now, let me close by reinforcing a central point: Thompson's "experiential" or "cultural" turn from "theory"—which marked the rise of the British New Left in the 1960s and which extends today to the troubled status of "cultural studies"—is effectively approached as a continued eighteenth-century arrangement.

This arrangement comprises the easy adequation Derrida wants to trouble between "responsibility," "knowledge," and collective "action," assumptions that I have traced from Thompson and Smith on the issue of "moral experience," to the former's inevitably embattled encounter with "theory." The abridged discussion below of Thompson's *The Making of the English Working Class* revisits the eighteenth-century crowd in the wake of the capitalist repeal of anti-forestalling legislation in 1772. In the extra-parliamentary activities of the 1790s Jacobin intellectual Dissenter and given the influence of Methodism on the working class, a by now familiar transposition between writing and collective agency emerges.[43] Even as he otherwise carefully susses out the contradictions of industrial England, Thompson takes the alliance between Thelwall's general "diffusion of knowledge" and mass political action at face value. This arrangement informs not only his own inescapable collision with Althusser, but a legacy of anti-"theoretical" thought whose coordinates precede us by some two hundred years.

Thompson's design in *The Making of the English Working Class* is to trace a fundamental shift in authority relations after the 1760s, from monarchical absolutism and client/gentry relations, to the rise of a morally informed public sphere which originated in the dissenting middle class (*MEWC*, 74).[44] Given on the one side new forms of industrial organization, and on the other an ambivalent Jacobin sympathy for the French Revolution within the middling sorts, Thompson seeks a " 'natural' alliance between an impatient radically minded industrial bourgeoisie and a formative proletariat" (*MEWC*, 177). The persecution of Jacobin sympathies as evident in Pitt's 1795 Test and Corporation Acts; the subsequent rounding up of the London Corresponding Society in 1798; and the anti-Jacobin nationalism emergent amongst the artisans and industrial laborers, rendered the broadly conceived revolutionary alliance against the aristocracy "broken as soon as it was formed" (*MEWC*, 178).

That this alliance would have required the integrity of propertied independence in its newer industrial form is left underexamined by Thompson in order to qualify the loss. What survives the failed revolutionary moment in the late eighteenth century becomes revolution's latest (and its only) hope. This is the same hope so vehemently presented in *The Poverty of Theory*: a transformation of the plebeian "mob" brought forth unobstructed by knowledge, by the will of that "arduous and rational tradition" against which is positioned the specter of "theory." In "the last, and greatest, period of popular agitation" (*MEWC*, 145) that Thompson sets out to recover, it is "not Pitt, but John Thelwall who [has] the last word" (*MEWC*, 185). This "last word," to recall with Thompson the legacy of Thomas Paine, is to put "faith in the free operation of opinion in [Paine's term] the 'open society'" (*MEWC*, 101). "Freedom of thought, of speech, . . . of conscience, . . . [and] moral consensus" (*MEWC*, 79) are for Thompson the proper limits within which the "mob" learns to operate as a "people" by the century's end.

In tracing the rise of the "open society" and the rational transformation of the eighteenth-century crowd, Thompson conjoins the emergence of Enlightened critical debate and "freedom of thought" (*MEWC*, 79) with the influence of Methodism among the laboring classes. The classical division between "structure" and "agency" in contemporary "cultural studies" manifests itself here, as elsewhere in his work, in the heroic reclamation of individual experience from power. Thompson challenges the "economistic" Weberian assessment of Puritan work discipline by offering a newly positivized account of transgressive appropriation. "The desolate inner landscape of Utilitarianism" (*MEWC*, 365) is set at a conveniently oppositional distance from the "self-discipline," "independence," and "self-consciousness," within which working-class struggle is prescribed to confine its future practice (*MEWC*, 397, 424).

The sublimation of mass agency to "moral earnestness" (*MEWC*, 739)—given all that the term "morality" denotes in the eighteenth century[45]—emerges here, at the crossroads of political and religious thought where Thompson's own anti-"theoretical" tenets originate: in the sobriety of various "institutes for the promulgation of knowledge amongst working people" (*MEWC*, 170), Thompson proclaims the task of middle-class dissent as being to "rescue the people from the imputation of being a 'mob'" (*MEWC*, 740). So it is with Methodist "morality," which added to plebeian "riot" the assumed complementary ingredient of an "earnestness to the pursuit of information" (*MEWC*, 739). For Thompson, what survives of the eighteenth-century crowd in its transition from a "mob" to "the people" is an order of knowledge, and one moreover increasingly dependent on "political print" (*MEWC*, 719). The eighteenth-century crowd attains its most effective form of agency above all in the guise of a "reading public" (*MEWC*, 719). So thorough is the combined effect of Methodist "earnestness towards information" and "the diffusion of knowledge," that by the first decades of the nineteenth century "the press [is made] the fulcrum of the Radical movement" (*MEWC*, 720).

In the process of the crowd's development from early-eighteenth-century "riot" to the "rescue" of mass political agency by knowledge, the loyalist Church-and-King mobs play for Thompson an essential role. Here Joseph Priestly figures, like Thelwall and Paine, as "the spirit of rational enlightenment" (*MEWC*, 26). The burning of his books by rioters in Birmingham in 1791 thus signifies a particularly important episode, given the crowd's imminent transformation by a print culture of debate. "The Priestly riots," Thompson suggests, "can be seen as a late backward eddy of the transitional mob, before Painite propaganda had started in earnest the formation of a new democratic consciousness" (*MEWC*, 74).

Late-eighteenth-century riot is anomalous in Thompson's more seamless account of rationalist "mob" evolution. This anomaly is allayed by the "transitional" or "backward"-looking function given to the Church-and-King riots. Such a formulation renders the whole history of eighteenth-century mass agency into a comfortable developmental sequence: from "violence" to "reason" having "smoothed out" Adam Smith's dreaded epistemological "gaps." Indeed, recalling Smith, peace in the capitalist socius is sought by the careful correspondence between word and object; between objects within classes and genera; and by extension, between morally correspondent subjects across class divides. Thompson's account of the eighteenth-century crowd in *The Making of the English Working Class* and in subsequent writings on the pre-1760s bread riots, characteristically reproduces the very order of knowledge it attempts to describe. Smith's philosophical mandate that thought proceeds from "violence" and "multiplicity" to "rational admiration" is found as an essential feature of the "mob's" becoming a "people" in Thompson's account. But, more incredibly, this mandate persists in Thompson's own writing: the crowd's historical assent to reason and to

"reading" as a condition of their own political best interest is redupli-
cated in his developmental history of the crowd.

An alternative history would show how Thompson's overly transparent, self-replicating correspondence between writing and collectivity
was itself a specific historical arrangement. This arrangement, as I want
to suggest in the paragraphs remaining, is forged in an exceedingly
complex and troublesome relation to the masses—not the seamless
and more reasonable extension of the crowd-into-knowledge that
Thompson presents.

Indeed by 1792, Joseph Priestly could elicit the protocols of writing
we find in Thompson and Smith as an effective governmental technique against the mobs who had razed his library the year before. In
the moments after Parliament had given the dissenters' case for religious tolerance its third, and most definitive rejection—the Test Act
would not be repealed until 1828—Priestly begins his *Appeal to the
Public*: "To be as candid and as impartial as I can, and the intelligent
reader will easily perceive whether I do or not, I shall divide the work
into two parts, Narrative and Reflections."[46] In the space between
"narrative" and "reflection," Priestly's reader is invited to initiate the
process of objectification and subjective correspondence that ensures
the disinterest and "[im]partiality" that Thompson would place at the
end of the crowd's Enlightened evolution. By writing the legitimacy of
authorial judgment itself into the revovery from riot, Priestly maintains
the innocence of cooperative reflection while eliciting the narrative
"smoothness" posited by Smith.

In a digression on the burning of his books, Priestly writes:

> The destruction of my library did not affect me so much on account of the
> money I had expended on it, as the choice of the books; having had
> particular objects of study, and having collected them with great care. It had
> also been my custom to read almost every book with a pencil in my hand,
> marking the essays that I wished to look back to, and of which I proposed to
> make particular use. . . . I have not only lost the books, but the cherished
> labor and judgment in reading them. . . . [I had lost] letters to friends that I
> had carefully arranged so that I could look back to them . . . as a memorial
> of former friendships. (*AP*, 41)

The sermon that Priestly rushed to compose the morning after the riot
was subtitled "Forgive them, for they know not what they do." By this
he meant, not that the crowd had no knowledge of the consequences
of their actions, but that they lacked a particular order of knowledge,
that they were the emblem of a certain epistemological disorder. This

distinction is secured by the opposition Priestly finds between the homogeneous effects of writing and his recollection shattered by riot. The crowd is situated by Priestly against the orderly organization of his feelings, and the correspondent fraternal reflections Adam Smith would call "rational admiration."

The sacking of Joseph Priestly's library is taken by Thompson as a supremely enabling moment in the 1790s transformation of the "mob" and its violence, to the "people's" faith in moral consensus. That the proliferation of writing mediated this heroic transformation is key. But it is precisely in opposition to riot that the order of writing Thompson seeks to recover—and to sustain in the name of a "people"—becomes possible. For Priestly, as for Thompson, the "mob" is writing's imma-nent cause: on the one hand, the hostile inversion of Enlightened self-recovery through the careful preservation of words; and on the other, the occasion by which writing itself recovers from the flames of "riot" in order to produce a more sociable order of thought. While the object of eighteenth-century writing is the masses, its objective as manifest in contemporary crowd history is to reproduce eighteenth-century proto-cols of thought.

Notes

Thinking for this chapter began in Clifford Siskin's various graduate seminars in Eighteenth-century Studies at SUNY Stony Brook during the early 1990s. I was also aided by attending a summer seminar, "Institutions of the Enlightenment," sponsored by the National Endowment for the Humanities and held at Stanford University in 1996. Thanks to Keith Baker and John Bender for hosting this event. I want to thank Laura Mendelson for comments on an earlier draft of this chapter.

1. Charles Tilly, *Popular Contention in Great Britain, 1758–1834* (Cambridge, MA: Harvard University Press, 1995).

2. Like E.P. Thompson, Charles and Louise Tilly have been placed within a "Marxist humanist" tradition. All three characteristically evoke the term "moral" to challenge what they perceive as the economistic tendencies of classical Marxism. See *Class Conflict and Collective Action*, eds. Charles and Louise Tilly (Beverly Hills: Sage, 1981). To the short list of contemporary crowd historians should be added George Rude, *The Crowd in the French Revolution* (London: Oxford University Press, 1959).

3. For an apt response to the backlash against "cultural studies" and an assessment of the latter's apparent excesses, see Lauren Berlant, "Collegiality, Crisis, and Cultural Studies," *ADE Bulletin* 117 (Fall 1997): 4–9.

4. A piece such as Richard Wilk's "When Theory is Everything, Scholarship Suffers," *Chronicle of Higher Education* (July 9, 1999) is not atypical. A more nuanced and sympath-etic take on the current moment of theory is Jeffrey Williams, "The Post-Theory Generation," *Symploke* 3.1 (1995): 55–76. See also Neil Larson, "Theory After the 'Theorists'," in ed. Peter Herman, *Day Late and a Dollar Short: The Next Generation and the New Academy* (Albany: SUNY Press, 2000).

5. Paul de Man's argument in "Resistance to Theory," *Yale French Studies* 63 (1982),

that theoretical work is measured precisely by the ways in which it inspires "resistance," would seem to bear on the debate over theory's troubled future.

6. For a more detailed account of the legacy of British "cultural studies" and its troubled status in the new corporate university, see my "Cultural Studies by Default," in *Class Issues*, ed. Amitava Kumar (New York: NYU Press, 1998).

7. Thompson placed a great deal of significance on his break with the British Communist Party in 1956, a time which saw a drop in party membership of 21 percent. See Brian Palmer, *The Making of E.P. Thompson: Marxism, Humanism, and History* (Toronto: Hogtown Press, 1981). Note, too, Stuart Hall's statement of "[coming] into Marxism backwards: against the Soviet Tanks in Budapest" as one of the legacies of cultural studies. See Hall, "Cultural Studies and its Theoretical Legacies," in *Cultural Studies*, eds. Lawrence Grossberg *et al.* (New York: Routledge, 1992).

8. See E. P. Thompson, *The Poverty of Theory* (New York: Monthly Review Press, 1978); Perry Anderson, *Arguments within Western Marxism* (London: Verso, 1980). In a 1985 speech, preferring to go no further in the argument—"bored" as he would have it—Thompson called his debate with Anderson "a draw." See Thompson, *Making History* (New York: The New Press, 1994), p. 360.

9. These essays were written when Thompson was awaiting proofs for *The Making of the English Working Class* (New York: Vintage Books, 1966). See "The Moral Economy Reviewed," in Thompson's *Customs in Common* (New York: New Press, 1993).

10. Indeed, Smith was Professor and Chair of Moral Philosophy at Glasgow. He persistently revised his first book, *Theory of Moral Sentiments*, half a dozen times until he died in 1790.

11. Thompson's work on British Romanticism renders "literature" what Terry Eagleton calls "the other of ideology" (141). See Eagleton, "The Poetry of E.P. Thompson," *Literature and History* 5.2 (1979): 139–45.

12. The former text was not widely available until 1963, the latter 1980.

13. Upon breaking with the Communist Party, Thompson, with John Sayville, launched the *New Reasoner*. This journal sought to challenge the "King Street" Marxism of *Modern Quarterly*. In choosing the title *New Reasoner*, Thompson was attempting to connect alternatively with the 1790s libertarian tradition of John Boone. Boone was chairman of the London Corresponding Society in 1808 and had founded his *Reasoner* to "plant the liberty tree" 150 years before the *New Reasoner*. See Palmer, *The Making of E.P. Thompson* (n. 4).

14. Jürgen Habermas, *The Structural Transformation of the Public Sphere* (Cambridge, MA: MIT Press, 1989).

15. "The Moral Economy of the English Crowd in the Eighteenth Century" (1971), reprinted in Thompson, *Customs in Common*, p. 188 (n. 6). Hereafter page references are cited in the text as "ME."

16. Elizabeth Fox Genovese rightly suggests, though with less specificity than I have here, that "both paternalism and liberalism have a moral base . . . [and] were both part of ruling class ideologies." (166). See Fox Genovese, "The Many Faces of Moral Economy," *Past and Present* 58 (February 1973): 161–8.

17. "Patricians and Plebes" (1974), reprinted with additions in *Customs in Common* (n. 6), 38. Hereafter page references cited in text as "PP."

18. Thirty years later Thompson sought to qualify himself from "overly consensual and holistic notions of the term 'cultural',," and likewise was concerned that "consensus . . . may serve to distract attention from social and cultural contradictions" (*Customs in Common*, 6). See "Introduction" in *Customs in Common* (n. 6). Thompson also sought to distance himself from the term "reciprocity" in revisiting the "moral economy argument," suggesting that this term "does not imply equity of burden or obligation" (343). See "The Moral Economy Reviewed," in *Customs in Common* (n. 6). These statements do not change the implications of the present argument in relation to Smith, whose prescription for capitalist morality could contain—indeed was designed precisely to contain—conflict and "correspondence" simultaneously. Page references to "The Moral Economy Reviewed" are hereafter cited in text as "MER."

19. See A.W. Coats's immediate suggestion to this effect in "Contrary Moralities: Plebes, Paternalists and Political Economists," *Past and Present* 54 (February 1972): 130–3.

20. See *Wealth and Virtue: The Shaping of Political Economy in the Scottish Enlightenment*, eds. Istvan Hont and Michael Ignatieff (London: Cambridge University Press, 1983).

21. See "Adam Smith as Civic Moralist," in *Wealth and Virtue* (n. 16). The term is J.G.A. Pocock's. See his "Cambridge Paradigms and Scotch Philosophers" in the same volume.

22. Smith, *The Wealth of Nations*, ed. Lawrence Dickey (Indianapolis: Hackett Publishing, 1993), p. 177. Hereafter pages are cited in the text as *WN*.

23. Indeed, Smith was reprimanded at Oxford for reading Locke, who was banned by the university in favor of Christian rationalism. See Athol Fitzgibbons, *Adam Smith's System of Liberty, Wealth, and Virtue: The Moral and Political Foundations of The Wealth of Nations* (Oxford: Clarendon, 1995).

24. Thus Smith uses the key term "frugality." Recognized by the capitalists' fellow men as "moral," frugality thus checks the unrestrained accumulation of capital. See *WN*, 67 ff. (n. 18). See Smith, *The Theory of Moral Sentiments* (Indianapolis: Liberty Fund Press, 1984). Page references to this book are hereafter cited as *TMS*.

25. See Dickey's essay in *WN* (n. 18), "Economics and Ethics in Smith's Theory of Capital Accumulation," pp. 213 ff.

26. Smith, *Lectures on Rhetoric and Belles Lettres* (Indianapolis: Liberty Fund Press, 1985), p. 10. Hereafter page references are cited as *LRBL*.

27. Getting aright our relation to sympathetic objects in thought, we then "voluntarily submit" and "render ourselves . . . proper objects" (*TMS*, 119).

28. Michel Foucault, *Discipline and Punish* (New York: Vintage, 1979).

29. Habermas, *Structural Transformation* (n. 10).

30. After the Act of Union with Scotland in 1707, Edinburgh saw a proliferation of spectatorial clubs and societies. See Pocock, "Cambridge Paradigms," p. 242 (n. 17). Before assuming his post in Glasgow in 1752, Smith was for four years a lecturer in rhetoric and belles lettres at Edinburgh. Direct references to Addison are found in several places in *TMS* as well.

31. *LRBL*, p. 61. Hereafter cited in text.

32. Smith, *The Principles which Lead and Direct Philosophical Inquiries*, in *Essays on Philosophical Subjects* (Indianapolis: Liberty Fund Press, 1982), p. 33. *The Principles* was published posthumously in 1795. Page references are cited hereafter as *EPS*.

33. In his few comments on the history of the novel, Smith cites Romance as an unnatural object in relation to which Richardson's formal realism creates the more stable standard. On the process of excess and recovery in the history of the novel, see Clifford Siskin, *The Work of Writing: Disciplinarity, Professionalism, and the Engendering of Literature in Britain 1700–1830* (Baltimore: Johns Hopkins University Press, 1997). I have written of this process as "the novelization of the multitudes" in "Towards a 'Materialist' Rhetoric: Contingency, Constraint, and the Eighteenth-Century Crowd," in *The Role of Rhetoric in an Anti-foundationalist World: Language, Culture, Pedagogy*, eds. Michael Bernard-Donalds and Richard Glejzer (New Haven: Yale University Press, 1998).

34. In this Smith is similar to his mentor, Henry Home, Lord Kames. For British influence on Smith's theory of interpretation, see Joel C. Weinsheimer, *Eighteenth-century Hermeneutics: Philosophy of Interpretation in England from Locke to Burke* (New Haven: Yale University Press, 1993).

35. See Karl Marx, *A Contribution to the Critique of Political Economy* in *The Marx-Engels Reader*, ed. Robert C. Tucker (2nd edn, New York: Norton, 1978), p. 5.

36. Sartre as quoted in Perry Anderson, *Arguments* (n. 7), p. 52. This is by no means to match Althusser with Sartre root and branch.

37. Althusser, *For Marx* (London: Verso, 1990 [1965]), p. 111. See Michael Sprinker's cogent summation of the concept of "last instance" in "Politics and Friendship," in *The Althusserian Legacy*, ed. Michael Sprinker and Ann Kaplan (London: Verso, 1993), p. 206.

38. Thompson, *The Poverty of Theory* (New York: Monthly Review Press, 1978), p. 5. Hereafter cited in page references as *POT*.

39. The origins of British cultural studies in eighteenth-century thought is spelled out fairly explicitly in *People's History and Socialist History*, ed. Raphael Samuel (London: Routledge, 1981), p. 4.

40. I have written at length on disciplinarity and genre in "Teaching, Writing, Changes: Disciplines, Genres, and the Errors of Professional Belief," in *Teaching in the Twenty-First Century*, eds Barbara Smith and Alice Robertson (New York: Garland, 1999).

41. One is tempted to surmise, as Anderson has, that part of the motivation for *The Poverty of Theory* was a change in editorial direction at *New Left Review* as regards the predominance of theory.

42. Etienne Balibar and Louis Althusser, *Reading Capital* (London: Verso, 1997 [1968]), p. 10. Cited hereafter as *RC*.

43. Focusing on provincial urban publics, Kathleen Wilson sets the rise of print much earlier in the 1760s. See her *The Sense of the People: Politics, Culture, and Imperialism in England, 1715–1785* (London: Cambridge University Press, 1995). On the proliferation of print in England generally, see Alvin Kernan, *Samuel Johnson and the Impact of Print* (New Jersey: Princeton University Press, 1987).

44. Nick Stevenson connects Habermas and Thompson in his *Culture, Ideology, and Socialism: Raymond Williams and E.P. Thompson* (New York: Avery, 1995).

45. Thompson is duly aware of the more insidious uses of "morality," for example, in Pitt's "moral lieutenant, Wilberforce, . . . [who] set up quasi official agencies for the 'enforcement of moral conduct'" (*MEWC*, 402). But it is the benevolent uses of the term and its commensurability with capitalism, for example Smith's "moral sympathy," that escapes Thompson's optimism for "the people."

46. Joseph Priestly, *Appeal to the Public on the Subjects of the Riots in Birmingham* (London: 1792), p. 6. Hereafter cited as *AP* in text.

12

Native Daughters in the Promised Land: Gender, Race, and the Question of Separate Spheres

You-me Park and Gayle Wald

On June 20, 1996, the regents of the University of California approved a now-infamous resolution mandating that as of 1997, the university would be forbidden from considering "race, religion, gender, color, ethnicity or national origin" as criteria of its admissions.[1] The issue of "race-based preferences"—the deliberately provocative phrase adopted by those opposed to affirmative action—was ultimately put to California voters, who in November voted to pass Proposition 209 (as the anti-affirmative action incentive was dubbed) by a margin of 54 to 46 percent. The effect of these changes, ostensibly designed to boost the percentage of students who gain admission to the university solely on the basis of academic achievement, has been immediate and chilling. A report about University of California law school admissions released in the spring of 1997 shows a radical drop in the numbers of admitted African American students, down from 104 admissions in 1995 to 21 in 1996. The group that so far has profited most dramatically from the new California policy is Caucasians, a fact that contradicts widely held expectations that Asian Americans would reap the greatest benefits. Ward Connerly, the African American regent who led the efforts to promote passage of the university resolution, told the *Los Angeles Times* that he "welcomed" such reports. "We are too politically correct to reach the conclusion: they are not as competitive to be lawyers and doctors. If we really want to help those black and Latino kids, we will give them some tough love and get them channeled back into being able to compete."[2]

We begin with this recitation of facts, at once familiar and yet dizzying in their implication, because the complex scenario that they point to raises issues that we explore in this chapter: issues of access to public institutions; of whose interests are represented within the public sphere of formal political participation; of the figuration of race and gender and the pitting of these against one another (since it often goes unnoticed that affirmative action has also benefited white women); of media representations that pit socially beleaguered and socially legitimated "minority" groups against one another; and of the privatization of certain interests and needs under the sign of a "tough love" policy that has little to do with love and even less to do with justice.

In this chapter, we intend to raise the following questions: how does "minority" literature represent the perceived boundaries of public/private spheres in the Unites States? How do these boundaries reinforce and overlap with class and gender lines? How does the nation/state become a factor in dictating how these boundaries are drawn? Rather than assuming that literary texts unproblematically reflect reality, we want to pay close attention to their strategies of representation. We want to ask how the private and public spheres are imagined and figured in these texts, how female subjects negotiate their positionality both in and between public/private spheres, where and how literary texts locate and represent the political and economic power that shapes, inscribes and sometimes nullifies the hopes, fears, and desires of these female subjects.

In what follows, we explore these issues more closely through an analysis of literary texts by two African American and two Asian American writers: Ann Petry's *The Street* (1946), Gwendolyn Brooks's *Maud Martha* (1953), Cynthia Kadohata's *Floating World* (1989) and Chang-Rae Lee's *Native Speaker* (1995). By looking at these texts, we explore the relationship between the public sphere and the simultaneously privatized and publicized subjectivities of black and Asian women. Our turn to these novels is strategic at a number of levels: most importantly, they enable us to conduct an investigation of how the "separate spheres" model is itself constitutive of gender and race discourses, and to do so not exclusively in abstract terms, but in terms that insist on the historical specificity of our own endeavor as well as the object of our investigation. Both of these sets of texts were produced at moments of perceived crisis in the discourses of race, gender, ethnicity, nationality and labor—"crises" that subsequently found social expression through the reordering of "public" and "private." It is through the lens of such reordering that both sets of novels elucidate

the particular plights of poor women of color—both "native" populations such as African Americans (who under segregation are explicitly
denied citizen rights within the formal public sphere) and immigrant
populations of Japanese and Korean Americans, whose citizenship
status, real or imagined, is subject to anxious scrutiny and policing
speculation.

The novels by Petry and Brooks, written in the wake of World War
Two, explicitly and implicitly portray the (re)domestication of women
workers confronting the return home (that is, to the nationalized
"domestic" sphere) of male citizen-soldiers. Both *The Street* and *Maud
Martha* are primarily concerned with the everyday struggles and aspirations of poor African American women—women who are not simply
victims of domesticity, but whose modes of access to the public sphere
are not simple either, entailing psychical or physical violation. Juxtaposed, respectively, against a romanticized representation of the "black
masses" and the figure of the masculinized citizen–soldier, Petry's and
Brooks's protagonists find no easy solutions to the problems posed by
their inability to gain meaningful control over the terms of their
publicity or privacy.

The novels by Lee and Kadohata address the issues of immigrants,
nationality, citizenry and domesticity in the context of the shifting
boundaries of internal and external national territories and public
spheres. These novels were produced during another moment of "crisis"—during the late 1980s and early 1990s, when anti–immigration
sentiments were fueled by collective anxiety around the perception of
limited resources and job opportunities for "legitimate" subject-
citizens. In *Native Speaker*, an acclaimed novel about the formation of
a Korean American subjectivity, Chang-Rae Lee deftly portrays how
the protagonist, Byongho, is shaped and defined by a sense of secrecy
and shame concerning his "difference": Asian looks, immigrant
parents who don't look or act like "normal parents" and, most importantly in the text, his compromised male sexuality *vis-à-vis* his white
wife, Lelia. The shadowy figures of Korean (-American) women disrupt
Lee's narrative, which mostly concerns itself with the legitimation of a
male immigrant subject in the public sphere. Tucked away in the
hyper-feminized private sphere which is sanctioned by both Korean
traditional ideals of domestic women and the U.S. cult around Asian
American "self-sufficiency" (read: "they don't ask for social welfare"),
these women are denied access to the public sphere conceived in any
meaningful way. In *The Floating World*, Kadohata's protagonist Olivia
lives through the period immediately following World War Two, trying

to negotiate both a domesticized femininity and a publicized "Japanese" identity. During World War Two, the public definition of Japanese American individuals as "Japanese," and thus enemy, subjects keeps Olivia and her family from taking root as "Americans." Their positionality as non-citizen subjects is signified in their failure to gain access to the private sphere.

By juxtaposing these two sets of texts culled from very different eras in postwar U.S. history, we intend to critique not only the binary logic of separate spheres but also the binary logic of race—the latter persists within the popular imagination even as late twentieth-century demographic shifts, combined with the emergence of new identity categories (such as "biracial" or "multiracial"), clearly signpost the inadequacy of such a black–white model. The juxtaposition of African American and Asian American texts presents particular opportunities and challenges for undermining the fetishistic separation of black and white racial "spheres" without retreating to easy (that is, romanticized) notions of hybridity. As recent events such as the 1992 Los Angeles uprisings and the murder trial of O.J. Simpson illustrate, even within the most patently "hybrid" social scenarios "blackness" can be made to function as a metaphor for "race" within cultural representation, not only obscuring the racialization of other U.S. minority populations, but keeping public discourse locked within the dominant logic of black and white. At the same time, the representation of bitter antagonisms between different racialized minority populations—another product of the LA uprisings, in which conflict between Korean American and African American publics was naturalized as the product of intractable *cultural* differences—has the effect of reinscribing racial polarity by reproducing a rhetoric of "whites" and "others." By focusing on the animosities between the Korean American and African American publics, the public discourse in effect reinforced a binary between the "minorities" or "others" who are mired in scuffles and "whites" who look on and regulate. The difficulty of thinking outside of a racial binary has important implications for how we organize knowledge within educational institutions—that is to say, not only in those public spheres constituted through media representation. In high school and college classrooms, on American literature syllabuses, and in anthologies of American literature, for example, African American and Asian American texts are often relegated to and analyzed within "separate spheres"—or if not, then lumped together under the potentially trivializing and de-legitimizing rubric of "minority" literature.

*

Since the early 1980s, the notion of separate and distinct "spheres" of modern social, cultural and economic life—on the one hand, a "private" sphere encompassing domestic life, "symbolic reproduction," and the "modern restricted nuclear family" and, on the other hand, a corresponding "public" sphere of "material reproduction," political participation, debate, and opinion formation"[3]—has been subject to rigorous and thoroughgoing critique, so much so that scholars have begun to question the usefulness of such a model for social and cultural analysis. Some of the most trenchant of these recent critiques have come from feminist critical theorists, who have argued that the separate spheres model naturalizes bourgeois male subjectivity even as it seeks to demonstrate that "the" bourgeois subject (understood as male, literate and landed) is the historical product of complex social changes wrought by European modernity and modernization. In several well-known essays, for example, Nancy Fraser has carefully criticized Jürgen Habermas's influential work on the public sphere and on the historical emergence of a public/private distinction (especially in *The Theory of Communicative Action* and *The Structural Transformation of the Public Sphere*), finding it methodologically and ideologically complicit with women's relegation to the less privileged, or private, side of the binary.[4] Complementing and extending Fraser's work, various feminist cultural historians and literary scholars have shown that gender cannot be tidily or consistently mapped onto the separate spheres model, as earlier work had suggested. Contending that the "public" and the "private" have never been wholly separate and that women's power cannot be adequately gauged according to the degree of their exclusion from the public (at least as conventionally defined), these scholars have established that even in the nineteenth century—the era, in the United States, of the publicly celebrated cult of domesticity and true womanhood—women were important social actors within various competing theaters of the public, now understood to include ladies' anti-slavery and temperance societies, organizations of working-class women, and popular literary culture.[5]

The relation of such recent feminist work to an orthodox separate spheres model is perhaps best characterized as critically collaborative—attentive to the model's utility (particularly for historicizing and de-universalizing key terms such as "domesticity" and "the family") and, at the same time, critically wary of its status as an ideological production that is largely silent about, and therefore potentially recuperative of, women's subordination within patriarchal social hierarchies of gender. As Kathy Peiss observes, although the separate spheres model "might seem consigned to the dustbin of historiography," nevertheless it "has retained its salience for feminist cultural historians as an ideology that organizes and gives meaning to social experience, a social construction that is contested and renegotiated over time" (817). That "separate spheres" is a social construction, in other words, does not negate the notion that "public" and "private" are also socially real insofar as they structure the terms of social agency and inclusion, the formation of social identities and subjectivities, and our capacity to imagine alternative or competing narratives of the social. The past few decades of critical analysis point to the emergence of a scholarly consensus about the need to deconstruct the hierarchical binary analytic of an orthodox separate spheres model, supplanting it with a model that acknowledges that public and private are not stable, unchangeable or natural polarities. Acknowledging the social pliability of separate spheres demands, on the one hand, that we stay alert to how the distinction between public and private has been vigilantly guarded and maintained through legal, cultural, and economic discourses. But it also obliges us to investigate the modes by which various "public interests" have tacitly or explicitly challenged these discourses, either by constructing alternative publics (or "counter-publics") or by imagining different ways of circulating and distributing power between public and private.

A strict separate spheres analytical framework, with its fetishistic and reductionist separation of the public and private, obscures crucial questions about mobility and agency across socially constructed lines of difference. The terms "public" and "private" have borne, and continue to bear, the inscription of ongoing struggles around questions of access to social power, where power is a function of one's location within a social geography of separate spheres. Our emphasis on mobility and access here is strategic as well as practical, given the intimate link between social subordination and social immobility. To cite one concrete example: even for the nineteenth-century bourgeois white female subject for whom the notion of a distinct, separate, and safeguarded private sphere has most relevance, the consequence of a discourse of separate spheres has never only or primarily centered on women's confinement to the private sphere or to a putatively inverse relation between female domesticity and modes of access to masculine "public" power.[6] As it imagines femininity in terms of a lack of agency, so the public/private model imagines masculinity in terms of an ability to access *both* the public and the private. As Fraser puts it, "in both spheres women are subordinated to men."[7] For those who have not enjoyed the privilege of crossing the line, or who have not been the beneficiaries of separate spheres, access to public sites of power is typically accompanied by self-mutilation, sacrifice or loss.

Alongside the fact that the private sphere has been as exclusionary as the public sphere to the "less deserved" of the country, we also need to remember that the coveted entrance into the public sphere by women might follow a patriarchal script rather than liberate these women from patriarchal restraints. As Doreen Massey argues in *Space, Place, and Gender*:

> Many women have had to *leave* home precisely to forge their own version of their identities, from Victorian Lady Travellers to Minnie Bruce Pratt. Moreover, in certain cultural quarters, the mobility of women does indeed seem to pose a threat to a settled patriarchal order. Whether it be the specific fact of *going out to* work in nineteenth-century England or the more general difficulty . . . of keeping track of women in the city. The relation to identity is again apparent.[8]

It is certainly true that, for some women (especially if those women have class privilege), leaving home has offered liberating potential. It is also true that an opportunity to become a "worker" rather than a domestic woman has enabled some working-class women to explore the possibility of defining themselves in a non-sexualizing way, the assumption being that, by eluding the ruthless sexualizing of their bodies, they will become less vulnerable to violation and violence. Yet the liberating potential of women's "posing a threat to a patriarchal order" when they emerge from the private sphere has been more than anticipated in most modern forms of patriarchy. This "threat" has been exaggerated and used to justify the confinement of women to the domestic sphere as well as the exploitation and persecution of women "out there." Hence the efficacy of patriarchy is predicated upon its mobility in weaving in and out of the boundaries between the private and public spheres, while maintaining the mirage of "separate spheres," where men and women each hold on to their own.

Given the centrality of questions of mobility to a discussion of separate spheres, it is all the more surprising that issues of race and ethnicity have figured so infrequently in recent feminist critiques of Habermasian social and cultural theory. It is patently obvious that the public sphere is implicitly and explicitly racialized as well as gendered (that is, normatively defined as masculine *and* white, and accessed via a privileged relation to patriarchal and white supremacist discourses).[9] Nineteenth-century abolitionist writers were explicitly concerned with elaborating the ways that the boundaries of public and private are

constituted by and through discourses of race as well as gender. Eager
to debunk the cult of true (white) womanhood, abolitionist authors
were at great pains to demonstrate that the sexualized violence associated with public rituals such as slave auctions and with the public
symbolism of white racial authority (most notably, the cowhide whip)
thoroughly permeated the "private" sphere. In their accounts of domestic bondage, writers such as Harriet Jacobs and Harriet Wilson took
great care to portray bourgeois white women not merely as the victims
of domestic enslavement but as the powerful "overseers" of their
households, as adept at enforcing the rule of racial and class superiority
as were plantation overseers charged with enforcing the will of the
slaveholding master. Not only does the conventional bourgeois distinction between public and private fall away in the face of such historical
evidence, but it is clear, too, from such examples that the subjective
value of public and private is radically contingent upon factors including gender, race, ethnicity, and citizenship. In short, such examples
invalidate the presumption of a necessary or essential coupling between
terms like "publicity" and "citizenship," "privacy," and "safety."[10]

Contemporary feminist scholarship has elaborated, extended, and
amplified these nineteenth-century critiques of the public/private
binary and its relation to the racialized and sexualized division of labor,
bringing such insights to bear on the experience of twentieth-century
immigrant and migrant female workers of color. "Black women's
experiences and those of other women of color have never fit [the
private/public] model," writes Patricia Hill Collins in *Black Feminist
Thought*. "Rather than trying to explain why Black women's work and
family patterns deviate from the alleged norm, a more fruitful approach
lies in challenging the very constructs of work and family themselves."[11]
Angela Davis's *Women, Race and Class* takes just such an approach,
noting that while black women have been able to circumvent many of
the conditions of patriarchal domesticity through their "outside work,"
in effect this "outside work" has itself been privatized, relegated to the
private sphere of white middle-class women.[12] "In 1910, when over half
of all Black females were working outside their homes," she writes,
"one-third of them were employed as domestic workers. By 1920 over
one-half were domestic servants, and in 1930 the proportion had risen
to three out of five" (237–8). As Davis demonstrates, the private sphere
of middle-class white women's domesticity was thus constructed
through the use of the labor of working women of color, including
(and perhaps especially) black women. Hence white middle-class
women's "privacy" and domestic comfort were dependent on the

"outside" labor of women of color, whose "public" sphere of work is the white middle-class women's private sphere.

The illusion of separate "public" and "private" spheres is reinforced through the fact that the entrance of women of color into the public sphere is often predicated upon the maintenance of the public/private divide. For example, Asian immigrant women found it much easier to assume identity as a "worker" when they remained within the domestic sphere. Hence their entry into the public sphere was compromised from the very beginning, since the moment they entered the "public" sphere, they were even more thoroughly defined as "private" beings who performed domestic labor primarily in middle-class white women's private space, where they were invisibilized. As Evelyn Nakano Glenn writes:

> For racial-ethnic women, then, employment in domestic service became a long-term proposition, not a temporary expedient. Their concentration in domestic service in turn reinforced their degraded status in society. They came to be seen as particularly suited for, and only suited for, degraded work. Racial-ethnic status and occupational position became more or less synonymous badges of inferiority. The black cleaning woman, the Mexican maid, the Japanese housecleaner, became stereotyped images that helped to rationalize and justify their subordination.[13]

The "public" and "private" spheres are thus not separate for these women laborers, but deliberately and persistently superimposed on each other. As a consequence, racial-ethnic women's identity within the public sphere is compromised by the demand that they maintain their "private" (i.e. degraded) identities even in the "public" sphere.

When contemporary feminist discourses assume a facile binary logic, the potential of these discourses to dismantle patriarchal definitions and regulations of women is seriously hampered. Women who don't fit conveniently into the conventional gender polarities of public/private—for example, women who are not "victims" in easily recognizable ways because they are not confined to the private sphere, or who are perceived as "workers" with access to the public—become, in effect, masculinized within feminist critique. That is to say, these women's very access to the public becomes a structural alibi for their invisibility *as women.* At the same time, and in a complementary way, feminist critique that works to destabilize the public/private binary by mapping gender onto it in effect renders gender the privileged, and hence public, term of analysis at the expense of issues of race, ethnicity, and nationality. Literally, once gender is recuperated from its position of invisibility within the Habermasian paradigm and made part of a public feminist scholarly conversation about the separate spheres model, terms like race and nation are rendered invisible, and hence privatized. Additive strategies of bringing terms like race and gender together within a critique of the separate spheres model inevitably transcribe and reinscribe the binary logic of public and private—that is to say, the very logic that such analyses propose to critique. In effect, the binary logic of public/private becomes the operative principle of such an additive model, in which previously privatized terms are added onto already existing models, leaving the models themselves intact. Instead of producing analyses that make visible the interconnectedness of terms like race and gender, the binary analytic of public/private initiates a process in which these terms eventually annul each other.

Such theoretical difficulties lend further urgency to the question of whether the public/private sphere distinction is ultimately another "solid" thing that will "melt into air." Our goal in the explorations of the literature that follow is not necessarily to transcend the public/private distinction, but to make these categories more historically responsible and responsive to the needs of subjects who have been marginalized by the separate spheres model. By "marginalized" subjects, we mean those who do not have the authority to negotiate the shifting boundaries of public and private, and who are unable to mobilize the discourse of publicity and privacy to articulate their needs, wishes and rights. Such authority is necessary if these subjects are to acquire autonomy over the way they are represented within the public sphere. Representation, in this context, is not mere abstraction; nor is it only an issue within the public sphere. Rather, representation has its own real power, and is in fact the way that power asserts itself within the public and private spheres alike.

Ann Petry's *The Street* and Chang-Rae Lee's *Native Speaker* (1995), despite the half-century that separates their publication, both offer us opportunities to investigate the precarious boundaries between the "public" and the "private" spheres, boundaries drawn and redrawn according to the alleged needs of privileged social groups. For the female subjects in the narratives of Petry and Lee, the private sphere in which they are entrapped is always already inscribed and saturated by the violent racialization and sexualization of their identities, bodies, and labor. Especially the fascination by and aversion towards the ruthlessly sexualized bodies of these women, exemplified by the real and threatened sexual violence against them in the private, domestic sphere, faithfully reinscribes the public perceptions and definitions of these women. Furthermore, female subjects of color in both novels are complicit with as well as victimized by the myth of bourgeois respectability and domesticity, which prohibits them from reaching out to alternative types of communities and public spheres. Reading Petry's *The Street* alongside Lee's *Native Speaker* allows us to reevaluate the paradigm of linear historical development in terms of women's negotiations with the public sphere: what if Petry's protagonist in *The Street* shares so much of the isolation, despair, hopes, and fantasies of Ajuma in Lee's *Native Speaker*?

The Street, Ann Petry's 1946 best-selling novel about the life of a poor unmarried black woman and mother living in Harlem in 1944, is primarily concerned with the ways in which racism, poverty, and the patriarchal sexualization of women condition the opportunities and the experiences of its protagonist, Lutie Johnson.[14] From its opening image of blustery November wind to its closing image of snow that settles on the "grime," "garbage," and "ugliness" of the New York streets, the novel characterizes Lutie's social and natural environments in terms of their assaultive force. The opening scenes of the novel find Lutie searching for an apartment for herself and her young son, Bub, but it becomes clear that domesticity offers no protection from the social; rather domestic spaces are those that interiorize the violence of the "outside," external world.

The cramped, dark and suffocating apartment of Lutie and Bub is a far cry from the houses that appear to Lutie to look "like something in the movies" (38). The physical deterioration of the apartment not only literalizes Lutie's emotional deterioration as she worries about her ability to pay the rent and protect Bub (without child care, these two intentions are sometimes mutually exclusive), but it also represents the interiorization of "urban decay," the cumulative effect of inadequate urban planning, population migrations, declining infrastructure, and large-scale economic deprivation. "The street" enters Lutie's home in more than one way, however. Bob Jones, a fellow tenant and supervisor of the building where she lives, embodies the interiorized, domesticated threat of sexual objectification and violation that conditions Lutie's experiences on the "outside"—at work, in the nightclubs where she occasionally sings, and on the city streets themselves. It would not be overstating the case to say that Lutie's everyday experience is defined as the attempt to avoid rape. Treated as if her body were public property, especially by men, Lutie finds little solace, privacy, or protection from sexual abuse in being able to afford a "room of her own." What privacy Lutie does have, moreover, bears the imprint of her powerlessness; it is a privacy imposed rather than chosen, an isolation Lutie suffers as a result of not having a "public of her own," a community that might offer her emotional nourishment and physical protection.

Farah Jasmine Griffin suggests that Lutie could discover such life-sustaining tonic in the voice of her grandmother and hence, metonymically, in a community of black female kin who are also survivors of racism and patriarchy. Such sources of community are, however, closer to home than Lutie's grandmother: they also lie in the various women—also black and also poor—who occupy Lutie's apartment building (especially Min, the woman who lives with Bob Jones but eventually musters the will to leave him). Petry makes it clear that Lutie's desperate attachment to an imagined ideal of bourgeois respectability hinders her potential ability to connect in meaningful ways with other women (and men). Although *The Street* is typically characterized as a naturalist novel in the tradition of earlier texts such as *Native Son* (1940), Petry resists depicting Lutie as a passive victim of environment and circumstance. Ironically, it is Lutie's own fidelity to the American Dream of meritocratic reward for individual effort—a dream exemplified in U.S. national mythology by Benjamin Franklin—that binds her to the street. Walking home with her groceries one evening, Lutie compares herself to Franklin, insisting (despite the fact that 116th Street in Harlem was not "Philadelphia a pretty long number of years ago") that "if Ben Franklin could live on a little bit of money and could prosper, then so could she" (64). Insofar as Lutie's American Dream enshrines wealth rather than social justice as the privileged object of individual ambition and the measure of civic virtue, *The Street* suggests, Lutie is ideologically entrapped, complicit with the social forces that oppress her and whose power lies largely beyond her individual control. While racism, in Lutie's experience, materializes as an all-but-unavoidable instrument of white social control—"Streets like the one she lived on were no accident. They were the North's lynch mobs" (323)—Lutie nevertheless bears responsibility for her investment in the professedly gender- and race-neutral ideology of the American Dream.

Petry's metaphor of urban milieux as Northern lynch mobs is telling for the way that it renders immaterial, "invisible" ideologies in material form. Indeed, the "street" of the novel's title refers not to a particular geographical location, but rather to a single, determining environment that renders obsolete conventional distinctions between "outside" and "inside," "street" and "home," "sacred" and "profane." And although black women were frequently the victims of Southern lynchings, Petry's metaphor includes and even centralizes black male subjects within the circle of her analysis. Lynching, as a performative spectacle, is intended to be read as a double-edged threat to masculinized African American subjects: first, as a violation of their physical integrity, and second, as the feminization of their bodies (male or female) so that they can be sexually assaulted and violated. Thus the trope of "lynch mobs" reveals the moment when Petry herself privileges the masculinized rendering of Lutie's plight and suffering and privatizes the issue of gender. Lutie's narrative becomes folded into the "larger" narrative of racial violence that doesn't read Lutie as a raced, gendered subject. Similarly, when Lutie inspects the names on the mail boxes of her future residence, she envisions herself as one facet of a collective subjectivity— a figure of the "black masses":

> She leaned over to look at the names on the mail boxes. Henry Lincoln Johnson lived here, too, just as he did in all the other houses she'd looked at. Either he or his blood brother. The Johnsons and the Jacksons were mighty prolific. Then she grinned, thinking who am I to talk, for I, too, belong to that great tribe, that mighty mighty tribe of Johnsons. (6–7)

The Street ends on a bitterly ironic note, as Lutie Johnson flees New York, leaving her son Bub to fend for himself in reform school. Petry's "solution" to her protagonist's struggle to discover a tolerable means out of poverty is ultimately to offer her movement without the promise of mobility, choice without the promise of agency. In a parodic reversal of the slave-narrative trope of emancipatory flight from Southern enslavement to Northern freedom, or of the migration-narrative trope of movement from rural Southern poverty to urban opportunity,[15] Lutie manages to flee domestic entrapment on a Chicago-bound train that "roar[s] into darkness" (436). This is hardly the utopian freedom of "the road" envisioned a few years later by Jack Kerouac and Neal Cassidy, whose novels celebrate and enshrine the fantasy of a masculinized American mobility predicated upon the evasion of the domesticating and entrapping "feminine" and an assumption of white male entitlement to inhabit the public spaces of "others." However dystopian *The Street*'s vision of the "road" for a penniless and unmarried African American woman in the late 1940s, Lutie's escape from the suffocation of the urban "street" at the end of the novel nevertheless substitutes for the certainty of imprisonment for the murder of Boots Smith, the egotistical henchman of the powerful slumlord Junto. The specter of imprisonment—the ultimate expression of state power over the individual—hangs heavily over the novel although its threat never materializes.[16]

*

In *Native Speaker*, it's not the specter of imprisonment but the realization of confinement that ultimately defeats the immigrant female subject. The male protagonist, Byongho, recollects the arrival of a Korean woman in his domestic space after his mother had passed away:

> I walked outside. A dim figure of a woman stood unmoving in the darkness next to my father's Chevrolet. . . . Beside her were two small bags and a cardboard box messily bound with the twine. When I got closer to her she lifted both bags and so I picked up the box; it was very heavy, full of glass jars and tins of pickled vegetables and meats. I realized she had transported homemade food thousands of miles, all the way from Korea, and the stench of overripe kimchee shot up through the cardboard flaps and I nearly dropped the whole thing. . . . This woman, I could see, had deep pockmarks stippling her high, fleshy cheeks, like the scarring from a mistreated bout of chickenpox or smallpox, and she stood much shorter than I first thought, barely five feet in her heeled shoes. Her ankles and wrists were as thick as posts. She waited for me to turn and start for the house before she followed several steps behind me. I was surprised that my father wasn't waiting in the doorway, to greet her or hold the door, and as I walked up the carpeted steps leading to the kitchen I saw that food and drink I had prepared had been cleared away.[17]

The woman, who is to replace Byongho's mother, has just arrived from Korea and been transported from the airport. As the protagonist's father explains later in the same chapter, she has been imported as part of a plan for the family's "move-up," a plan that includes moving into "big house and yard" [*sic*] in a ritzy neighborhood shortly after the woman's arrival.

It is no coincidence that the acquisition of a private residence, a prominent marker of class mobility especially for Asian American immigrants, is planned to occur alongside the arrival of the woman. In patriarchal imagination, Korean and American alike, the private sphere will not have been procured until the physical domestic space is complemented by female labor and sexuality that is always handily available. In the context of the immigrant domestic sphere, the burden on women can be twofold in that they are also required to retrieve and re-create the domestic rituals associated with distinctly Korean domesticity. The woman in the text knows only too well what's expected of her: she has risked the scrutiny of customs officers and brought jars of kimchee and pickled meat all the way from Korea. In the name of preserving national culture—a project that is sometimes touted as patriotism or at other times simply evoked as nostalgia—Korean immigrants' versions of nationalism exact an unreasonable amount of women's labor. Thus female immigrants in the Korean American community are assigned the role of the preserver of national traditions and spirits *in the private sphere*. Surprisingly yet also understandably similar to the operation of national movements and sentiments in colonial and postcolonial Korea, women are imagined to exist in a private sphere that is sanctioned by and also preserves national tradition. It is not enough to note that, relegated to the private sphere, these immigrant women will not have the mobility that will allow them access to the public sphere where political, economic, and cultural power is supposedly negotiated and distributed. As a flip side of the nationalist and traditionalist ideology, these women are also burdened by the shame and (self-)hatred that Korean immigrants harbor toward the part of their own Koreanness that would refuse to become part of "real" Americanness. In *Native Speaker*, the description of the woman's pockmarked face, embarrassingly short stature, and ankles and wrists "thick as posts" not only betrays Byongho's loathing of her but also anticipates and legitimates her relegation to thorough isolation in "her own space" until the very end, when she makes her genuine debut in the outside world on a hospital deathbed.

The woman's "place" even within the domestic sphere is firmly defined at the very moment of her arrival. She knows she won't be greeted by the patriarch and that she doesn't deserve the "food and drink" Byongho would normally serve male guests. As a symbolic gesture as well as an economic principle, Byongho shouldn't perform any kind of labor for the woman. The much-touted Asian hospitality, which only has currency as a principle that regulates the privatized yet formalized exchange between the public and private spheres, is easily overridden by the patriarchal rules concerning labor and class in the domestic sphere.

Once she is established in the domestic sphere, Byongho "understood that her two rooms, the tiny bathroom adjoining them, and the kitchen and pantry, constituted the sphere of her influence"(65). Contrary to Byongho's facile reading of her "sphere of influence" based on the separate spheres model, he senses that she doesn't assume authority over her own body, let alone the domestic sphere that she performs labor in.

> Sometimes I thought she was some kind of zombie. When she wasn't cleaning or cooking or folding clothes she was barely present; she never whistled or hummed or made any noise, and it seemed to me as if she only partly possessed her own body, and preferred it that way. (65)

Byongho dimly perceives that the woman's body itself has become co-opted and incorporated into the structure of the domestic sphere so that she cannot assume full authority over it. Rendered identical to the domestic labor that she performs, the woman has no access to any cultural, political, or "economical" encounters with American society. As she doesn't watch television ("she always turned them [soap operas] off after a few minutes"), or go shopping by herself (Byongho's father would "take her to the mall and buy her some clothes and shoes"), the woman who is not properly named throughout the text remains as "Ah-ju-ma," a Korean name for a woman of no significance (similar to the term "Auntie" in the U.S.), without ever being interpellated by the "outside" world. Whether she actually "preferred it that way" remains unclarified and unclarifiable, as the reader never gets a glimpse into her consciousness. Denied interiority, "Ah-ju-ma" in the text occupies a curious (but predictable in the tradition of invisibilized domestic workers) mode of hyperprivatized existence in which she has no access to individualized, hence public, subjectivity.

Thus *Native Speaker*, a text that mainly concerns itself with the Korean American male protagonist's sexual anxiety concerning his white wife and his agony over his privatized identity, introduces the reader early on to a Korean woman who leads her entire life in a highly claustro-phobic domestic sphere. The issues raised by the main plot of the novel, such as immigrant subjectivity, cultural interpretation of the American public sphere, and publicity and access to political power, have to be read against the backdrop of the figures of numberless and nameless Ah-ju-mas. During the present period of perceived "crisis," when immigrant communities feel beleaguered by anti–immigrant sentiments and legislation, Korean immigrants' negotiations over the boundaries of the public and private spheres in the United States, especially in terms of their needs and rights (to be educated, to work, and so on), tend to be carried out in masculinized terms that persist-ently invisibilize women "working" in the domestic sphere and opt to "forget" their desires and needs.

Unlike *The Street* and *Native Speaker*, Gwendolyn Brooks's *Maud Martha* explicitly focuses on the protagonist's *gendered* subjectivity in the con-text of her negotiation of "minority" status in the U.S. public sphere. Maud Martha's desires and needs are presented to the reader in an unequivocally gendered form, particularly through the interiorized expression of her hopes as a mother and her fantasies as a domestic sexualized woman. For example, the final pages of the novel, a story of the title character's development from childhood to adulthood (defined through marriage and childbirth), find Maud Martha optimis-tically contemplating both the end of World War Two and her own pregnancy: not only are U.S. soldiers returning home and life is returning to "normal," but "in the meantime, she was going to have another baby" (180). Brooks's juxtaposition of these two events—the one staged within the hypermasculinized "public" sphere of war, the other staged within the "private" sphere of Maud Martha's own body— simultaneously draws our attention to the mid-century masculinization of national citizenship and to the ways that women are both accorded and denied access to the "privileges" of such citizenship via their sexuality. Although black soldiers participated in all American wars, historically World War Two marked the moment when African American men began to organize politically around the war effort to demand their rights as "citizens." In early postwar civil rights discourse, full citizenship for black men was (re)imagined as a reward for their wartime contributions, as black civil rights leaders successfully mobilized collective outrage that African Americans who had "defended democracy" abroad (that is, in the public sphere of war) could not enjoy the fruits of that democracy in their own "home" country. Such slogans were not only effective in rallying people on the "battlefield" of civil rights—which could now be publicly reinterpreted as "the war at home," in language that contracted the public and private spheres; these slogans were also instrumental in publicizing black struggles for citizenship as struggles to defend black masculinity. Whereas African Americans had always understood segregation and the various limitations imposed on black enfranchisement as affronts to their constitutionally guaranteed citizenship (in contrast to the U.S. Supreme Court, which in its 1896 *Plessy* decision had shamefully enshrined the shibboleth of "separate but equal" as the prevailing legal alibi for such denial of citizenship), these affronts were now reconfigured in gendered terms, specifically as insults to black "manhood." The modern civil rights movement was thus initiated, at least in part and in the collective imagination, through a discourse of the citizen-soldier which conflated issues of race, masculinity, and publicity, and which used these issues to foreground the denial of citizenship to black men.

The end of World War Two thus produced a demand for two parallel reorderings of the public/private divide: on the one hand, a gendered demand that women of all races step aside to allow men to reassume their roles as workers and as citizens, and, on the other hand, a racialized demand that black noncitizen-subjects be accorded full citizenship rights in light of the wartime contributions of black men. But where, in the face of such demands, were black women's desires for citizenship or for mobility within and between the "separate spheres" represented? On what imaginary battleground, conceived within the newly masculinized discourse of civil rights, were black women's civil rights to be fought for? Or, as Brooks's protagonist says to herself at the end of the novel, "What, *what*, am I to do with all of this life?" (178). It is significant that this question, like most of Maud Martha's other questions and observations, remains interiorized and unvoiced in Brooks's text. From childhood, Maud Martha has struggled to access publicity in the socially sanctioned way: by attaining "proper" femininity, like the "pale and pompadoured" women displayed as icons of black female "achievement" on the covers of the Negro press, or like her sister Helen, who has the requisite "long lashes, the grace, the little ways with the hands and feet" (3). The privatization of Maud Martha's very subjectivity—given formal expression in the novel as a kind of unrelenting narrative interiority—operates in at least two ways: denied entrance into the public as a legitimate worker on account of gender, she is also refused such entrance via her sexuality on account of race. As a black woman and "a thing of ordinary allurements" (20), Maud Martha cannot mobilize normative beauty culture in the interests of her own power, and thus she falls back upon reproduction as a way of producing and proliferating her "self."

If we define daily experience through the rubric of publicity, then it could be said that very little "happens" to Maud Martha in the course of the novel: she grows up, attends school, goes out on dates, marries, moves with her new husband to an apartment, establishes her identity as a "wife," and has her first child.[18] Of course, Maud Martha's experience is more than just a collection of the sorts of "events" that construct women's biographies according to the rites of marriage and reproduction. Yet, in the end, *Maud Martha*'s conclusion poses more questions than it answers. In the novel's final line, Maud eagerly anticipates future movement—"the weather was bidding her bon voyage" (180)—and yet it is unclear whether she will ever be able to construct the imagined or wished-for mobility that might provide her a way out of her kitchenette apartment. The promise of a child may be joyful, but at the same time there seems little likelihood that maternity will produce the conditions necessary for such a journey out of the domestic. Rather Brooks's novel hints that Maud Martha's subjective interiority will continue to find expression in her confinement to literal interiors—the word "confinement" here resonating, at the novel's end, with its nineteenth-century associations with "childbirth." It seems more likely, in other words, that as in Petry's novel, the actual experience of domesticity will continue to have a dialectical bearing upon Maud

Martha's subjectivity, leading her simultaneously to rejoice at the thought of men "back from the wars!" and to domesticate her own ambitions.

As in *Maud Martha*, Cynthia Kadohata's *The Floating World* is situated at the postwar moment when national identity and public/private sphere distinctions are being reordered.[19] We close this section with Kadohata's novel because it is a contemporary work that looks back at an earlier period of "crisis" with an eye toward understanding contemporary "crises" (such as violent anti-immigrant sentiments and policymaking) by reaping a historical lesson from earlier representations. It also provides a means of exploring an alternative model of female subjectivity in relation to work, domesticity, and sexuality. How do we imagine an immigrant woman who is not relegated to the domestic sphere or rendered "publicized" and vulnerable in the "public" sphere? When does she assume autonomy over her body and work in the public and private spheres alike? How does she assume discursive and political authority to negotiate the boundaries of her privacy and publicity? *The Floating World* emphasizes the possible refiguring of the public/private spheres in a way that neither relegates women of color into the private sphere nor publicizes them and hence makes them vulnerable.

The Floating World's protagonist, Olivia, grows up in transit, as it were, following her parents as they look for work and social and emotional stability. She "explains" their life in these terms:

> We sometimes traveled in the Pacific states with one or two other young Japanese families, heading for jobs the fathers had heard of. We moved often for three reasons. One was bad luck—the businesses my father worked for happened to go under, or the next job we headed to evaporated while we were in transit. Also, it could be hard even into the fifties and sixties for Japanese to get good jobs. Nothing was ever quite the position my father felt he deserved. The third reason was that my parents were dissatisfied with their marriage, and somehow, moving seemed to give vent to that dissatisfaction. It was hard to leave our homes, but once we started traveling, a part of me loved that life. . . . I remember how fine it was to drive through the passage of light from morning to noon to night. (4)

The perspective of the young Olivia is retained in this quote and the family's predicament is presented as stemming from three disparate causes: inscrutable "bad luck" in terms of job security, the "accident" of their Japanese identity, and the conflict within the familial/private sphere. The three "causes" roughly coincide with the conflicts that

Japanese immigrants had to deal with in the postwar United States: the economic crisis brought about by the need to adjust to a slower pace of growth, the racializing nationalist discourse that defines Japanese Americans only as objectionable "Japanese" subjects, and the reconfiguring of gender relations within family structures. The book can be read as a narrative of the process by which these seemingly unrelated factors are reinterpreted by the older Olivia so that she can come up with a deeper understanding of each domain and also attain a synthesized view of her own social reality: how a perceived crisis in the U.S. economy fuels exclusionary nationalist sentiments, how the pressure to assimilate puts strain on the most private and intimate relationships, and how changes in employment patterns in the public sphere and daily rituals and gender roles in the private sphere influence each other.

The fact that Olivia's family is always on the run undoubtedly attests to their uprootedness and social instability. Yet the evocation of fine moments when the family drives "through the passage of light from morning to noon to night" makes the reader believe that there is more to this recollection than the narrator's nostalgia for her childhood. Learning to make a home out of motels and cars, Olivia also has access to the more flexibly imagined boundaries between the public and private spheres. Far from idealizing such possibilities, however, the text shows us how Olivia struggles with a claustrophobic sense of tightly knit family ties (the fact that they don't have stable links to the outside world seems to intensify the interdependency among family members) and a sense of estrangement from the "outside world." Nevertheless, such experiences and an understanding of shifting public/private boundaries together empower Olivia to shape and define her identity as a gendered worker-subject. At a hatchery in a little town in Arkansas, Olivia learns about workers' solidarity as well as their cruelty and exclusionary politics vis-à-vis people whom they perceive to be misfits and deviants. In the end, she opts to leave her family and the hatchery in order to carve out a space where she can draw boundaries for her privacy as well as for her public existence as a worker.

Traveling to repair and restock the vending machines in the Pacific states where she used to travel with her parents, she reckons with the "ghost" of her father (Jack) and her life, which hitherto has been defined by him and what he represents: family legacy, disillusionment, racialized subjecthood, and patriarchy. After she has "situated" the father as a worker "as young as herself" and "worked silently together" (159) with him, she feels that she can now move on: "The dry air smelled faintly of gasoline. I still had another stop, and for a moment I began to worry about my work and forgot about Jack. I tried to calculate from the night sky what time it was, but then I gave up. It didn't matter; it was high time I left" (161). This final paragraph of the novel, despite its inevitable visionary nature, doesn't merely level out the conflicts and contradictions concerning gendered/racialized subjectivities and the public discourses that represent and regulate them. For example, Olivia's sense of resolution at the end of the novel has more to do with her holding her ground as a second-generation immigrant–worker–woman subject than with a facile reconciliation with the outside world. Her achievement of mobility and "freedom" at the end attains significance only in the context of carefully represented conflicts in both the public and private spheres throughout the novel. It goes without saying that not every immigrant woman can become freed from racial and gender conflicts by becoming a self-employed caretaker of vending machines. Yet the novel, through the portrayal of Olivia's struggle to attain autonomy and mobility, allows us to take a critical and closer look at the ways the concepts of immigrants, women, workers, family, racism and patriarchy define, shape, and relate to each other.

Kadohata's *The Floating World* is an attempt to explore the possibilities for an Asian American female subject to define herself outside of the ruthlessly sexualizing and racializing gaze of the dominant culture. We are not arguing here that the liberating potentials that the text imagines should be the model for "minority" culture in general. To do so would be lapsing back into the binary logic of "whites" and "minorities," a logic that lumps the different aspirations and ambitions of various minority publics into a messy jumble. Rather, we are interested in performing a consciously limited yet focused reading of a cultural text that addresses the issues of the public/private spheres, women's work and female sexuality. We do so with a view to coming up with a piece of the puzzle that we need to put together in order to understand the collective imagination of raced and gendered subjects that underlies our legal discourses as well as our daily rituals. Ultimately, the puzzle will need to be completed not only by the "pieces" provided by the stories of African Americans and Asian Americans, but by the "pieces" that bear the stories of, for example, Hispanic American women and Native American women. This list should continue to grow as we learn to discern the operation of race/gender politics.

Nancy Fraser starts her article "What's Critical about Critical Theory? The Case of Habermas and Gender" with Marx's definition of critical theory as "the self-clarification of the struggles and wishes of the age." In her subsequent argument for the need to centralize the issue of gender in our understanding of the separate spheres model, Fraser fails to explore the relationships and the possible distinctions between "struggles" and "wishes." What if the concept of "struggles" itself implies a certain public nature, a privileged relation to the public? And what if the concept of "wishes" similarly implies desire that is privatized? How do we link these two terms when struggles are waged at the level of wishes, as is the case in texts discussed here? It goes without saying that wishing well and struggling well must not be relegated to separate spheres, but must instead support each other within a dialectical relationship. Looking at the nationalized and masculinized public sphere in the United States from the perspective of women of color, who need to negotiate a skewed and uneven relationship with the public sphere, we have attempted to address questions concerning citizenship, family, labor, mobility, and agency. Although we have attempted to situate these texts "in conversation" with one another, we are not constructing a linear narrative that follows a predictably optimistic trajectory: from Lutie's sense of entrapment to Olivia's departure. Rather, we have attempted to scrutinize the narrativization of *both* the struggles *and* the wishes of African American and Asian American female subjects.

The juxtaposition of these two sets of texts enables us to be historically specific about the ways that immigrant and native minority "publics"[20] differently negotiate the challenge of constructing power and recognition within and across the public/private binary. Our analysis reveals that the discourse of "separate spheres" organizes these groups dialectically. For example, African Americans are still the most visible of "minority" groups within U.S. society, whereas Asian Americans' presence here is often obscured, the product of an imaginative "amnesia" that derives from the tenacity of the black/white polarity. In media representation, Asian Americans typically "earn" publicity through sanctioned forms of economic or cultural achievement (including assimilation); by contrast, African American "failure" is relentlessly publicized and spectacularized through media accounts of "black" crime and poverty (recalling Petry's text). Within a culture that fetishizes the mobility of the impoverished but hardworking immigrant (to the disadvantage of African Americans, for whom immigration is less likely to figure as a central aspect of "American" experience), Asian Americans are widely lauded for "taking care of themselves." As *Native Speaker* makes clear, Asian Americans are socially rewarded as "model" minorities to the degree that their "problems" remain private—in this case, unloaded onto the backs of economically vulnerable Korean American women. African Americans' "problems" are, by contrast, revealed in the full glare of the media spotlight, where the most impoverished citizens are not only subject to withering and hostile public scrutiny, but are also represented as presenting their "problems" to a weakened and vulnerable welfare state which *they*, in their helplessness and poverty, victimize.[21] Because public institutions historically have been more progressive in allowing black participation, they have been relatively dependable sources of black employment; hence African Americans have traditionally found work in post offices and federal government offices, as social workers or teachers, and in the military. African Americans confront the particular dilemma born of having labored to build the American nation and yet been relegated to the status of non-citizen, a condition of such absurdity that W.E.B. DuBois used the phrase "double-consciousness" to characterize it.[22] Automatic linkage of the terms "worker" and "citizen" is similarly denied to Asian Americans, who on the one hand are seen to be models of industry contributing to the health of the U.S. economy and on the other hand are perpetually denied recognition as citizens. Asian Americans have come to occupy "model" minority status in part because of beliefs that they are willing to work without demanding the civic corollary of work—recognition as citizen-subjects. One of the known "merits" of Asian Americans is that they are not interested in running for office and do not vote.

It is significant that while African Americans and Asian Americans are seen as inhabiting, respectively, "public" and "private" positions within the U.S. popular imagination of race, *both* groups are feminized (in the sense of being marked under the sign of the feminine). Indeed, it is under the rubric of gender—and, in particular, of women's *labor*— that the relation of these differently racialized publics is best elucidated. Although it is more common for the plights of Latinas and African American women to be linked (perhaps because of Asian Americans' distinction as the "model minority"), in fact, both Asian American and African American women have served as primary sources of U.S. domestic labor, where sexual violence is the "inevitable" consequence of their domestication and sexualization. It comes as no surprise, given such affinities, that today "immigrants" (often coded as Asian) and "welfare mothers" (often coded as black) define the terrain upon which the most recent political assaults on public resources have been waged.

Notes

1. The regents didn't stop with university admissions, but rather extended these criteria to cover decisions in hiring and contracting. What was thus largely represented in the media as a student issue was therefore also an issue that directly affects labor.

2. Kenneth R. Weiss, "UC Law Schools' New Rules Cost Minorities Spots," *Los Angeles Times*, May 15, 1997. This article was pulled from the newspaper's web site, at http://www.latimes.com.

3. Nancy Fraser, "What's Critical About Critical Theory? The Case of Habermas and Gender," in *Unruly Practices: Power, Discourse and Gender in Contemporary Social Theory* (Minneapolis: University of Minnesota Press, 1989), p. 119.

4. Ibid.; Nancy Fraser, "Rethinking the Public Sphere: A Contribution to the Critique of Actually Existing Democracy," in *The Phantom Public Sphere*, ed. Bruce Robbins (Minneapolis: University of Minnesota Press, 1993), pp. 1–32.

5. See Kathy Peiss, "Going Public: Women in Nineteenth-century Cultural History," *American Literary History* 3, 4 (Winter 1991): 817–28; and Mary P. Ryan, "Gender and Public Access: Women's Politics in Nineteenth-century America," in *Habermas and the Public Sphere*, ed. Craig Calhoun (Cambridge, MA: MIT Press, 1992), pp. 259–88.

6. For an argument that nineteenth-century bourgeois women actually exercised considerable influence and power despite their relegation to the "private," see Ann Douglas, *The Feminization of American Culture* (New York: Knopf, 1977).

7. Fraser, "What's Critical," p. 119.

8. See Doreen Massey, *Space, Place and Gender* (Minneapolis: University of Minnesota Press, 1994), p. 11.

9. Michael Hanchard makes a similar point about the domain of the public sphere in Brazil in his "Black Cinderella?: Race and the Public Sphere in Brazil," in *The Black Public Sphere*, ed. The Black Public Sphere Collective (Chicago: University of Chicago Press, 1995), p. 171.

10. In a provocative reading of the Senate judicial confirmation hearings of (then) Supreme Court justice nominee Clarence Thomas, Fraser similarly observes that "categories of privacy and publicity are not simply gendered categories; they are racialized categories as well. Historically blacks have been denied privacy in the sense of domesticity. As a result, black women have been highly vulnerable to sexual harassment at the hands of masters, overseers, bosses, and supervisors. At the same time, they have lacked the public standing to claim state protection against abuse, whether suffered at work or at home" (606). The potential of these insights into the interarticulation of race and gender within the "separate sphere" model notwithstanding, Fraser is left at the end of the article calling, somewhat defensively and resignedly, for additional work. "In any event," she notes, foreclosing further discussion within her own essay, "we need more work that theorizes the racial subtext of categories of privacy and publicity and its intersection with the gender subtext" (606). See Nancy Fraser, "Sex, Lies and the Public Sphere: Some Reflections on the Confirmation of Clarence Thomas," *Critical Inquiry* 18 (Spring 1992): 595–612.

11. Patricia Hill Collins, *Black Feminist Thought: Knowledge, Consciousness, and the Politics of Empowerment* (London: Unwin Hyman, 1990), p. 47.

12. Angela Y. Davis, *Women, Race and Class* (New York: Vintage, 1981).

13. Evelyn Nakano Glenn, *Issei, Nisei, War Bride* (Philadelphia: Temple University Press, 1986), p. 5.

14. Ann Petry, *The Street* (1946; Boston: Houghton Mifflin, 1974). See also Barbara Christian, *Black Women Novelists: The Development of a Tradition, 1892–1976* (Westport: Greenwood Press, 1980).

15. Within the African American slave narrative tradition, the trope of the slave's flight to freedom is well known. On images of mobility in black migration narratives, see Farah Jasmine Griffin, *Who Set You Flowin? The African-American Migration Narrative* (New York: Oxford, 1995).

16. Particularly for African American men, prison is a "public" institution that bears the traces of a dialectical relation both to the "street" and to "home." In prison, not only individuality but actual citizenship is eviscerated, while at the same time the "individual" is reconstituted through new discourses of punishment and rehabilitation. Moreover, while the disciplinary norms of state prisons demand the radical elimination of individual privacy (in shared cells and bathroom facilities, activities that otherwise would be designated "private" on the "outside" are made public and collective), prisons mediate the publicity of African American "deviance."

The threat of imprisonment is prefigured in the text when Lutie, a live-in domestic for the Chandlers, a wealthy white family, is present one Christmas morning when Jonathan Chandler commits suicide in the living room. From this incident Lutie learns not only that violence permeates the "private" lives of white elites, but more importantly that wealth and status confer the opportunity to enforce a nominal separation of "private" and "public" affairs.

17. Chang-Rae Lee, *Native Speaker* (New York: Riverhead, 1995), p. 62.

18. In an introductory African American literature course, students reading the novel for the first time have often complained that they are put off by Brooks's modernist style and "bored" because "nothing happens" in the plot.

19. Cynthia Kadohata, *The Floating World* (New York: Ballantine Books, 1989).

20. In "Sex, Lies and the Public Sphere," Nancy Fraser makes an enabling distinction between the term "communities"—which falsely implies consensus and univocality within groups—and "publics"—a term that indicates heterogeneity, and that retains the implication of unity-through-struggle. See "Sex, Lies and the Public Sphere," p. 611.

21. See Patricia Williams, *The Alchemy of Race and Rights* (Cambridge, MA: Harvard University Press, 1988). Ironically, Fraser's reading of Clarence Thomas's confirmation hearings overlooks the fact that this and other recent highly mediated juridical spectacles (such as the Rodney King beating and Simi Valley trial and the murder trial of O.J. Simpson)—spectacles often falsely touted as facilitating "public discourse" about race and citizenship—attest to the generally intense public scrutiny that attaches to "minority" (particularly African American) attainments and failure—especially failure.

22. Here is W.E.B. DuBois: "After the Egyptian and the Indian, the Greek and the Roman, the Teuton and Mongolian, the Negro is a sort of seventh son, born with a veil, and gifted with second-sight in this American world—a world which yields him no true self-consciousness, but only lets him see himself through the revelation of the other world. It is a peculiar sensation, this double-consciousness. . . . One ever feels his two-ness—an American, a Negro; two souls, two thoughts, two unreconciled strivings; two warring ideals in one dark body, whose dogged strength alone keeps it from being torn asunder." From DuBois, *The Souls of Black Folk* (1903; New York: Penguin, 1989), p. 5.

13

Counter-Public Spheres and the Role of Educators as Public Intellectuals: Paulo Freire's Cultural Politics

Henry A. Giroux

> It is a spirit in opposition, rather than in accommodation, that grips me because the romance, the interest, the challenge of intellectual life is to be found in dissent against the status quo at a time when the struggle on behalf of underrepresented and disadvantaged groups seems weighted against them.
>
> —Edward Said[1]

> Taking an interest in the world as a whole and feeling an increased sense of responsibility for it, intellectuals often yield to the temptation to try to grasp the world as a whole, to explain it entirely and offer universal solutions to its problems.
>
> —Václav Havel[2]

These are hard times for public intellectuals on the left in the United States. Fueled by an attack on the welfare state, many conservatives and liberals have joined forces in dismantling all those public spheres not governed by the imperatives of the market.[3] One consequence has been an ongoing and relentless attack on those non-commodified public spaces that provide intellectuals with the opportunity to "openly debate issues of vital public concern, publish tracts and newspapers, engage in heated, but civic-spirited discussions in public spaces"[4] and deploy political practices that help keep alive, as the poet Robert Haas puts it, "the idea of justice, which is going dead in us all the time."[5] But the threat to critical intellectual work is evident not only in attempts to eliminate counter-public spheres that connect educators, artists, and other cultural workers to an insurgent cultural politics.[6] The very notion of culture as a terrain of struggle, that is, the recognition of culture and power as a constitutive political and pedagogical practice, is also under attack by a growing number of left-oriented progressives. The value of this current attack is that it points to the necessity to revive Jürgen Habermas's notion of the public sphere and its emphasis on the political struggle to address the decline of civil society as a site for the struggle over freedom, rationality, and democracy. What makes this issue even more complicated is the necessity to move beyond Habermas's definition of the public sphere as defined largely within the culture of the communicative practices of the white, male, bourgeois subject. Theorists such as Nancy Fraser, Chantal Mouffe, Iris Marion Young, and Oskar Negt and Alexander Kluge[7] have radically modified Habermas's insight about the public sphere and have not only pluralized the concept but have extended its call for equality to the demands of marginalized groups and cultures in order to make visible the relationship between social equality and cultural difference. This chapter is animated by these insights.

In what follows, I want to address how the attack on both counter-public spheres and the politics of culture is expressed through an assault on public education. What is at stake here is the very idea of the public sphere as a place for engaging important social issues as part of the learning process itself as well as the role that educators might play as public intellectuals through such a practice. I will conclude by arguing that the work of Paulo Freire offers a challenge to both of these positions by addressing the role cultural workers assume as public intellectuals who refuse to define themselves either through the language of the market or through a discourse that abstracts the political from the cultural sphere. This appropriation of cultural workers as public intellectuals suggests both a critical analysis of the relationship between the political and the pedagogical, and a redefinition of educators and other cultural workers as border crossers and border intellectuals who engage in intertextual negotiations across different sites of cultural production. The concepts of border crossing and border intellectual at work here foreground not only the shifting nature of counter-public spheres and the problems they pose in naming and articulating the locations of identity-formation, politics, and struggle; they also draw attention to the kinds of cultural work that increasingly take place in the border space between "high" and popular culture; between the institution and the street; between the public and the private. Intellectual work in this instance becomes both theoretical and performative; that is, it is marked by forms of invention, specificity, and critique as well as by an ongoing recognition of public space as partial, fluid, and open to the incessant tensions and contradictions that inform the educator's own location, ideology, and authority in relation to particular communities.

Erasing Schooling as a Counter-Public Sphere

Besieged by the growing forces of vocationalism and the culture wars, prospective and existing classroom teachers are caught in an ideological crossfire regarding the civic and political responsibilities they might assume through their roles as engaged critics and public intellectuals. Asked to define themselves either through the language of the marketplace or through a discourse that abstracts the political from the realm of the cultural or the sphere of the social, educators are increasingly being pressured to become either servants of corporate power or disengaged specialists wedded to the imperatives of a resurgent and debasing academic professionalism.

According to right-wing advocates of school–business partnerships, schools should be viewed as a private rather than a public good, tied to the dictates of the marketplace and run just like any other business. For many who support this position, schools should either be turned over to for-profit corporations—exercising complete control over their organization, curricula, and classroom practices—or be organized through strategies that favor educational choice, vouchers, and private charter schools. Within the language of privatization and market reforms, there is a strong emphasis on standards, measurement of outcomes, and holding teachers and students more accountable. Privatization is an appealing prospect for legislators who do not want to spend money on schools and for those Americans who do not want to support public education through increased taxes. Such appeals are reductive in nature and hollow in substance. Not only do they abstract questions of equity and equality from the discourse of standards, they appropriate the democratic rhetoric of choice and freedom without addressing issues of power and inequality.

Conservatives exhibit little concern over who has access to the resources, wealth, and power that make the range of choices available more viable for some groups than others. The ideas and images that permeate this corporate model of schooling reek with the rhetoric of insincerity and the politics of social indifference. Stripped of a language of social responsibility, the advocates of privatization reject the assumption that school failure might be better understood within the political, economic, and social dynamics of poverty, joblessness, sexism, race and class discrimination, unequal funding, or a diminished tax base. Rather, student failure, especially the failure of poor minority-group students, is often attributed to a genetically encoded lack of intelligence, a culture of deprivation, or simply pathology. Most important, within this attack on public education, there is an equally sustained critique of the assumption that educators can assume the role of critically engaged public intellectuals capable of combining theoretical rigor and social relevance in addressing important political, economic, and social problems. What is disturbing about this conservative attack on public education is that it not only separates culture from politics, it also attempts to erase the contradictions and spaces within dominant institutions that open up political and social possibilities for contesting domination, for doing critical work within the schools and other public spheres, or for furthering the capacities for students and others to question dominant authority and the operations of power.

Even more surprising is the growing army of progressives who remove culture from the play of power and politics and in so doing dissolve the possibility for understanding how learning is linked to social change, how the struggle over identities, meanings, and desires takes place across a whole spectrum of social practices, or how social authority is wielded to make it difficult for subaltern groups to participate in such struggles in ways that carry any legitimacy or weight. Within this discourse, progressives such as Todd Gitlin, Michael Tomasky, and Jim Sleeper pit the alleged "real" material issues of class and labor against a fragmenting and marginalizing politics which falsely assumes that culture is a sphere where effective political struggles can be waged over broad visions of social justice.[8] Within the narrow confines of this discourse, "culture and identity are opposed to the real material issues of class,"[9] cultural politics is tantamount to the politics of difference and victim politics, and the university and public schools do not qualify as viable public spheres in which to wage political battles. For theorists such as Gitlin and others, the political does not include sites that trade in pedagogy, knowledge, and the production of meaning. In what follows, I highlight some of the more repeated arguments made by this group by focusing on the work of Todd Gitlin, one of its most prolific and public representatives.

For Gitlin, contemporary cultural struggles, especially those taken up by social movements organized around sexuality, gender, race, the politics of representation, and, more broadly, multiculturalism, are nothing more than a weak substitute for "real world" politics, notably a politics that focuses on class, labor, and economic inequality.[10] According to Gitlin, social movements that refuse the primacy of class give politics a bad name; they serve primarily to splinter the left into identity sects, fail "to address questions of economic equity and redistribution,"[11] and offer no unifying vision of the common good capable of challenging corporate power and right-wing ideologues.

Gitlin's critique of social movements rests on a number of erasures and evasions. First, in presupposing that class is a transcendent and universal category that can unite the left, Gitlin fails to acknowledge a history in which class politics was used to demean and domesticate the modalities of race, gender, and sexual orientation. Its leading practitioners expressed the conviction that race and gender considerations could not contribute to a general notion of emancipation, and in doing so ignored a legacy of class-based politics marked by a history of subordination and exclusion toward marginalized social movements. Moreover, it was precisely because of the subordination and smothering of difference that social groups, in part, organized to articulate their respective goals, histories, and interests outside of the orthodoxy of class politics. Judith Butler is right in arguing, "How quickly we forget that new social movements based on democratic principles became articulated against a hegemonic Left as well as a complicitous liberal center and a truly threatening right wing."[12] Moreover, not only does Gitlin limit social agency to the pristine category of class, he can only imagine class as a unified, pregiven subject position, rather than a shifting, negotiated space marked by historical, symbolic, and social mediations, including the complex negotiations of race and gender. Within this discourse, the history of class-based sectarianism is forgotten, the category of class is essentialized, and politics is so narrowly defined as to freeze the open-ended and shifting relationship between culture and power.[13]

Second, by reducing all social movements to the most essentialistic and rigid forms of identity politics, Gitlin cannot understand how class is actually lived through what Stuart Hall has called the modalities of race and gender. In Gitlin's discourse, social movements are nothing but particularistic; hence it is impossible for him to "conceive of social movements as essential to a class-based politics."[14] For instance, Robin Kelley points out the failure of Gitlin and others to recognize how ACT UP made AIDS visible as a deadly disease that is now taking its greatest toll among poor black women.[15] Nor is there any recognition of how the feminist movement made visible the dynamics of sexual abuse, particularly as it raged through the communities of poor black and white households. Nor is there any understanding of how a whole generation of young people might be educated to recognize the racist ideologies that permeate representations in advertising, films, and other aspects of media culture that flood daily life.

Third, Gitlin's appeal to majoritarian principles slips easily into the reactionary tactic of blaming minorities for the white backlash that characterizes the present moment, going so far as to argue that because the followers of identity politics abandoned a concern for materialist issues, they opened up the door for an all-out attack on labor and the poor by the right. At the same time, identity politics bears the burden in Gitlin's discourse for allowing the right to attack "racialized rhetoric as a way of diverting attention from the economic restructuring that has been hurting most Americans."[16] Thoughtlessly aligning himself with the right, Gitlin seems unwilling to acknowledge how the historical legacy of slavery, imperialism, urban ghettoization, segregation, the extermination of Native Americans, the war against immigrants, and the discrimination against Jews as it has been rewritten back into the discourse of American history may upset a majoritarian population that finds it more convenient to blame subordinate groups for their problems than to engage their own complicity.[17]

Against this form of historical amnesia, the call to patriotism, majoritarian values, and unity shares an ignoble relationship to a past in which such principles were rooted in the ideology of white supremacy, the presumption that the public sphere was white, and the prioritizing of a "racially cleansed notion of class."[18] If identity politics poses a threat to the endearing (because transcendent and universal) category that class represents to some critics, as the historian Robin Kelley argues, either it may be because such critics fail to understand how class is lived through race, sexual orientation, and gender or it may be that the return to a form of class warfare against corporate power represents simply another form of identity politics, that is, an identity-based campaign that stems from the anxiety and revulsion of white males who cannot imagine participating in movements led by African Americans, women, Latinos, or gays and lesbians speaking for the whole or even embracing radical humanism.[19]

Finally, Gitlin's materialism finds its antithesis in a version of cultural studies that is pure caricature. According to Gitlin, cultural studies is a form of populism intent on finding resistance in the most mundane of cultural practices, ignoring the ever-deepening economic inequities, land dispensing entirely with material relations of power. Banal in its refusal to discriminate between a culture of excellence and consumer culture, cultural studies becomes a symbol of bad faith and political irresponsibility. For theorists in cultural studies, Gitlin argues, it is irrelevant that African Americans suffer gross material injustice since what really matters is that "they have rap."[20] It seems that, for Gitlin, cultural studies should "free itself of the burden of imagining itself to be a political practice"[21] since the locus of much of its work is the university—a thoroughly delegitimated site for intellectuals to address the most pressing questions of our age and take responsibility for what Stuart Hall calls "translating knowledge into the practice of culture."[22]

Gitlin's model of politics is characteristic of a resurgent economism rooted in a totalizing concept of class in which it is argued that "we can do class or culture, but not both."[23] Within this discourse, social movements are dismissed as merely cultural, and how we might understand and engage the political is removed from considering the cultural sphere as a serious terrain of struggle. Little attention is paid in this perspective to a notion of politics that addresses how meaning, ideas, and beliefs mobilize desires, speak to human needs, and provide the ground for hope, social engagement, and collective transformation. Ellen Willis rightly argues in opposition to positions such as Gitlin's that if people "are not ready to defend their right to freedom and equality in their personal relations, they will not fight consistently for their economic interests, either."[24] Questions of agency or resistance in Gitlin's version of cultural studies are dismissed as retrograde forms of populism while cultural pedagogy is traded for an anti-intellectual and anti-theoretical incitement to organizing and pamphleteering.

It is against the current onslaught on cultural politics and its attempt to discredit the role that educators might play as public intellectuals working in a diverse range of public spheres that Paulo Freire's work provides an important theoretical and political service.

Toward a Politics of Hope

Freire's belief in the ability of people to resist and transform the weight of oppressive institutions and ideologies has been forged in a spirit of struggle tempered both by the grim realities of his own imprisonment and exile and by a profound sense of humility, compassion, and hope. Acutely aware that many contemporary versions of hope were not anchored in practice and lacked a historical concreteness, Freire has repeatedly denounced such romantic fantasies and has been passionate about recovering and rearticulating hope through, in his words, an "understanding of history as opportunity and not determinism."[25] Hope, for Freire, is a practice of witnessing, an act of moral imagination that encourages progressive educators and others to stand at the edge of society, to think beyond existing configurations of power in order to imagine the unthinkable in terms of how they might live with dignity, justice, and freedom. Hope demands an anchoring in transformative practices, and one of the tasks of the progressive educator is to "unveil opportunities for hope, no matter what the obstacles may be."[26]

Underlying Freire's politics of hope is a view of radical pedagogy that locates itself on the dividing lines where the relations between domination and oppression, power and powerlessness continue to be produced and reproduced. Freire argues that radical democracy demands the ongoing production of and struggle over knowledge, skills, values, and social relations in order to develop dynamic pedagogical practices that are faithful to the spirit of open and democratic forms of insurgent citizenship. A radical pedagogy, in part, means listening to and working with the poor, oppressed, and other subordinate groups so that they might speak and act in order to change the concrete material and social conditions that exploit and oppress them.

Freire's politics of hope is grounded in a project that refuses both the sectarianism of the orthodox left and the authoritarianism of a retrograde conservatism. According to Freire, material oppression and the affective investments that tie oppressed groups to the logic of domination cannot be grasped in all of their complexity within the singular logic of class struggle.[27] Moreover the mechanisms of domination, both economic and ideological, cannot be understood without engaging with how the oppressed in many instances actually become complicitous and participate in their own oppression. As Stanley Aronowitz has pointed out, Freire recognizes that "the oppressed are situated within an economic and social structure and tied to it not only by their labor but also by the conditions of their psychological being."[28]

For Freire, the prophetic nature of politics and pedagogy lies in a notion of cultural politics in which culture provides the constitutive framework for making the pedagogical political—recognizing that how we come to learn and what we learn is imminently tied to strategies of understanding, representation, and disruption that offer the possibilities and opportunities for individuals to engage and transform when necessary the ideological and material circumstances that shape their lives. One of Freire's lasting contributions has been, in addition, to make the political more pedagogical. By repeatedly pointing to the diverse ways in which culture is related to power and how and where it functions both symbolically and institutionally as an educational, political, and economic force, Freire provocatively argues that cultural pedagogy is the outcome of particular struggles over specific representations, identifications, and forms of agency. According to Freire, culture is constitutive of agency(ies) and politics because it provides the resources through which individuals learn how to relate to themselves, others, and the world around them. For Freire, culture is neither free-floating nor does it stand still. Amplifying the relationship between learning and social change, Freire insists that cultural workers deepen the meaning of the political by producing pedagogical practices that engage and challenge those representational strategies, material machineries and technologies of power that condition and are conditioned by the indeterminate play of power, conflict, and oppression within society. Culture is the social field where power repeatedly mutates, identities are constantly in transit, and agency is often located where it is least acknowledged. Agency in this discourse is neither prefigured nor always in place but subject to negotiation and struggle and open for creating new democratic possibilities, configurations, and transformations. How one "deals with the place of cultural politics" remains essential to any viable notion of politics concerned with how subjects are situated within historical, social, economic, and cultural relations.[29] Within this context, learning itself becomes the means not only for the acquisition of agency but for the imaginary of social change itself.

Making the Pedagogical More Political

> The role of an educator who is pedagogically and critically radical is to avoid being indifferent. . . . On the contrary, a better way to proceed is to assume the authority as a teacher whose direction of education includes helping learners get involved in planning education, helping them create the critical capacity to consider and participate in the direction and dreams of education, rather than merely following blindly.[30]

Unfortunately, many of Freire's followers have reduced his pedagogy to a methodology or set of teaching techniques emphasizing dialogue, the affirmation of student experience, and the decentralization of power in the classroom.[31] What has been lost in this analysis is Freire's legacy of revolutionary politics. For Freire, "problem posing education is a revolutionary futurity,"[32] an observation that suggests not a methodology but a social theory whose aim is the liberation of individuals and groups as historical subjects through a critical educational process that involves making the pedagogical more political and the political more pedagogical. For Freire, pedagogy is political in that its task is to revitalize questions of individual and social agency as well as critically engage with how power is produced, applied, and resisted across a range of histories, social formations, institutions, and signifying practices.

Pedagogy, according to Freire, is concerned not simply with self-improvement but with social transformation aimed at creating the conditions for the oppressed to overcome material, ideological, and psychological forms of domination while reviving and expanding the fabric of democratic institutions. In this discourse, pedagogy and politics mutually inform each other as part of a broader project that requires the addressing of citizenship as "a social invention that demands a certain political knowledge, a knowledge born of the struggle for and the reflection on citizenship itself."[33] Freire's call for political self-determination and for the oppressed to become agents not only expresses a move away from a certain vanguardism that marked his early work, but signals the need for educators to address the vast range of experiences that inform the values, histories, and experiences that students bring with them to the classroom and other educational sites. According to Freire, critical educators must always be attentive to the specific and the contingent; one of their primary undertakings is to recover and rethink the ways in which culture is related to power and how and where it functions both symbolically and institutionally as an educational, political, and economic force. For Freire, culture and power must be organized through an understanding of how the political becomes pedagogical; that is, how the very processes of learning constitute the political mechanisms through which identities are shaped, desires are mobilized, and experiences take on form and meaning. Pedagogy in this sense becomes central to the task of making knowledge meaningful in order to make it critical and transformative. For Freire, pedagogy is always the outcome of conflicts that are historically specific, and "the sites, goals, and forms of struggle must be understood contextually."[34] Such struggles are defined by projects that cannot be given beforehand, they emerge in response to specific formations, they address where people are, how they actually live their lives, and what it might mean to open up "new imagined possibilities for changing [such] contexts."[35] Echoing Antonio Gramsci's insight that "Every relationship of 'hegemony' is necessarily an educational relationship,"[36] Freire reminds us that pedagogy takes place in multiple sites, and he signals how students and others are constructed as subjects and subjected to relations of power within and across a variety of public spaces.

Freire consistently informs us that political struggles are won and lost in those specific yet hybridized spaces that link narratives of everyday experience with the social gravity and material force of institutional power. Any radical pedagogy that calls itself Freirean has to acknowledge the centrality of the particular and contingent in shaping historical contexts and political projects. Always taking seriously what it means to link political struggle with the contexts that give rise to pressing social problems, Freire develops pedagogical practices forged in the specificities of the struggles he addresses. For Freire, politics is about the making and the changing of contexts, and pedagogy is not simply the practical application of such politics but a performative struggle in which teaching and learning reflect the need for subordinate and marginalized groups to develop their languages, histories, and cultures as a meaningful and critical condition for developing their own sense of agency in political struggles.

Committed to the specific and contextual, Freire offers no recipes for those in need of instant theoretical and political fixes. Nor does he wish to affirm and romanticize the experiences of students or subordinate groups. Freire refuses to reduce knowledge and politics either to biography or to a fetishizing of marginality. More important, pedagogy is strategic and performative, and at its best moves beyond simply detailing models of domination and resistance by providing a discourse and politics of articulation and transformation. Considered as part of a broader political practice for democratic change, radical pedagogy cannot be viewed as an *a priori* discourse to be reasserted, a methodology to be implemented, or a mantra to affirm uncritically the voices of the oppressed. On the contrary, for Freire pedagogy is a theoretically rigorous, political, and performative act organized around the "instructive ambivalence of disrupted borders,"[37] a practice of bafflement, interruption, and intervention that is the result of ongoing historical, social, and economic struggles.

In Freire's radical educational theory, critical pedagogical practice means shifting power from the teacher to students, but rather than suggesting that radical educators abandon authority, Freire calls upon teachers to assert authority in the service of creating a participatory and democratic classroom. He shuns the role of the educator as facilitator who turns all authority over to students, an educator who by default becomes silent in the face of injustice. Freire also rejects using the authority of the teacher in order to collapse the political into the personal. The purpose of teacher authority in this case is to provide students with forms of therapy that focus largely on uplifting their self-esteem and making them feel good. As a form of pedagogical uplift, which transposes an all-knowing teacher against a victimized, vulnerable student, this type of pedagogical authority and practice represents for Freire "the false generosity of the oppressor."[38] Freire argues against the exercise of teacher authority in the service of a pedagogical model that positions students as fragile, delicate victims of a dominant culture "in need of protection."[39]

For Freire, educators have an obligation to dream and work toward, with their students the conditions necessary to live, as he puts it, in "a world that is less oppressive and more humane toward the oppressed."[40] Radical educators also have a responsibility to present students with critical choices about the places they might inhabit in the larger society.

Freire forcefully acknowledges that educators can never impose their views on students or, as he puts it, "transform the learner's presence into a shadow of the educator's presence."[41] But this should not be seen as merely a defense of teaching multiple perspectives or as an endorsement of what Gerald Graff refers to as "teaching the conflicts."[42] On the contrary, Freire argues that educators must develop critical pedagogical practices grounded in existing concrete realities and social problems, and exhibit for students "an active presence in educational practice."[43] According to Freire, educators must fashion their pedagogical practices within a democratic social project, and seize authority in order "to stimulate learners to live a critically conscious presence in the pedagogical and historical process."[44] In this pedagogical project, the role of the educator is directive and theoretically informed. Critical educators cannot impose their views on students by telling them what to think, but they can "teach them the importance of taking a stance that is rooted in rigorous engagement with the full range of ideas about a topic,"[45] while stressing the social and not merely individualistic character of learning and struggle.

Radical pedagogy in Freire's discourse insists that learners become subjects in their own education by critically engaging through dialogue and debate the historical, social, and economic conditions that both limit and enable their own understanding of knowledge as power. According to Freire, engaging authority critically cannot be referenced or justified in exclusively methodological terms, as in a call to teach the conflicts or to simply dialogue. In exercising and defending teacher authority, educators must be able to name their own location, openly articulate their project and vision, reveal their partialities, refuse to silence students, and open their own problematic and use of authority to critical debate.

Freire also challenges the separation of culture from politics by calling attention to how diverse technologies of power work pedagogically within institutions to produce, regulate, and legitimate particular forms of knowing, belonging, feeling, and desiring. But Freire does not make the mistake of many of his contemporaries of conflating culture with the politics of textuality. Politics is more than a gesture of translation, representation, and dialogue; it is also about mobilizing social movements against the oppressive economic, racial, and sexist practices put into place by colonization, global capitalism, and other oppressive structures of power. A critical theory of literacy and culture is central to Freire's radical educational project, but it cannot be understood outside of the equally important registers of the material economy of power, resources, and means. Freire repeatedly emphasizes culture as an important site of political struggle, but he also insists that if such a sphere is to have any radical pedagogical relevance, it has to be taken up critically by students and others in order to intervene in the material circumstances that have shaped their lives. For Freire, a cultural politics that lacks a historical dimension or ignores the machineries of power that shape the relations among schools, everyday life, and discourse fails to address the revolutionary potential of critical pedagogy and undermines the project of social reconstruction.

Refusing the comfort of master narratives, Freire's work is always unsettled and unsettling, restless yet engaging. Unlike so much of the politically arid and morally vacuous academic and public prose that characterizes much of contemporary educational discourse, Freire's work is consistently fueled by a healthy rage over the needless oppression and suffering he witnessed as he traveled all over the globe. His work exhibits a vibrant and dynamic quality that allows it to grow, refuse easy formulas, and open itself to new political realities and projects. Freire's gift was to elaborate a theory of social change and engagement that is neither vanguardist nor populist. He has a profound faith in the ability of ordinary people to become critical agents in shaping history, but he also refuses to romanticize the culture and experiences of those that bore the weight of oppressive social conditions. Combining theoretical rigor, social relevance, and moral compassion, Freire's work and politics give new meaning to the registers of daily life while affirming the importance of critical theory and radical pedagogy in opening up counter-public spheres marked by critique, possibility, and practice. Theory and language are tools of struggle and possibility that give experience meaning and give action a political direction, and any attempt to reproduce the binarism of theory versus politics has been repeatedly condemned by Freire.[46]

Freire's work has enormous relevance for how educators and other cultural workers define themselves as public intellectuals and make pedagogy a defining principle of politics, and for how they assert the importance of schools as democratic public spheres. At a time when both public and higher education are being either deracinated or vocationalized because they represent one of the few places left where democracy can be experienced or at least acknowledged as central to educating students for the future, Freire's passionate defense of radical democracy provides a crucial resource for public intellectuals to reclaim public education as a site of democratic education and struggle. Against the elitism of Allan Bloom, William Bennett, Diane Ravitch, and E.D. Hirsch, Freire offers a passionate defense of popular culture as a pedagogical starting point for developing multiple vocabularies and literacies that enable students and others to negotiate the public realm, take seriously the imperatives of creating a transnational democracy, and expand individual and collective capacities for social engagement. Freire never abstracts his methods from a larger vision of freedom and never relents in his advocacy of an international sense of responsibility; because of this he offers his readers a language of critique and possibility that reinvigorates the meaning of what it means to be a public intellectual constituted across multiple borders and willing to fight and struggle for social change while learning to "live a critically conscious presence in the pedagogical and historical process."[47]

Notes

1. Edward Said, *Representations of the Intellectual* (New York: Pantheon, 1994), p. xvii.

2. Václav Havel, "The Responsibility of Intellectuals," *New York Review of Books* (June 22, 1995), p. 37.

3. My use of the term "public sphere" draws primarily from the following: Jürgen Habermas, *The Structural Transformation of the Public Sphere*, trans. Thomas Burger (Cambridge, MA: MIT Press, 1989); various papers collected in *Habermas and the Public Sphere*, ed. Craig Calhoun (Cambridge, MA: MIT Press, 1992), especially Nancy Fraser, "Rethinking the Public Sphere: A Contribution to the Critique of Actually Existing Democracy," pp. 99–108; Oscar Negt and Alexander Kluge, *Public Sphere and Experience: Toward an*

Analysis of the Bourgeois and Proletarian Public Sphere (Minneapolis: University of Minnesota Press, 1993); Chantal Mouffe, *The Return of the Political* (London: Verso, 1993); *The Phantom Public Sphere*, ed. Bruce Robbins (Minneapolis: University of Minnesota Press, 1993).

4. Stanley Aronowitz, "The Situation of the Left in the United States," *Socialist Review* 23:3 (1994): 59.

5. Sarah Pollock, "Robert Haas," *Mother Jones* (March/April 1997): 22.

6. My notion of the counter-public sphere is developed in Negt and Kluge, *Public Sphere and Experience*; see also Henry A. Giroux, *Border Crossings: Cultural Workers and the Politics of Education* (New York: Routledge, 1992), and Stanley Aronowitz and Henry A. Giroux, *Education Still under Siege* (Westport: Bergin and Garvey, 1993).

7. See Fraser, "Rethinking the Public Sphere," pp. 99–108; Mouffe, *The Return of the Political*; Iris Marion Young, *Justice and the Politics of Difference* (Princeton: Princeton University Press, 1990); Negt and Kluge, *Public Sphere and Experience*.

8. See Todd Gitlin, *Twilight of Our Common Dreams* (New York: Metropolitan Books, 1995); Michael Tomasky, *Left for Dead: The Life, Death and Possible Resurrection of Progressive Politics in America* (New York: Free Press, 1996); Jim Sleeper, *The Closest of Strangers* (New York: W.W. Norton, 1990).

9. Iris Marion Young, "Iris Young Replies to Todd Gitlin," *Dissent* (Spring 1997): 93–4.

10. Gitlin's most sustained development of this argument can be found in *Twilight of Our Common Dreams*.

11. Judith Butler, "Merely Cultural," *Social Text* 15: 52–5 (Fall/Winter 1997): 266.

12. Ibid., p. 268.

13. For an insightful analysis of this position, see Lawrence Grossberg, "Cultural Studies: What's in a Name?" in his *Bringing It All Back Home: Essays on Cultural Studies* (Durham: Duke University Press, 1997), pp. 245–71.

14. Robin D.G. Kelley, *Yo' Mama's Disfunktional! Fighting the Culture Wars in Urban America* (Boston: Beacon Press, 1997), pp. 113–14.

15. Ibid.

16. Iris Marion Young, "The Complexities of Coalition," *Dissent* (Winter 1997): 67.

17. Although Habermas does not dismiss identity politics as reductionistically as Gitlin does, he argues for a universalized notion of juridical ethics based on a liberal notion of consensus and a defense of Enlightenment rationality that does not allow the "Other" as a complex, enunciatory subject to be theorized within the specificity of diverse cultural formations, social contexts and historical configurations. Hence there is an undertheorization of how democracy gets translated differently in diverse cultural landscapes or how the constraints on agency, not to mention communicative action and deliberative possibilities, are structured differently among marginalized groups. For example, Habermas's notion of communicative rationality and juridical ethics has little to contribute theoretically and politically to an understanding of how the racial state actively participates in eliminating an entire generation of black youth who are being imprisoned at an alarming rate by the criminal justice system in the United States; nor does it hold any implications for addressing and challenging Enlightenment forms of rationality that are unmindful of the colonial legacy that is central to their development. See Jürgen Habermas, "Struggles for Recognition in the Democratic Constitutional State," in *Multiculturalism*, ed. Amy Gutman (Princeton: Princeton University Press, 1994), pp. 107–48.

18. Butler, "Merely Cultural," p. 268.

19. Kelley, *Yo' Mama's Disfunktional!*

20. Todd Gitlin, "The Anti-Political Populism of Cultural Studies," *Dissent* (Spring 1997): p. 81.

21. Ibid., p. 82.

22. Stuart Hall, "The Emergence of Cultural Studies and the Crisis of the Humanities," *October*, No. 53 (summer 1990): 18.

23. Ellen Willis, "We Need a Radical Left," *Nation* (June 29, 1998): 19.

24. Ibid.

25. Paulo Freire, *Pedagogy of Hope* (New York: Continuum Press, 1994), p. 91.

26. Ibid., p. 9.

27. Of course, this position is clearly articulated in Freire's early work, such as *Pedagogy of the Oppressed*, but can also be found in his later work as well.

28. Stanley Aronowitz, "Paulo Freire's Democratic Humanism," in *Paulo Freire: A Critical Encounter*, eds. Peter McLaren and Peter Leonard (New York: Routledge, 1993), p. 17.

29. Stuart Hall, "Subjects in History: Making Diasporic Identities," in *The House That Race Built*, ed. Wahneema Lubiano (New York: Pantheon, 1997), p. 289.

30. Paulo Freire and Donaldo Macedo, "A Dialogue: Culture, Language and Race," *Breaking Free: The Transformative Power of Critical Pedagogy*, eds. Pepi Leistyna, Arlie Woodrum, Stephen A. Sherblom (Cambridge, MA: Harvard Educational Review, 1996), p. 202.

31. One recent example of this can be found in Alice McIntyre, *Making Meaning of Whiteness* (Albany: SUNY Press, 1997), pp. 19–20. McIntyre refers to Freire's work as a "methodology for learning" as if such a "methodology" can be understood outside of the specific historical context, radical political theory, and specific set of social formations and conditions that produced it. The refusal to contextualize Freire's work betrays a positivist refusal to deal with the relationship between political projects and the emergence of specific pedagogical formations.

32. Paulo Freire, *Pedagogy of the Oppressed*, trans. Myra Bergman Ramos (New York: Seabury Press, 1973), p. 72.

33. Paulo Freire, *Letters to Christina: Reflections on My Life and Work* (New York: Routledge, 1996), pp. 113–14.

34. Grossberg, *Bringing It All Back Home*, p. 264.

35. Ibid., p. 262.

36. Antonio Gramsci, *Selections From the Prison Notebooks*, trans. Q. Hoare and G. Smith (New York: International Press, 1971), p. 350.

37. Homi Bhabha, "The Enchantment of Art," in *The Artists in Society*, eds. Carol Becker and Ann Wiens (Chicago: New Art Examiner, 1994), p. 28.

38. Freire, *Pedagogy of the Oppressed*, p. 142.

39. Jane Gallop, *Feminist Accused of Sexual Harassment* (Durham and London: Duke University Press, 1997), p. 62. Gallop relates a chilling story about her own colleagues who opposed a conference she was organizing on the grounds that it would make students "unhappy or remind them of painful experiences." Gallop rightly criticizes this position and argues that, "We who were planning the conference considered it our primary duty to foster knowledge. Inasmuch as we were teachers, it was our responsibility to expose students to as much learning as possible. Protecting students from knowledge that would make them uncomfortable seemed ultimately a failure to teach them, placing some other relationship above our duty as their teachers. . . . We . . . assumed that what women most need is knowledge and that women students are tough enough to learn" (pp. 61–2). While this critique is applied to some versions of feminist pedagogy, the notion that the pedagogical goal of making students feel good—and conversely not making them uncomfortable in the learning process—has become one of the defining features of a number of strands of critical pedagogy. I would argue such a position is the ideological and pedagogical antithesis of what Freire had in mind when he talked about dialogue and sharing power with students.

40. Freire cited in Freire and Macedo, "A Dialogue: Culture, Language, and Race," p. 214.

41. Ibid., p. 202.

42. Gerald Graff, *Beyond the Culture Wars: How Teaching the Conflicts Can Revitalize American Education* (New York: Norton, 1992). For an insightful rebuttal of Graff's attack on radical pedagogy, see Freire and Macedo, "A Dialogue: Culture, Language, and Race," pp. 188–228.

43. Freire, cited in Freire and Macedo, "A Dialogue: Culture, Language, and Race," p. 202.

44. Ibid.

45. bell hooks, "Black Students Who Reject Feminism," *Chronicle of Higher Education* (July 13, 1994): A44. hooks also provides an excellent feminist analysis of Paulo Freire's pedagogy in bell hooks, "Bell Hooks Speaking About Paulo Freire—The Man, His Work," in *Paulo Freire: A Critical Encounter*, eds. McLaren and Leonard, pp. 146–54.

46. Surely Freire would have agreed wholeheartedly with Stuart Hall's insight that: "It is only through the way in which we represent and imagine ourselves that we come to know how we are constituted and who we are. There is no escape from the politics of representation." Stuart Hall, "What is this 'Black' in Popular Culture?" in *Black Popular Culture*, ed. Gina Dent (Seattle: Bay Press, 1992), p. 30. At the same time, Freire was as much concerned with what educators do with language as with decoding its meanings.

47. Freire cited in Freire and Macedo, "A Dialogue: Culture, Language, and Race," p. 202.

Notes on Contributors

Stanley Aronowitz is Professor of Sociology at the Graduate School of CUNY. He is the author of *The Knowledge Factory: Dismantling the Corporate University and Creating True Higher Learning* and *From the Ashes of the Old: American Labor and America's Future*.

Etienne Balibar is Professor of Philosophy at the Université de Paris X. His recent works include *Race, Nation, and Class* and *Spinoza and Politics*.

Crystal Bartolovich is Assistant Professor of English and Textual Studies at Syracuse University. She is co-editor of *Marxism, Modernity, Postcolonial Studies* (forthcoming).

Jamie Owen Daniel is Assistant Professor of English at the University of Illinois at Chicago, and editor of *Not Yet: Reconsidering Ernst Bloch*.

Henry Giroux is Waterbury Chair Professor of Education at Pennsylvania State University. He is the author of *Counternarratives: Cultural Studies and Critical Pedagogies in Postmodern Spaces* and *Critical Education in the New Information Age* (Critical Perspective Series).

Michael Hardt is Assistant Professor of Literature at Duke University. He is the author of *An Apprenticeship in Philosophy*, and, with Antonio Negri, *Empire*.

Mike Hill is Assistant Professor of English at SUNY Albany, and editor of *Whiteness: A Critical Reader*.

David McInerney is a doctoral candidate in Political Science at the Australian National University. He is the author of several essays on Marxism and postcolonialism.

Warren Montag is Associate Professor of English at Occidental College. He is the author of *Bodies, Masses, Power: Spinoza and His Contemporaries*.

You-me Park is Assistant Professor of English, George Washington University. She is the co-editor of *The Postcolonial Jane Austen*.

Erin Post is a graduate student in Literature at Duke University.

Ted Stolze of California State University, Hayward, is co-editor of *The New Spinoza*.

Raúl H. Villa, Associate Professor of English at Occidental College, is the author of *Barrio-Logos: The Dialectic of Space and Place in Urban Chicano Literature and Culture* (History, Culture, and Society Series).

Gayle Wald is Assistant Professor of English at George Washington University, and author of *Crossing the Line: Racial Passing in Twentieth-Century U.S. Literature and Culture* (New Americanists).

Acknowledgments

Grateful acknowledgment is made to the original publishers for permission to reprint the following previously published material, which appears in this book in slightly different form. Michael Hardt, "The Withering of Social Society," first published in *Social Text* 45, Winter 1995; Mike Hill, "Of Multitudes and Moral Sympathy: E. P. Thompson, Althusser, and Adam Smith," *English Literary History* (forthcoming; portions reprinted here with kind permission from Johns Hopkins University Press); You-me Park and Gayle Wald, "Native Daughters in the Promised Land: Gender, Race and the Question of Separate Spheres," first published in *American Literature*, vol. 70, no. 3, September 1998.

The editors wish to express much gratitude to Sarah Johnson and Cynthia Marugg, without whose assistance this volume would have been far longer in the making.

Index